WRONGLY DIVIDING THE WORD OF TRUTH

WRONGLY DIVIDING THE WORD OF TRUTH

A Critique of Dispensationalism

JOHN H. GERSTNER, Ph.D.

Foreword by R.C. Sproul

Wolgemuth & Hyatt, Publishers, Inc.
Brentwood, Tennessee

The mission of Wolgemuth & Hyatt, Publishers, Inc. is to publish and dis-
tribute books that lead individuals toward:

- A personal faith in the one true God: Father, Son, and Holy Spirit;
- A lifestyle of practical discipleship; and
- A worldview that is consistent with the historic, Christian faith.

Moreover, the company endeavors to accomplish this mission at a reasonable profit and in a manner which glorifies God and serves His Kingdom.

© 1991 by John Gerstner. All rights reserved.
Published May 1991. First edition.
Printed in the United States of America.
97 96 95 94 93 92 91   8 7 6 5 4 3

Scripture quotations marked NASB are from the New American Standard
Bible © 1960, 1962, 1963, 1968, 1971, 1972, 1973, 1975, 1977 by The Lockman
Foundation and are used by permission.

Scripture quotations marked NIV are from the Holy Bible, New International Version, © 1973, 1978, 1984 by International Bible Society. Used
by permission of Zondervan Bible Publishers.

Wolgemuth & Hyatt, Publishers, Inc.
1749 Mallory Lane, Suite 110, Brentwood, Tennessee 37027.

Printed in the United States of America.

Library of Congress Cataloging-in-Publication Data

Gerstner, John H.
    Wrongly dividing the word of truth : a critique of
dispensationalism / John H. Gerstner. — 1st ed.
        p.   cm.
    Includes bibliographical references.
    ISBN 1-56121-021-8
    1. Dispensationalism — Controversial literature.   2. Calvinism.
3. Evangelicalism.   I. Title.
BT157.G47   1991
230'.046 — dc20   91-517
                                                                    CIP

CONTENTS

FOREWORD

When Karl Barth's *Epistle To the Romans (Romerbrief)* was published in 1918, it was said that it exploded like a bomb on the playground of theologians. This current work on Dispensationalism by Dr. John H. Gerstner will be equally explosive on the American evangelical scene. This bomb — unlike missiles that suffer from dubious guidance systems and are liable to land on civilian populations wreaking havoc indiscriminately — is delivered with pinpoint accuracy into the laps of dispensational scholars.

It is a hard book, not in the sense of theological difficulty, but in that it hits hard against a theological system that in all probability is the majority report among current American evangelicals. Gerstner does not have a reputation for dueling with gentility; he asks no quarter and gives none. Yet Gerstner is not interested in substituting vitriolic polemic for hard debate. Rather, he is convinced that nothing less than the gospel is at stake here and hence it is not a time for pussy-footing timidity.

As a debater Gerstner is steeped in the tradition of Paul, Luther, Calvin, and Edwards where the issues are of such importance that it is imperative that those who go to the mat are dealt with not as weaker brothers, but as able-bodied, indeed, formidable opponents. In this sense the book is hard and not for the weak-minded.

As a world-class historian, Gerstner has done his homework. The book is a result of years of careful and painstaking research. Gerstner has examined in the minutest detail the works of the most important historic dispensational theologians. He has canvassed scholarly journals and Ph.D. dissertations. He has been in repeated dialogue and debate with contemporary dispensational scholars. The current publication is the crystalized essence of over one thousand typescript pages of Gerstner's research and conclusions.

In most modern discussions about Dispensationalism, the issues usually brought into sharp focus are eschatology and the "Lordship Salvation" question. Gerstner gives a close analysis of these matters. The scope of the book, however, goes far beyond these issues. Gerstner's chief criticism is directed at Dispensationalism's entire structure (classic and current) of soteriology.

Historic Dispensationalism tends to view itself as an innovative and modified form of Reformed Theology. It frequently claims to be a four-point type of Calvinism, embracing 80 percent of the acrostic T-U-L-I-P, which summarized the Reformed response at the Synod of Dordt to the chief objections leveled by the Remonstrants. Dispensationalists tend to affirm total depravity, unconditional election, irresistible grace, and perseverance of the saints, while demuring on the doctrine of limited atonement.

Gerstner not only responds to those who would beat the "L" out of "TULIP" (in the process taking some of his own Reformed colleagues to task) but charges that in reality Dispensationalism, closely studied, actually deviates from all five points, crushing the flower altogether. Perhaps most significant in this portion of the book, is Gerstner's tight critique of Dispensationalism's view of regeneration. This touches a core issue between Reformed Theology and other theologies.

One of the most serious charges Gerstner levels at Dispensationalism is the charge that its system of theology is inherently antinomian. Though Antinomianism is at the heart of the Lordship Salvation debate, it is not limited to it.

The Biblical doctrine of sanctification has been imperiled in every generation. It is a difficult task to steer between the Scylla of legalism and the Charybdis of Antinomianism. It is rare that a legalist ever calls himself a legalist; it is perhaps even more rare for an antinomian to call himself antinomian.

Even the king of modern antinomians, Joseph Fletcher, goes to extraordinary lengths in his book, *Situation Ethics*, to show how he escapes the charge. Likewise dispensationalists cringe at the charge of Antinomianism and repeatedly deny it. Gerstner insists, protests to the contrary, that the dispensational system of theology is inherently and inescapably antinomian. Surely dispensationalists do not desire to be antinomian any more than they want to be neo-nomists or legalists. What Gerstner suggests, however, is that if dispensationalists avoid Antinomianism personally, they do it by a happy inconsistency—not because of their theology but in spite of it. For Gerstner, when a dispensationalist eschews Antinomianism, he is, in effect, eschewing Dispensationalism. It is by embracing the *ism* that one becomes an *ist*.

I am convinced that dispensationalist theologians will be exceedingly distressed by this book. Surely many will cry "foul!" They will claim that Gerstner is either unfair or inaccurate in his assessments and evaluations. They will argue that Gerstner erects a straw man and then demolishes it.

Anyone familiar with Gerstner's work knows that he is not interested in building scarecrows. Scarecrows are for the birds not for serious theologians. If a dispensationalist reads this book and honestly says, "This is not what I believe," nothing would please Gerstner more.

Is it possible that Gerstner has misunderstood dispensational theology and consequently misrepresented it? We must surely hold to this possibility. Knowing Gerstner, I am confident that he would prefer torture or death to intentionally distorting or misrepresenting anyone's position. This would be particularly true in the case of dispensationalists because he has such a high regard for their relentless and uncompromising adherence and defense of the inerrancy of Scripture.

If Gerstner is inaccurate—if he has failed to understand dispensational theology correctly—then he owes many a profound apology. But first he must be shown where and how he is in error. This is the challenge of the book. If Gerstner is accurate, then Dispensationalism should be discarded as being a serious deviation from Biblical Christianity. The issues here are not trifles; they touch on the *cor ecclesia*.

My hope is that this book will spark earnest debate. Recent years have witnessed cordial and helpful dialogue between Reformed theologians and dispensational theologians. In that dialogue much has been accomplished. This book will escalate the debate. It will surely generate heat. My hope is that in the heat there will be light and that in mature debate our understanding of the gospel will be sharpened and not obscured.

R. C. SPROUL
Orlando, FL
Good Friday—1991

INTRODUCTION

How I have come to write this book is a story in itself. My conversion came about, I believe, through the witness of a dispensationalist. As I grew older in years and in the faith, I realized, however, that Dispensationalism as a system of doctrine was not sound, though it retained the elements of truth by which I came to know Jesus Christ savingly. About Him I learned more soundly two years later. For the following fifty years, I have taught the Reformed faith, leaving Dispensationalism on the back burner of my attention except for occasional references and a seminary course.

Although I had become aware of its serious departure from Biblical teaching, I had not really realized how serious it was until I was teaching a survey course in church history at the Campus Crusade Summer Institute in Fort Collins some years ago. Before that, I had delivered the Griffith-Thomas Lectures at Dallas Theological Seminary and had tried, on various occasions, to persuade some of the professors of Dispensationalism's non-Calvinistic character. Even then, I had not fully realized that the divergence was far more serious than that. Finally, questions from the Campus Crusade students concerning Antinomianism, and particularly the anti-Lordship teaching of Charles Ryrie, brought home to me the realization that contemporary Dispensationalism, like past Dispensationalism, is still committed to the non-negotiable doctrine of Antinomianism.

Not being quite able to believe this, I corresponded with Dr. Ryrie. Troubled by his response, in spite of his sincere denials that he and others were guilty of this deep anti-evangelical heresy, I felt constrained to publish a little *Primer on Dispensationalism* in 1982.

The only serious responses I have had to the *Primer* have argued that Dispensationalism as seen, for example, in Ryrie's *Dispensationalism Today*, is no longer where I located it. This larger work of mine is written to show that there has been no *essential* change. Dispensationalism today, as yesterday, is spurious Calvinism and dubious evangelicalism. If it does not refute my charges and the charges of many others, it cannot long continue to be considered an essentially Christian movement. As John MacArthur says, "There is no salvation except Lordship Salvation."[1]

This is not to say that there is not a great deal of truth being proclaimed by dispensationalists. Dispensationalism affirms the inerrancy of Scripture and the deity of Jesus Christ along with many other important and indispensable verities of the Christian religion.

However, the more truth an *essentially* unsound movement teaches, the more dangerous it becomes — especially for lay Christians. The little ones of Christ's flock hear in Dispensationalism so much of what their Shepherd *does say* that they are terribly confused when they hear the same voice uttering what they know the true Shepherd would *never say.* Liberalism, cults, and the occult do not deceive the sheep because these movements explicitly deny Christ. Dispensationalists are bewildering because they are faithful to such an extent that many simply cannot believe that such people could end up denying Christ. But the sheep must listen carefully. If they do not, they will prove to be little bears rather than little sheep. "My sheep hear my voice," says the Great Shepherd.

No one disputes, of course, that there have been some changes in Dispensationalism, especially in this century and in this country. Changes are evident, for example, in the progression of dispensational study Bibles from *The Scofield Reference Bible* (1909) through *The Scofield Reference Bible* (1917), *The New Scofield Reference Bible*

---

1. Real dispensationalists reciprocate this view. Zane Hodges, for example, does not hesitate to call an attack on Dispensationalism an attack on Christianity. See his *The Gospel Under Siege* (Dallas: Redencion Viva, 1981). Charles Ryrie is also direct. "The message of faith only and the message of faith plus commitment of life cannot both be the gospel; therefore, one of them is *false and comes under the curse of perverting the gospel or preaching another gospel* (Galatians 1:6-9)" [*Balancing the Christian Life* (Chicago: Moody, 1969), p. 170 (emphasis mine)]. That this is not a correct statement of Lordship teaching does not relieve Dr. Ryrie of the responsibility for anathematizing what goes by that name, correctly understood.

This is strong but honest language on both sides. If Calvinism is what dispensationalists say it is, it is a curse. If Dispensationalism is what Calvinists say it is, it is a curse. The present vogue of confounding the meaning of Calvinism and Dispensationalism only delays the inevitable reckoning. The Bible teaches Dispensationalism or Calvinism. It cannot teach both and be the infallibly true Word of God. True dispensationalists and true Calvinists agree on *that.*

(1967), and *The Ryrie Study Bible* (1978). In my opinion, all of the little changes are for the better. Nevertheless, they are minor and their significance lies only in their pointing in a certain direction. But, until Dispensationalism moves instead of merely timidly pointing, it will have to be recognized as spurious Calvinism and dubious or false evangelicalism.

I am grateful to many libraries with which I have had the privilege of consulting while preparing this work. The British Museum and other London libraries were valuable in the English background to which I give only passing attention. The Speer Library of Princeton Theological Seminary had many sources for Plymouth Brethrenism as well as American Dispensationalism. Dallas Theological Seminary Library was, of course, especially valuable, particularly its hundreds of masters and doctoral dissertations. The Roberts Library of Southwestern Baptist Seminary was also useful. While serving as a Yale Divinity School Research Fellow, I had access to the riches of the Sterling and Yale Divinity School libraries. Capital Bible Seminary has also been helpful. All of these and many other shrines of learning were invariably kind and helpful in every way. Along the way, some students helped me in aspects of this research, among whom I would mention David F. Coffin with particular gratitude. John Dulling has helped in gathering bibliographical data. James M. Boice very graciously, thoroughly, and critically read this work. I am deeply grateful to him, though he is in no way responsible for what I have written here. The "Gerstner Project," R. C. Sproul, Robert D. Love, and Bill and Jeanne McKelvey have, by their generous assistance, sped up the production of this work, as has my wife, Edna, by her complete cooperation. Ron Kilpatrick has made especially valuable contributions concerning recent dispensational literature of the eighties. The Rev. John Wilson has also been helpful in research.

PART I

HISTORICAL SKETCH OF DISPENSATIONALISM

ONE

ANTECEDENTS
OF MODERN
DISPENSATIONALISM

I t has been said that, to keep abreast of the times, one must first get abreast the times. In other words, an awareness of the past is crucial if we wish to understand the present and the future. Dispensationalism, a school of thought with a penchant for dividing history into dispensations or epochs, has its own "dispensations," its own history. In this chapter, we will briefly survey anticipations of Dispensationalism prior to the nineteenth century. Subsequent chapters will deal with the definitive development of Dispensationalism in England under John Nelson Darby and with its spread to Europe, Asia, and the United States. Attention will also be paid to the development of Ultra- or consistent Dispensationalism.

The Early Church

There is little point in closely surveying early church history for anticipations of Dispensationalism proper. Dispensationalists themselves claim novelty for their system. They recognize that it was mainly a nineteenth-century phenomenon. Nevertheless, some elements of the system are very old, while, of course, the specific combination is new. Some dispensationalists, such as A. D. Ehlert, claim antiquity for their system.[1]

---

1. Arnold D. Ehlert, "A Bibliography of Dispensationalism," *Bibliotheca Sacra* 101 (1944):319–328, 447–460; *A Bibliographic History of Dispensationalism* (Grand Rapids:

Unfortunately, Ehlert views anyone who used the term *dispensation* as a dispensationalist and thus his bibliography (which cites such foes of Dispensationalism as Jonathan Edwards and Charles Hodge) is almost worthless as a proper bibliography of Dispensationalism.

Still, there is genuine antiquity to some of the various features found in dispensational theology. To point out every occurrence of items in dispensational theory would be very tedious and only slightly profitable. We shall restrict ourselves to one indispensable feature of all Dispensationalism — premillennialism. Every dispensationalist regards this as an indispensable element in his theology.

Indeed, he does more than that by arguing that, in Dispensationalism, premillennialism has its only and necessary logical and systematic support. In other words, consistent premillennialism, the dispensationalist says, implies Dispensationalism. Non-dispensational premillennialists, whom we will call classical or historic premillennialists, do not admit this. All do agree, however, that you cannot have Dispensationalism without premillennialism. Therefore, the presence of premillennialism admits the *possibility* of the presence of Dispensationalism. Conversely, the absence of premillennialism almost proves the absence of Dispensationalism.

The Second Century

Most dispensationalists are prone to claim the whole sub-apostolic age for premillennialism. For example, John Walvoord calmly states that "the most ancient view, that of the church of the first few centuries, was what is known as premillennialism or chiliasm."[2] Such an ambitious statement goes far beyond the evidence. While we grant that Justin Martyr, Hermas, Papias, and Irenaeus may have been premillenarians and that many regard the Epistle of Barnabas as also premillennial, the following considerations need to be noted.

First, it can be shown with respect even to some of these that their theology was clearly not dispensational. For example, Justin and Irenaeus[3]

Baker, 1965). Ehlert later wrote a more precise bibliography: *Brethren Writers, A Checklist with an Introduction to British Literature and Additional Lists* (Grand Rapids: Baker, 1969).

2. John F. Walvoord, "Postribulationism Today, Part II: The Rapture and the Day of the Lord in 1 Thessalonians," *Bibliotheca Sacra* 139 (1982):4.

3. Justin Martyr, "Dialogue with Trypho," in *The Ante-Nicene Fathers*, ed. Alexander Roberts and James Donaldson (Grand Rapids: Eerdmans, 1952; reprint ed.), 1:260–267. Irenaeus, "Against Heresies," in *The Ante-Nicene Fathers*, ed. Alexander Roberts and James Donaldson (Grand Rapids: Eerdmans, 1952; reprint ed.), 1:511, 562.

regarded the church as the fulfillment of the new covenant of Jeremiah 31:31. This fact precludes their Dispensationalism because Dispensationalism regards the church age as not predicted by the Old Testament prophets.

Second, Justin Martyr, though a premillennialist, did not regard premillennialism as a test of orthodoxy, but admitted that some right-minded Christians did not agree with his view on this subject.[4]

Third, it should also be pointed out that chiliasm was widely held among the heretics. Agreeing with the great German church historian (and Jewish convert to Christianity) August Neander, W. G. T. Shedd noted that the premillennialism in Christian churches was just a revival of a Jewish belief that flourished especially between A.D. 160 and A.D. 250. "Chiliasm never formed a part of the general creed of the church. It was diffused from one country (Phrygia), and from a single fountainhead."[5] The arch-heretics Cerinthus, Marcion, and Montanus were premillennialists, as were the apocalyptic books of *Enoch*, *The Twelve Patriarchs*, and the *Sibylline Books*.

Fourth, as intimated by Neander, premillennialism was not the doctrine of the catholic creeds. Furthermore, the creeds appear to be distinctly anti-chiliastic. The Apostles' and Nicene Creeds leave no room for a millennium, and, speaking of Christ's kingdom, the Council of Constantinople affirmed that "of whose kingdom there shall be no end." The Athanasian Creed states: "at whose coming all men shall rise again with their bodies and shall give account for their own works, and they that have done good shall go into life everlasting, and they that have done evil into everlasting fire."[6] Thus, the eschatology of these early creeds is better characterized as amillennial or postmillennial.[7]

Finally, the millennialism of the first few centuries is itself rather ambiguously premillennial. One of the ablest recent premillennial writers, D. H. Kromminga, claims far less for ancient millennialism. He finds Barnabas to be, not only not a premillenarian, but "The

---

4. Justin, "Dialogue," p. 239.

5. W. G. T. Shedd, *A History of Doctrine*, 2 vols. (Minneapolis, Minn.: Klock & Klock, 1978; reprint ed.), 2:642. See also Emil Schurer, *A History of the Jewish People in the Time of Jesus Christ*, 3 vols. in 5 (New York: Scribner, 1896), II/2:170–177.

6. Philip Schaff, ed., *The Creeds of Christendom*, 6th ed., 3 vols. (Grand Rapids: Baker, 1990; reprint ed.), 2:45, 59, 69–70.

7. See James H. Snowden, *The Coming of the Lord* (New York: MacMillan, 1919), p. 20. From a survey of the early creeds, Snowden concludes that they are "postmillennial." This, however, was because he entertained no alternative to premillennialism except postmillennialism.

Father of Amillennial understanding."[8] Of the Apostolic Fathers, Kromminga claims only Papias as a millenarian, but does not find the evidence in his case conclusive.[9] He grants that Justin and Irenaeus acknowledge the presence of millennial eschatologies in the church.[10] He notes that Justin laid the foundation for the Reformed doctrine of the covenants and that he was not a premillennialist.[11] Speaking generally, he says:

> So far as the available evidence goes, there is no ground for ascertaining that Millenarianism was prevalent in the church during the apostolic period, ending with the year 150 A.D. Not only was there very little of it, so far as the literature indicates but what little there was can be traced rather definitely to un-christian Jewish apocalyptic sources.[12]

Others take a similar view of premillennialism in the early church. W. Masselink, for example, finds no chiliasm in Clement of Rome, Ignatius, Polycarp, Athanasius, or Theophilus.[13] Louis Berkhof writes, "It is not correct to say, as Premillenarians do, that it was generally accepted in the first three centuries. The truth of the matter is that the adherents of this doctrine were a rather limited number."[14]

An important treatment of this period by a dispensationalist is found in the Dallas Seminary thesis by Allan P. Boyd.[15] This work indicts the statement by Charles Ryrie that "Premillennialism is the historic faith of the Church."[16] Citing noted dispensationalists Dwight Pentecost, John Walvoord, and others, Boyd points out that the assumption of "continuative premillennialism" is general among dispensationalists. Focusing on Ryrie, Boyd shows that his "premillennialism"

---

8. D. H. Kromminga, *The Millennium in the Church* (Grand Rapids: Eerdmans, 1945), p. 37.

9. Ibid., pp. 43, 48.

10. Ibid., p. 43.

11. Ibid., p. 49. We will see later that Reformed covenants are quite different from dispensational covenants. See Harold O. J. Brown, "Covenant and Dispensation," *Trinity Journal* NS 2 (1981):69–70.

12. Ibid., p. 41.

13. W. Masselink, *Why a Thousand Years?* (Grand Rapids: Eerdmans, 1930), p. 27.

14. Louis Berkhof, *The History of Christian Doctrines* (Grand Rapids: Eerdmans, 1953), p. 270.

15. Allan P. Boyd, "A Dispensational Premillennial Analysis of the Eschatology of the Post-Apostolic Fathers (Until the Death of Justin Martyr)" (Th.M. thesis, Dallas Theological Seminary, 1977).

16. Charles Caldwell Ryrie, *The Basis of the Premillennial Faith* (New York: Loizeaux, 1953), p. 17.

includes rapture thinking, the division of Israel and church, Dispensationalism, literalism, and pretribulationism.

After carefully surveying and citing the texts of the early church fathers, Boyd ends by saying, "It is the conclusion of this thesis that Dr. Ryrie's statement is historically invalid within the chronological framework of this thesis."[17] "These early churchmen were not literalistic; drew no essential distinction between Israel and the Church; did not have a dispensational view of history; though Papias and Justin had a thousand-year kingdom, that was the only similarity to Dispensationalism; did not hold to imminency and pretribulationism; and their eschatological chronology was not synonymous with Dispensationalism's."[18] In fact, the early eschatology was "inimical" to Dispensationalism and was "perhaps" a seminal amillennialism.[19]

What was Ryrie's response? Boyd comments in the preface that, "on the basis of classroom and private discussion, . . . Dr. Charles Ryrie, whose statements regarding the historicity of dispensational premillennialism in the Church Fathers are carefully scrutinized in this thesis, has changed his opinion on these matters. Unfortunately, he has not published these clarifications, and it is hoped that he will do so in the near future."[20]

The Third Century and Beyond

In the period leading up to the Council of Nicea (A.D. 325), millenarianism is not especially conspicuous. Millenarians themselves, who have often made excessive claims for the preceding period, see this time as one when their faith began to wane as the church became more worldly. Nevertheless, there were some strong premillennial voices in this era. Commodus, early third-century bishop, anticipated a thousand years during which the Christians were to be served by sinners. This era was to follow upon the defeat of the Antichrist by Christ. Methodius, an opponent of Origen and his excessive spiritualizing of all prophecy, is often claimed by premillennialists, but Kromminga finds the case for his chiliasm no stronger than for that of Barnabas.[21]

---

17. Boyd, "Analysis," p. 89.
18. Ibid.
19. Ibid., p. 91.
20. Ibid., preface. Larry Crutchfield has tried to offset this somewhat by his study of later church fathers in "Israel and the Church in the Ante-Nicene Fathers," *Bibliotheca Sacra*, 144 (1987):254–276.
21. Kromminga, *Millennium*, p. 71.

On the other hand, Lactantius was, according to Kromminga, the last great representative of premillennialism. "His views are so much like modern premillennial views, that it must be acknowledged, that these were in all their essentials current in the ancient church."[22] Over against these men were anti-millenarians such as Origen, Hippolytus, and Victorinus.

With the coming of Constantine and the favoring of the Christian church, we note a more complete turning from premillennialism. In Tyconius and Augustine, this reached the stage of complete repudiation, though the latter held to the six ages of the world.[23] The Donatist Tyconius was more of an eschatological specialist than Augustine, and his commentary on the book of Revelation influenced Augustine profoundly. But, since most of his essential ideas are taken up and popularized by Augustine, we will consider the latter rather than the former.[24]

Augustine put a virtual end to millennialism for a millennium of church history. Although he had once held to chiliasm, Augustine rejected it because of its carnal features. He did not object particularly to the idea of the Millennium and the saints enjoying it; rather, he insisted that the joys were to be purely spiritual. Fundamentally, however, the Millennium was to be understood as the reign of the saints with Christ during the interadvent period. The first resurrection in Revelation 20:5 refers to regeneration, and only the second to the physical resurrection. Satan's being restrained refers to his inability to prevent the church from gathering souls from the nations. His binding took place at the first coming of Christ which began the world conquest by the gospel. The church is the kingdom. Here, the saints reign with Christ over their own lusts and their church.[25] The millennial thinking of Pope Gregory the Great, who is generally known as the popularizer of Augustine, and through whom Augustine strongly influenced the Middle Ages, followed the basic pattern of the Bishop of Hippo in expecting the end of the church age to issue in immortality.

---

22. Ibid., p. 76.
23. Aurelius Augustine, "On the Catechising of the Uninstructed," trans. S. D. F. Salmond, in *A Select Library of the Nicene & Post-Nicene Fathers of the Christian Church*, first series, Philip Schaff, ed. (Grand Rapids: Eerdmans, 1977; reprint ed.), 3:282–314.
24. For the work of Tyconius, see LeRoy Edwin Froom, *The Prophetic Faith of Our Fathers*, 4 vols. (Washington, D.C.: Review and Herald, 1950), 1:465–473.
25. See Aurelius Augustine, "City of God," trans. Marcus Dods, in *A Select Library of the Nicene & Post-Nicene Fathers of the Christian Church*, first series, Philip Schaff, ed. (Grand Rapids: Eerdmans, 1977; reprint ed.), 2:421–451.

Glancing back at the early church we note that there was some premillennialism which, while clearly existing at first, died out after Augustine. We must also note that the chiliasm of the early church can in no way be characterized as *dispensational* premillennialism. Advocates of premillennialism in the early church lacked dispensational eschatological distinctives such as the notion of a pretribulational rapture. Furthermore, they affirmed beliefs, such as the nature of the relationship between Israel and the church, which are fundamentally incompatible with Dispensationalism.

The Middle Ages

The medieval period was not noted for its eschatological writings although we will consider a few typical positions taken during this era. Some theologians, such as Thomas Aquinas, saw the reign of the church as the millennial glory. In direct opposition to this, the Franciscan Spirituals, such as Ubertino of Casale and Peter Olivi, regarded the "Babylon" of Revelation 18 to be the church and the "Beast" as the papacy. This view became rather prominent during the latter part of the medieval period. Some, such as Hildegard, looked for the fulfillment of apocalyptic hopes in the reform of the church.

Most notable of the eschatologists was the Cistercian monk Joachim of Flora (c. A.D. 1135–1202). He saw history as three ages — the age of the Father (the law), the age of the Son (the gospel), and the age of the Holy Spirit (monasticism with its spiritual earnestness). This last period was the proper fulfillment of Christ's promise of the coming of the Holy Spirit. His position was opposed by Aquinas, and in 1260 (the very year that the third age was to begin according to Joachim) his writings were condemned at the Council of Arles. These views lived on, however, among the Joachimites and the Spiritual Franciscans. Donnino, for example, saw the age of the Spirit in the mendicant orders and regarded Joachim's writings as the eternal gospel.

The Reformation Period

With the Reformation came a resurgence of eschatological thinking and preaching, but the Reformation-era creeds were substantially the same with regard to eschatology as the creeds of the early church. They usually affirmed that Christ would return to judge the living and the dead and then establish the eternal state. This is true of such creeds as the Tetrapolitan Confession, the First and Second Confessions of Basle, the Second Helvetic Confession, the Heidelberg Catechism, the Belgic Confession, the Canons of Trent, the Orthodox Confession of 1642, the Westminster Confession of Faith, and the Thirty-Nine Articles of the Church of England. Article seventeen of the Lutheran Augsburg Confession condemned the "Jewish notion" that, before the resurrection, the saints should occupy this world, as does the Reformed Second Helvetic Confession: "We also do reject the Jewish dream of a Millennium, or golden age on earth, before the last judgment."[26]

The Second Helvetic also affirms that

> "Christ will come again to judgment, when the wickedness of the world shall have reached the highest point, and Antichrist corrupted the true religion. He will destroy Antichrist, and judge the quick and the dead (II Thess. ii. 8; Acts xvii. 51,52; I Thess. iv. 17). The believers will enter into the mansions of the blessed; the unbelievers, with the devil and his angels, will be cast into everlasting torment (Matt. xxv. 41; II Tim. ii. 11; II Pet. iii. 7)."[27]

John Calvin himself may never have written a commentary on the book of Revelation but that does not imply indifference to apocalyptic notions. According to Calvin, the numbers "144 thousand" (Revelation 7:4, 14:1), "666" (Revelation 13:18) and "one thousand" (Revelation 20:2) were not to be taken literally. Of those who did so construe them, "their fiction is too puerile to deserve refutation." Calvin dismissed such teaching as a childish fantasy without scriptural support.

The Post-Reformation Period

The modern period has seen a great deal of eschatological activity, especially in the form of the resurgence of premillennialism. While the Lutheran, Reformed, and Roman Catholic traditions remained fundamentally a- or postmillennial, premillennialism gained standing within these traditions. Johannes Bengel, for example, made premillennialism respectable in the Lutheran church because he took away the imminency doctrine often associated with it. Jung-Stilling effectively introduced premillennialism into the Reformed communions. The Jesuit Ribera,

---

26. Second Helvetic Confession, chapter 11.
27. Ibid.

who died in 1591, expected the Antichrist to come as a Jew who would reign three and a half years.

John Alsted, one of the great seventeenth-century Reformed theologians, wrote a solid volume defending premillennialism. His prestige tended to overcome suspicion arising from his deviation from amillennial orthodoxy. This tends to prove that, though chiliasm was not a standard feature of Calvinism (detested, as we saw, by Calvin), it could be accommodated within the school. Since that time, it has become much more common.

Johannes Cocceius (1603–1669), was especially significant. Kromminga enumerates quite a number of dispensational features. First, he posited seven dispensations (which, however, differ widely from those of Scofield). Second, he placed great stress on the prophetic literature. Third, he felt that there is a one-to-one correspondence between prophetic prediction and its historical fulfillment. Fourth, he stressed typology. Fifth, he was especially interested in unfulfilled prophecy. Sixth, he did not regard the Sabbath as binding (though this position has been taken by many non-dispensationalists, it is *always* held by dispensationalists). Seventh, he distinguished between *aphesis* (the forgiveness of sin) and the *paresis* (the overlooking of sin) of Romans 3:25, believing that the Old Testament saints had an imperfect justification. Eighth, he was tinged with chiliasm. Ninth, he believed that peace will come, the Jews will be converted, Babel (the Roman Catholic church) will perish, the kingdom of Christ will appear in which all the nations will serve, and the gospel will be preached in all the world. All this is to come suddenly at the time when the anti-Christian power will have reached its highest point.[28]

Our comment on all this is that it hardly proves Cocceius to be a modern dispensationalist. Many of these features have been held by classical premillennialists. He comes closest to Dispensationalism in his stress on the difference between *aphesis* and *paresis* and his insistence that the Old Testament saints, who had received only the *paresis* of their sins, were not fully justified. But, even at this point, we recognize that Romanists, Lutherans, Episcopalians, and others (believing that the Old Testament saints were not ready at death to go to heaven because Christ had not yet offered up the sacrifice of Himself), seem to

---

28. Kromminga, *Millennium*, pp. 204ff. See also C. S. McCoy, "Johannes Cocceius: Federal Theologian," *Scottish Journal of Theology* 16 (1963):352–370; "The Covenant Theology of Johannes Cocceius (Ph.D. Dissertation, Yale University, 1957). See also Michael A. Harbin, "The Hermeneutics of Covenant Theology," *Bibliotheca Sacra* 143 (1986):246–259.

be assuming a kind of imperfect justification of the Old Testament saints. Nevertheless, Cocceius' combination of so many features characteristically found in Dispensationalism, while hardly justifying Kromminga's term "father of dispensationalism," does make him very significant in its history.[29]

Kromminga seems to find other forerunners of modern Dispensationalism as well. F. A. Lampe, the eighteenth-century theologian, is regarded as a dispensationalist. He, too, had dispensations but more than this is necessary to prove the presence of Dispensationalism. Attention must also be paid to the *theology* which underlies an historical schema of dispensations.

While premillennialism in the eighteenth century was becoming more prominent, it was free of the modern dispensational theology. Unfortunately, this point has been missed by those who seek to enlist eighteenth-century figures such as Isaac Watts as dispensationalists. Ehlert, commenting on Watts' *The Harmony of all the Religions which God ever Prescribed to Men and all Dispensations Toward Them*, remarked that here we find "exactly the outline of the first six dispensations that have been widely publicized by the late Dr. C. I. Scofield in his notes."[30] Ehlert does not show, however, that the dispensational *theology* of Scofield underlay the divisions of Watts. Dr. Ryrie quotes similarly from Watts. He also notes that, except for the Millennium, it is exactly like *The Scofield Reference Bible*. Ryrie concludes, "This was a period of developing dispensationalism."[31]

Rather than proving Watts' alleged Dispensationalism, the work in question shows how pure a *covenant* theologian Isaac Watts was. Thus, it is not surprising that Watts calls the "Mosaical dispensation, or the Jewish Religion" nothing less than "a fourth edition of the covenant of grace."[32] Writing as if he were forewarning of John Nelson

---

29. Rutgers' evaluation is probably more appropriate: "As a more representative characterization of this novel doctrine [Dispensationalism] I would prefer to style it Coccejanism run riot . . . several covenants, each one representing a specific method of God's dealing with men during that particular period." William H. Rutgers, *Premillennialism in America* (Goes, Holland: Oosterbaan & Le Cointre, 1930), p. 172. C. Norman Kraus, *Dispensationalism in America* (Richmond: John Knox, 1958), pp. 57–59, notes Cocceius' significant departures from Reformed orthodoxy as follows: first, many covenants of which the covenant of grace is only one; second, the covenant of grace is not said to be one and the same in all dispensations; third, the church is not the climax of redemptive history.

30. Ehlert, "Bibliography," p. 454.

31. Charles Caldwell Ryrie, *Dispensationalism Today* (Chicago: Moody, 1965), p. 73.

32. Ibid., p. 55.

Darby and his Dispensationalism, Watts observes about our present "Christian dispensation" that "this is the last *edition of the covenant of grace.*"[33]

A great weakness of Ehlert's *Bibliography* and of C. F. Lincoln's "The Development of the Covenant Theory" is the failure to demonstrate the real points at issue.[34] Both seem to be ready to settle for the mere occurrence of certain terms as proof of a great deal more than the mere terms necessarily signify. As we have seen, Augustine spoke of six ages and Jonathan Edwards had more.

L. S. Chafer also suffered from this inexplicable misunderstanding of Edwards when he wrote, "in his day dispensational distinctions were a living topic of theological discussion."[35] This is true but rather irrelevant. More to the point is Edwards' contention that "the work of redemption is a work that God carries on from the fall of man to the end of the world."[36] This "work" is done at different times, periods, ages, dispensations, but all are the redemption of God's elect, the church, through the covenant of grace.

While it is highly doubtful that we have any real dispensationalists in this period before the nineteenth century, we certainly have a goodly number of premillennialists. Indeed, premillennialism became very prominent and even dominant among many who stressed eschatology and wrote on it.

As we conclude this brief survey of millennialism prior to the nineteenth century, we observe its general character in contrast to dispensational millenarianism. It is worth noting that dispensational premillennialism represents quite an innovation over against historic premillennialism and traditional Christian eschatology in general.

One area of innovation is in the interpretation of the book of Revelation. Dispensationalism uniformly follows the futurist interpretation. Everything from Revelation chapter 4 through the end of the book is yet to be fulfilled. While classic millenarians have seen the prophecies of Revelation fulfilled in various historical men and movements, dispensationalists regard the Beast, Antichrist, seals and trumpets, and so forth as yet to be manifested.

---

33. Ibid., p. 562 (emphasis mine).

34. Charles Fred Lincoln, "The Development of the Covenant Theory," in *Bibliotheca Sacra* 100 (1943):134–135.

35. L. S. Chafer, "Dispensationalism," *Bibliotheca Sacra* 93 (1936):392–393.

36. *The Works of Jonathan Edwards, with a Memoir by Sereno E. Dwight*, 2 vols., rev. and corrected by Edward Hickman (Edinburgh: The Banner of Truth Trust, 1987; reprint ed.), 1:534.

The dispensational tendency toward innovation is also seen in the details of its eschatology. While classical premillenarians agreed with post- and amillennialists that the church would suffer through the Tribulation, virtually all dispensationalists are pretribulationists. That is, dispensationalists believe that Christ will return *secretly* for His saints prior to the onset of the Tribulation. This doctrine of a pretribulational return leads dispensationalists to speak in reality of three comings of Christ—the Incarnation, the coming of Christ *for* His saints (the Rapture), and the return of Christ *with* His saints (the Revelation). This stands in marked contrast to the historic view, held by all except dispensationalists, that there would be only two comings—the Incarnation and the return or Second Advent.

Another dispensational innovation is evident in its anti-covenantalism. This is a peculiar way to designate this new view for it is pro-covenantal in a sense. It rejects the traditional two-covenant schema of law and grace in favor of many covenants and dispensations. While the traditional view sees the covenant of works as ended by the fall of Adam from his probation and the covenant of grace as then initiated and continued through the Old and New Testaments and into eternity, Dispensationalism finds many covenants and regards this unity of the covenant of grace in different dispensations as a fundamental error.

There are really more than new factors here—this is a new system of theology. It can hardly be said that the eschatological is even the most important element in the system, although it is the most discussed and the most conspicuous. As we shall see in our study of this movement, it has a new theology, anthropology, soteriology, ecclesiology, eschatology, and a new systematic arrangement of all of these as well.[37] Dr. Wick Broomall, in an unpublished syllabus entitled "The Bible and the Future," gives a helpful list of ten distinguishing features of modern Dispensationalism as over against the older premillennialism:

1. Older premillennialism taught that the church was in the forevision of the Old Testament prophecy; Dispensationalism teaches that the church is hardly, if at all, in the Old Testament prophets.

2. Older premillennialism taught that the great burden of Old Testament prophecy was the coming of Christ to die (at the First Advent) and the kingdom age (at the Second Advent). Dispensationalism says that the great burden of Old Testament prophecy is the kingdom of the Jews.

---

37. See Kromminga, *Millennium*, pp. 242, 252, 302, 303.

3. Older premillennialism taught that the First Advent was the specific time for Christ to die for man's sin; Dispensationalism teaches that the kingdom (earthly) should have been set up at the First Advent for that was the predicted time of its coming.

4. Older premillennialism taught that the present age of grace was designed by God and predicted in the Old Testament; Dispensationalism holds that the present age was unforeseen in the Old Testament and thus is a "great parenthesis" introduced because the Jews rejected the kingdom.

5. Older premillennialism taught that one may divide time in any way desirable so long as one allows for a millennium after the Second Advent; Dispensationalism maintains that the only allowable way to divide time is in seven dispensations. The present age is the sixth such dispensation; the last one will be the millennial age after the Second Advent. It is from this division of time that Dispensationalism gets its name.

6. Older premillennialism taught that the Second Advent was to be one event; Dispensationalism holds that the Second Advent will be in two sections—"the Rapture" and "the Revelation." Between these two events they put the (to them) unfulfilled seventieth week (seven years) of Daniel 9:23–27, which they call "the Great Tribulation."

7. Older premillennialism taught that certain signs must precede the Second Advent; Dispensationalism teaches that no sign precedes the "rapture-stage" of the Second Advent, which may occur "at any moment." However, there are signs that precede the "revelation-stage" of the Second Advent. The "Rapture" could occur "at any moment," but the "Revelation" must take place after the seven years of the Great Tribulation. The first stage is undated and unannounced; the second stage is dated and announced.

8. Older premillennialism had two resurrections—the righteous before the Millennium; the unrighteous after the Millennium. Dispensationalism has introduced a third resurrection—"tribulation-saints" at the "revelation-stage" of the Second Advent.

9. Older premillennialism usually held what is called the "historical-symbolic" view of the book of Revelation. This view makes Revelation a picture in symbolic form of the main events in the present age. Dispensationalism holds generally to the "futurist" view of the book of Revelation, which view makes almost the whole book (especially chapters 4 to 19) a literal description of events to take place during "the Great Tribulation" or Daniel's seventieth week, which Dispensationalism considers as yet unfulfilled.

10. The general attitude of older premillennialism was on the whole mild and reverent in its approach to Scripture. There have been some outstanding scholars who have been persuaded that the premillennial is the correct view. In contrast, Dispensationalism has assumed a far more dogmatic attitude. It has introduced a number of novelties in prophetic interpretation that the church never heard of until about a century ago.

TWO

MODERN DISPENSATIONALISM IN ENGLAND

The Plymouth Brethren movement, from which modern Dispensationalism arose, began in the second decade of the nineteenth century.[1] From one perspective, it may be seen as part of the general Independent movement which had been firmly established in England since the Puritan period. Like the earlier Independents, who viewed the established Church of England as either apostate or severely defective, the Brethren were also a reaction against the established church.

Precursors of the Brethren Movement

A specific independent movement, known as the Walkerite group, began in 1804 when a Mr. Walker left the Anglican Church. Though

---

1. Napoleon Noel, *The History of the Brethren*, 2 vols. (Denver: Knapp, 1936), 1:20. Historical investigation is more difficult because secondary works are neither numerous, nor easily accessible, nor written with much documentation. We shall rely primarily, though critically, on Noel's work. Other important sources for this chapter include W. Blair Neatby, *The History of the Plymouth Brethren* (London: Hodder & Stoughton, 1901); H. A. Ironside, *A Historical Sketch of the Brethren Movement* (Grand Rapids: Zondervan, 1942); and W. G. Turner, *John Nelson Darby* (London: C. A. Hammond, 1951). Attention should also be drawn to other helpful studies including F. Roy Coad, *A History of the Brethren Movement* (Exeter: Paternoster, 1968); Harold Hamlyn Rowden, *Who Are the Brethren and Does It Matter?* (Exeter: Paternoster, 1986); and

his movement lapsed after a decade, his ideas lived on in the Dublin area. Furthermore, it seems that this spirit of dissatisfaction with existing forms of organized religion was fairly widespread. It has been observed by Noel, Ironside, and others that from 1812 to 1820 a correspondence was carried on between believers in New York City and Great Britain who were dissatisfied with the contemporary condition of the organized churches.[2]

Rennie has a neat summary of other factors present at this time:

> As historicist pre-millennialists and all pre-millennialists were such between 1815 and 1830—they saw a number of signs that indicated the Second Coming. And it appeared as if these signs were being fulfilled before their eyes. One sign was the conversion of Jews, and the aggressive ministry after 1815 of the L.S.P.G.J. with its trickle of Jewish converts convinced many that the turning of the Jews as a whole to Christ was about to take place. . . . Another sign of the Second Advent was the preaching of the Gospel throughout the world, and the partial decline, at least, of opposing forces. The modern missionary movement provided the former, although the pre-millennialists were not as imaginatively exuberant about its achievement as other Evangelicals. Events in Ireland also suggested that God was calling many out of the Roman Catholic Church. During the 1820's many Irish Roman Catholic children began to attend schools provided and directed by Protestants where the Bible was taught.[3]

The movement which concerns us seems to have been precipitated by the dissatisfaction of one man with an Independent church in Dublin. Dr. Edward Cronin, who had been converted from Roman Catholicism, had at first enjoyed the fellowship of this independent church. However, when it came time to take communion, he discovered that he was not considered qualified until he joined some visible and independent church. It did not seem right to him that he was welcome to fellowship but not to the communion service. Cronin then withdrew together with Edward Wilson, and these were later joined by H. Hutch-

---

Graham Carter and Brian Mills, *The Brethren Today, A Factual Survey* (Exeter: Paternoster, 1980). See also Nathan DeLynn, *Roots, Renewal and the Brethren* (Pasadena: Hope Publishing House, 1986); G. H. Lang, *Anthony Norris Groves* (Miami Springs, Fl.: Schoettle, 1988); and Robert H. Krapohl, "A Search for Purity, the Controversial Life of John Nelson Darby" (Ph.D. dissertation, Baylor University, 1980).

    2. Noel, *History*, 1:20; Ironside, *Historical Sketch*, p. 8.

    3. Ian S. Rennie, "Nineteenth-Century Roots," in *Handbook of Biblical Prophecy*, ed. Carl E. Armerding and W. Ward Gasque (Grand Rapids: Baker, 1977), p. 46.

inson, William Stokes, J. Parnell, J. G. Bellett, and J. N. Darby. They fellowshiped apart from an organized Christian community.

This would appear to be the actual beginning of the Plymouth Brethren as they were later to be called. One of their foremost principles was already in evidence—where two or three are gathered together in Christ's name, there is He in the midst of them. This gathering together of believers is the only church there actually is. That no ordained minister was necessary was a second of their principles. Only the third fundamental principle of early Brethrenism was still lacking—the breaking of bread together by those who had thus assembled in the name of Jesus.

The Influence of John Nelson Darby

When the first breaking of bread by this group took place is not easily determined. Some think it was prior to the appearance of John Nelson Darby among them. Others argue that he introduced this feature. Andrew Miller is quoted approvingly by Napoleon Noel, who is a strong advocate of the primacy of Darby in the founding of the movement:

> So the first breaking of bread was in 1826, and the first formal meeting for that purpose was in a private house in Dublin in 1827 (as Mr. Andrew Miller says), and the first meeting in a public meeting place was in 1830.[4]

Nevertheless, Darby did not join the group before 1827 at the earliest, and some think it was not until 1828. Still, Noel argues strenuously that it was Darby who introduced the practice of breaking of bread by these assemblies. "Nothing is easier to prove," Noel writes, "than that it was at Mr. Darby's suggestion that they broke bread together."[5] Noel himself seems inconsistent in saying that the Brethren were breaking bread together in 1826, although Darby, who was supposed to have introduced the practice, did not join them until 1827. In the light of this inconsistency in Noel's evidence, we incline to believe that Darby was not the innovator at this point, and that the movement was under way before he joined it in its early years.

---

4. Noel, *History*, 1:25.
5. Ibid., p. 54.

This fact, however, does not vitiate Noel's contention that Darby was in a real sense the founder of the movement. As we shall see, it was Darby's views on ecclesiology, communion, and eschatology which shaped the Brethren movement. Noel writes:

> Mr. W. Blair Neatby's view is similar to that of another, who claims that Dr. Cronin learned certain things before J. N. Darby, "but only in the germ and much simplicity." But could every person who had watched the steam raise the lid of a boiling tea kettle claim to be the inventor of the steam engine?[6]

There may still be some question whether Darby was the founder or only the chief systematizer and teacher of the movement; there is, however, no question whatever that he was the leading figure and has remained to this day the chief influence. We turn, therefore, our attention to his story and how he came to be related to the movement and quickly rose to the leadership of it.[7]

The youngest son of John Darby, of Leap Castle, Ireland, John Nelson Darby was born in London in 1800, the same year as Pusey, Newman, and Macaulay. Following his father's wishes, he studied law at Westminster College, and he received his B.A. degree from Trinity College, Dublin. A change in career plans led him to study for the ministry, and he was ordained to the Anglican priesthood in 1826.

Assigned to a primitive parish in the mountainous country of county Wicklow in Ireland, Darby was an earnest priest but grew increasingly dissatisfied with the church he served. The formality and externalism of the church were depressing to him, and he concluded that "Christendom, as seen externally was really the world and could not be considered as 'the church.' "[8]

---

6. Ibid., pp. 54–56.

7. In addition to the standard life by W. G. Turner (see note 1 above), we call attention to the recent brief studies by William Cox, *An Examination of Dispensationalism* (Phillipsburg, New Jersey: Presbyterian and Reformed, 1979); Clarence B. Bass, *Backgrounds to Dispensationalism: Its Historical Genesis and Ecclesiastical Implications* (Grand Rapids: Baker, 1960). Particularly interesting is the evaluation by E. E. Whitfield, "Plymouth Brethren," *The New Schaff-Herzog Encyclopedia of Religious Knowledge*. We note that this writer sees Darby as the main Plymouth Brethren influence and that in their eyes Augustine, Luther, and Calvin were "mere ciphers." See also L. V. Crutchfield, "The Doctrine of Ages and Dispensations as the Foundation of the Published Works of John Nelson Darby (1800–1881) (Ph.D. dissertation, Drew University, 1985).

8. J. N. Darby, letter to F. A. G. Tholuck quoted in Noel, *History*, 1:35.

Darby's thoughts on these matters were further crystallized by a statement, to which Darby took great exception, from the Anglican Archbishop of Dublin, calling for the establishment of the Anglican Church as the state church of Ireland. This was a transparent attempt to protect the interests of Protestants in Ireland, and Darby could not understand, as J. G. Bellett noted, why "Ministers of Christ in doing their business as witnesses against the world for a rejected Jesus, should, on meeting resistance from the enemy, turn round and seek security from the world."[9]

About this time (1827–28), Darby fell from his horse and, while convalescing in Dublin, he came into contact with the little band of original Brethren.[10] As indicated above, it is difficult to ascertain whether the Lord's Supper was already being celebrated or whether Darby himself introduced the practice to the group. It is also not clear whether Darby at this time left the Anglican Church, nor is it apparent exactly when he left Ireland.[11] We do know that he went to Oxford, Plymouth, and Paris in the following years.

In 1831, the first Powerscourt meeting, a sort of symposium on Biblical prophecy, was hosted by the wealthy Lady Powerscourt. These meetings, of which several were held, had a great impact on Darby's developing thought on this subject. Darby resided at Oxford for a time before moving to Plymouth where he worked with B. W. Newton, another Brethren leader. The influence of the Brethren at Plymouth was apparently profound on Darby. He wrote a short while later that "Plymouth has altered the face of Christianity to me."[12]

The year 1831 also saw the beginning of Darby's extensive publishing efforts in the field of prophetic interpretation. We know that he began his considerations of the Second Coming the following year although the origins of his "secret Rapture" doctrine are unclear. The doctrine itself seems to have emerged at the Powerscourt prophetic conferences although who actually originated it is a matter of debate. Darby's prominence at the Powerscourt meetings has led to the supposition that he is responsible for it but, Clarence Bass questions this. Jon Zens

9. J. G. Bellett, quoted in Noel, *History*, 1:29.

10. See Turner, *Darby*, p. 17.

11. Neatby, *History*, p. 17, thinks this is the probable year. See also Friedrich Loofs, "Darby, John Nelson," *Realencyklopaedie fuer Protestantische Theologie und Kirche*.

12. John Nelson Darby, *Letters of J. N. D.*, 3 vols. (London: G. Morrish, 1914–15), 3:492. Loofs, *Realencyklopaedie*, p. 487, considers the importance of Plymouth so great for Darby that he writes, "So far from Darby being the originator of the Plymouth Brethren, they showed him the way."

attributes the idea of a secret, pretribulational Rapture to Edward Irving while Dave MacPherson concludes that it arose through the charismatic prophecies of Margaret MacDonald, a visionary in the Irvingite group, though Darby· later concluded that she was deluded.[13]

As the numbers of Brethren increased, the scope of Darby's ministry also widened. In 1833, Darby came into contact with George Mueller, of Bristol orphanage fame, who was also an early brother. Darby's relation to the Anglican church at this point is still not clear. Darby does indicate that, in 1833, he still attended the Church of England ministry.[14] It is probable, at this point, that Brethren weddings and funerals were still done by ministers.

During this period, Darby, who had been disinherited by his father, received his uncle's legacy.[15] This inheritance subsequently allowed Darby to devote his considerable energies and talents to his ministry without further monetary worries.

In 1837, Darby travelled on the continent, visiting Switzerland, eastern France, and possibly Geneva before returning to Plymouth. His labors in Europe began to show fruit, and a Brethren *Gemeinde* (congregation) was formed in 1839 in Elbersfeld, Germany.

Returning to Plymouth in 1845, Darby found a developed clericalism in the Brethren assembly there. B. W. Newton and J. L. Harris were recognized as elders, and they alternated Sabbaths in their preaching. After considerable controversy, Darby and others withdrew from the Plymouth assembly on the last Sabbath of 1845. Establishing a pattern that was soon to be played out repeatedly, the split spread to other Brethren groups in England. The embers of this controversy were again fanned into flames in 1848 when the Bethesda assembly in Bristol received some members from the Plymouth assembly. Darby, arguing for a strict principle of "separation," maintained that this act constituted a toleration of the Plymouth errors and that such toleration tainted the Bristol assembly. This controversy was the origin of the

---

13. Bass, *Backgrounds*, p. 41; Jon Zens, *Dispensationalism: A Reformed Inquiry Into Its Leading Figures and Features* (Phillipsburg, N.J.: Presbyterian and Reformed, 1980), p. 18; Dave MacPherson, *The Unbelievable Pre-Trib Origin* (Kansas City, Mo.: Heart of America Bible Society, 1973) and *The Incredible Cover-Up* (Medford, Oreg.: Omega Publications, 1975). Thomas Ice responds, from a dispensational perspective, to MacPherson's claims in "Why the Doctrine of the Pretribulational Rapture Did Not Begin with Margaret MacDonald," *Bibliotheca Sacra* 147 (1990):155–168. Robert H. Gundry gives a rather detailed history of the rise of pretribulationism in *The Church and the Tribulation* (Grand Rapids: Zondervan, 1973), p. 185f.

14. Darby, *Letters*, 1:20.

15. Loofs, *Realencyklopaedie*, p. 474.

split, which continues to the present, between the so-called "Open" and the "Closed" or exclusive Brethren.

Darby continued his extensive ministry of writing and speaking, and he travelled extensively in England and Europe. In 1864–65, he visited the United States twice. Through these visits, the 16th and Walnut Avenue Presbyterian Church, which was pastored by James H. Brookes, became a chief center for the dissemination of Dispensationalism in America.

In 1866 a rift developed between Darby and some of his friends over his peculiar views on the sufferings of Christ (these will be considered later when we consider the soteriology of Dispensationalism). This was only one of many Brethren conflicts which occurred during this period over a variety of church order and doctrinal issues.

Darby died in 1882 in Bournemouth, England, and he was buried there with eight to ten thousand persons present at the service. Seven hundred exclusive congregations existed at the time of his death—a remarkable testimony to Darby's energy and dedication.

The personal legacy of Darby is mixed. He is universally recognized as a man of exceptional talents and industry. His favorable financial condition permitted him to cultivate both, and he gave himself generously and influentially in the service of the Brethren. On the other hand, Darby showed little patience with those who disagreed with him or who failed to understand his arguments. That he could be ungracious and scathing in his criticism is evident in the incident where, when the great evangelist Dwight L. Moody failed to grasp a point, Darby turned to a bystander and remarked, "I am here to supply exposition not brains."[16] This kind of episode explains why Darby was seen to possess both Adams in force.

Brethren History—Dissension and Schism

Having glanced at the life of J. N. Darby, we turn back now to pick up the more general history of the movement. As we have seen, the Plymouth group was the prominent branch of the new Brethren assemblies for the first decade and a half of the movement's existence. By the year 1845, when B. W. Newton was the leading spirit in this assembly, it had reached an attendance of twelve hundred. It had not only an imposing membership, but also an outstanding leader in Newton.

---

16. Turner, *Darby*, p. 21.

B. W. Newton and the Issue of Clericalism

B. W. Newton stood for the better things in the denominations from which most of the Brethren had come. For one thing, he recognized the need for church order and discipline. He himself seemed capable of leading and was recognized as such by most of the people at Plymouth. Alternating with J. L. Harris, he preached regularly. Impromptu speaking (into which the Spirit may have been thought to have led others) was discouraged. The very arrangement of the assembly room revealed this "clericalism" of Newton.

In another and even more important respect, Newton attempted to preserve the sounder tradition of the denominations from which the Brethren had come. That is to say, he tried to prevent the virus of dispensational thinking from fatally infecting the Brethren movement at the outset. Newton was, in fact, a classical or historic premillennialist. Some of his antidispensational doctrines include the following. First, the church consists of the body of the redeemed throughout all ages and includes both the Old and New Testament saints. Second, the church's New Testament form was definitely predicted in the Old Testament and was not a mystery in the sense of being utterly unknown before the revelation through the Apostle Paul. Third, Daniel's seventieth week was fulfilled in Christ's life and death and did not await its fulfillment after the Rapture. Fourth, the church would go through the Great Tribulation. In addition to these fundamental differences from later dispensational ecclesiology and eschatology, Newton's soteriology also differed, at least from Darby.

J. N. Darby and some others, after futile efforts to change the situation at the Ebrington Street assembly, withdrew near the end of 1845. In April of 1846, a meeting of Brethren from various places was held in London and again in 1847. These meetings definitely denounced the situation at Plymouth and insisted on separation from it.[17] Newton himself came to London in 1848 and taught in the Compton Street assembly, but he continued occasionally to return to Plymouth.

Bethesda and the Issue of Separation

If the first major split of the Brethren history is considered as having occurred in 1846 at Plymouth, this rift widened considerably two years later at Bethesda. Some members from Plymouth who had not sepa-

---

17. See Noel, *History* 1:211, note.

rated with Darby came to Bristol. They were received into the fellowship of the Bethesda assembly there, but the elders withdrew in protest, contending that the receiving of these persons was a condoning of the Plymouth error. The *Letter of the Ten* was written in reply to this charge, arguing that the persons received into the Bristol fellowship had not been in agreement with developments at Plymouth and therefore were not contaminated by them.[18] In the meantime, Darby had returned from France and wrote his *Bethesda Circular.* He rejected the position of the Ten as compromise, arguing that it was a duty not only to disapprove of Plymouth, but to separate from it and to have nothing to do with those who did not separate from it. Brethren leader George Mueller, who had been a friend of Newton, defended the *Letter of the Ten*, and the majority of the Bristol congregation also did. About fifty or sixty members withdrew, however, and the division extended throughout the fellowships. This was the origin of the "Open" versus the "Closed" or exclusive Brethren.

In spite of all the divisions, the Brethren movement continued to grow. Revivals in England tended to benefit the more scripturally oriented Brethren as theological liberalism tended to weaken the established churches. Church of England losses often became Brethren gains.

The Darbyites have continued to the present day. Holding to exclusive principles, they remain one of the two major divisions of the Brethren movement, the Bethesda or Open Brethren being the other and somewhat larger division. The principles which are still championed by the exclusive Brethren are that every church should have elders who decide the time of meeting and who are qualified to say whether what is said is true or not. Discipline, however, is to be settled by the whole assembly. The Lord's Supper is received weekly and liberty of ministry is associated with it.[19] The exclusives, although smaller in membership and lesser in activity than the Open Brethren, have had the outstanding teachers in men such as Darby, William Kelly, and C. H. Mackintosh. All of these were gifted men, but Charles Haddon Spurgeon could say of Kelly what was true of all, "Kelly, a man for the universe has narrowed his mind by Darbyism."[20]

Exclusivism is based on 2 John 10-11, and is applied to those in error and all in any way related to them.[21] Noel states their outlook in no uncertain terms:

---

18. See Ironside, *Historical Sketch*, p. 60 for the text of this statement.
19. Neatby, *History*, pp. 58–59.
20. Cited in Turner, *Darby*, p. 51.
21. See Neatby, *History*, p. 186.

"Exclusive" here [those separating from Plymouth at the time of Newton] means the corporate position and unity of all scripturally gathered assemblies, meeting in separation from iniquity and from vessels to dishonor. (See 2 Tim. 2:19–22; 2 John 10, 11). They collectively and effectively exclude evil.[22]

The Bethesda group has continued, grown, and divided. It represents today the largest wing of the Brethren movement, and it has not had quite as many divisions as its exclusive rival. The three major offshoots are the F. Vernal group, the Philip Mauro group, and the Needed Truth movement. The Open Brethren have spread extensively and have been quite active in missions. Today they are found in Britain, China, India, the Straits Settlements, Africa, New Zealand, Europe, and North and South America.

While they are considered much looser than the Closed Brethren, they hold tenaciously to the general principles of the movement and can divide on some extremely fine points. For example, Harry Ironside, who was at one time a member, tells us that the use of a platform has torn some of these assemblies apart because some have thought the platform is a symbol of the dreaded clericalism.[23] They have also put out members for "adultery," which is defined as attending some meeting for Christian testimony other than a Brethren assembly.[24]

In spite of their fear of clericalism and insistence on not being a church or having a ministry, they carefully select their leaders before the meeting.[25] Harry Ironside bluntly notes the irony of this:

And each fellowship of Brethren is as truly a system as any other body of believers. If any one doubts it let him venture to act on his own initiative or as he believes the Spirit leads, contrary to custom, and he will soon find out how sectarian an unsectarian company of Christians can be. . . . In their protest against sectarianism they have become the narrowest and most bigoted sect on earth, and are truly described in Scriptures as living in malice and envy, hateful, and hating one another.[26]

---

22. Noel, *History*, 1:219.
23. Ironside, *Historical Sketch*, p. 137.
24. Ibid., p. 141.
25. Ibid., p. 137.
26. Ibid., pp. 174, 197.

Ramsgate — The Separation Principle Extended

The Ramsgate division of 1881 was the next important schism. There had, however, been separations of individuals in the intervening years between 1848 and 1881. For example, in 1866 Hall and Dorman had separated from Darby because of his views on the sufferings of Christ wherein he denied that the first few hours on the cross were atoning. The Ramsgate matter was, like the Bethesda division, based not on doctrinal or theological principles but on church government or order. It is ironic how many divisions in their group (which itself divided from the organized churches to avoid organization) have come about on matters of church government and discipline. It also represents a further development of the principle of separation involved in the Bethesda affair.

At Ramsgate in Kent, a Mr. Jull excommunicated the whole Kennington assembly because it was vacillating about the treatment of Edward Cronin, the elderly original brother, who had gone clandestinely to Ryde and, on his own initiative, set up a table there against the judgment of Darby and others. Since not everyone was of the same opinion as Jull about the propriety of excommunicating a whole assembly for this reason, there was a split at Ramsgate. The division spread across the Atlantic, and Darby himself was quite distressed by it, especially because of his friend Kelly, with whom he did not agree but from whom he did not want to separate. The groups involved in this division were finally reconciled in 1926. The matter involved in this dispute represents an extension of the Bethesda principle. The latter involved the rightness of tolerating one who tolerated an offender; the former, the rightness of tolerating one who tolerated a vacillator.

F. W. Grant and Soteriological Dissension

A much more serious division, the Grant affair, occurred two years after Darby's death. Frederick W. Grant was born in England but had moved to Canada and, while still young, had come to live in Plainfield, New Jersey. It is conceded, even by the exclusives, that his life at first was useful in the gospel. But he came to hold some views which were out of line with Darby's, and he had a controversy with the aged and frail leader at Darby's last public gathering at Croydon, England. He is reported to have said, before leaving England, that he would advocate his views after Darby had passed on. It does appear that he began seriously to press them in 1883, the year after the death of Darby. Matters came to a head in Montreal, where a few had been affected by his views. Lord Adalbert P. Cecil, a faithful Darbyite, came over from England to deal with the situation. Grant defended his views, and he and his supporters could not be dissuaded from their position. Since they could not win all the Brethren, a division followed. The group meeting at Natural History Hall in Montreal finally severed the Grant faction from fellowship, while the latter denied the legitimacy of the Lord's Table at the History Hall assembly.[27]

It is clear, from the literature surrounding this controversy, that substantial doctrinal issues were at stake. Grant propounded four doctrines which diverged from Darbyite "orthodoxy." First, he maintained that the Old Testament saints enjoyed the full bestowal of eternal life and union with Christ rather than a partial and provisional redemption. Second, he maintained that there was no temporal distinction between regeneration and the "sealing of the Holy Spirit." Third, Grant argued that Romans 7:15–25 describes the experience of the Christian who has been sealed by the Spirit. Finally, with regard to assurance of salvation, Grant maintained that a genuine believer may not always be conscious of God's favor.[28]

Ironside relates an incident which occurred in the course of the controversy that illuminates the nature of the doctrinal struggle. A young man had been converted on a sick bed, and he then asked to receive communion. The assembly examined him and it was judged that he truly believed in Christ. But that was not enough to admit him to the Lord's Supper. The sealing of the Spirit was also necessary, and the young man had not been sealed.[29] Grant was appalled by the pastoral consequences of such a doctrine, and he argued strenuously that the sealing of the Spirit accompanies the saving exercise of faith.

It is clear that Grant's position, in general, was really the position of the Anglican and other Reformed churches from which the Brethren had originally separated. The assembly in Montreal rightly sensed that it was a defection from the principles of Darby and the Brethren. We see it as the Holy Spirit calling those zealous but erring Brethren back to the church they had left and inflicting upon them, because of their stubborn refusal to be entreated, a further division. As might be expected, the Grant controversy spread and assemblies in England as well as America were split.

---

27. See Noel, *History*, 1:334–335.
28. Noel, *History*, 1:336.
29. See Ironside, *Historical Sketch*, pp. 99–100.

C. E. Stuart and the Doctrine of Justification

The third major division in five years occurred under Clarence Esme Stuart in 1885. He was expelled from the London Darbyites for his teaching that the standing of a Christian (i.e., justification) is complete through faith in the Atonement, independent of personal union with Christ. Union with Christ was considered a condition of added privilege, an improved condition but not an improved standing. The standing with God was achieved when faith was exercised while a better condition was effected by this union with Christ. James Butler Stoney and C. H. Mackintosh, leaders of the Closed Brethren, attacked Stuart's teaching, maintaining that justification itself was found in the risen Christ.[30] Stoney argued that *standing* (both groups accepted the terminology of *standing* and *condition* which is standard in Brethrenism) consists of "removal of the First Man from under the eye of God" while *condition* depends upon "the Spirit's work forming Christ within."[31] Stuart and his followers were excommunicated and they formed their own assembly. In time, they broke the Darbyite discipline and admitted members freely in the Open Brethren manner.

F. E. Raven and Christological Heresy

The next major division of the Brethren, who were not supposed to have any organized or visible churches, was the Raven schism of 1890. Frederick E. Raven was a government official of a mystical temperament, and his mysticism led him into heresy concerning the person of Christ.[32] We have noticed that a number of the earlier divisions of the Brethren were occasioned by men trying to return to a sounder view from which the Brethren had originally separated. In Raven, however, we see the outbreak of explicit heresy which had been long condemned by the church. It is clear that Raven adopted a view of the person of Christ which is associated with Apollinaris of Laodicea, a fourth-century bishop whose views were condemned by the Council of Constantinople in A.D. 381. The fault of Apollinaris lay in his refusal to ascribe a full and complete humanity to Jesus Christ by denying the presence

---

30. Neatby, *History*, pp. 311–313.
31. See Ironside, *Historical Sketch*, p. 114. The importance of the theological issue at stake here should not be underestimated. The faith which "justifies" does so in that it apprehends its object, the person of Jesus Christ. The Reformed faith has always confessed that mere assent is no saving faith at all.
32. Ibid., p. 130.

of a human soul. Raven apparently went even further than the fourth century heretic in that Raven was not willing to affirm any genuine humanity in Christ. He was, therefore, taking a Docetic view—arguing that Christ only "seemed" to be human. Furthermore, according to Noel, he denied that Christ was eternally the Son of God or the Word (which would have scandalized even the Docetists).[33]

In addition to this particular separation, there have been a number of other smaller ones and two larger ones connected with the names of John Taylor and Russell Elliott. By this time, however, the patterns of dissension and schism are no doubt clear to the reader, and it is neither profitable nor edifying to proceed further with the details of the story.

Never has one body of Christians split so often, in such a short period of time, and over such minute points of difference. The Brethren themselves used to ask in 1881, "To what section of the disorganization do *you* belong."[34] This is fissiparousness in the purity of its expression and, tragic as it is in itself, it also teaches most emphatically the evils of unnecessary separation from the visible church of Christ.

Reasons for this tendency toward schism are not difficult to find. The Brethren exaltation of the notion of the "invisible church" at the expense of "visible church" structure, organized ministry, and credal continuity could only result, given the nature of the human condition, in the sort of splintering we have seen in this chapter. There is an even deeper theological problem involved. Darby's view of the activity of the "new nature" in the believer who has been sealed by the Spirit served to foster an attitude of spiritual arrogance and inflexibility on the part of those who claimed such sealing. A denial of the activity of the old man within the Christian can only lead to a failure, on the part of that Christian, to recognize the effects of that sinful humanity when they inevitably manifest themselves. The implicit Perfectionism involved in Darby's views at this point will be discussed in a later chapter. Theological error cannot but issue in negative practical consequences.

The Spread of the Brethren Movement

Given the movement's tendency to fragment, the growth that the early Brethren did achieve is rather remarkable. There can be no doubt that the movement was able to tap into the enormous revival of millennial interest that swept England, Europe, and America in the early nine-

---

33. Noel, *History*, 2:595ff.
34. Neatby, *History*, p. 322.

teenth century. From this perspective, the Brethren were only one of a number of eschatologically oriented groups whose number also included the Irvingites in England and the various Adventist groups in America.[35]

Social factors also contributed. Much of the early success of the movement was attributed to its aristocratic membership. Darby admitted this, and the feature has continued in a lesser degree to characterize the Brethren.[36] The bar and military service are forbidden vocations and, since medicine and dentistry are virtually the only professions approved, the large number of doctors among them is not surprising.[37] The society has also tended to follow the personal conduct principles of Darby who was opposed to voting, holding office, using musical instruments, and taking exercise.

Brethrenism has never been so extensive outside England, but, from Darby on, it has made efforts to expand. As already noted, the Open Brethren were more missionary-minded. In any case we find the movement in south and central Africa, Egypt, the West Indies, Guiana, India, Burma, and Japan as well as in Europe and America.

Switzerland was probably the land of most significant early growth outside Britain. Darby visited there before 1838. An influential member of the state church had invited him to fight Methodism which was beginning to draw people away from the establishment. It soon became apparent, however, that Darbyism was opposed to the Reformed state church as well as the Methodists, and the opposition of Swiss evangelicals limited the spread of the Brethren in Switzerland.[38]

From Switzerland, Brethrenism spread to France. Darby was especially active in the southern area of France around Montpelier. The Brethren in this region were called *Derbists* after the leader of the movement who had converted them.[39]

George Mueller, as well as Darby, was instrumental in bringing Brethrenism to Germany. While Darby was especially active around Elbersfeld, Mueller was invited to Stuttgart by an official of the government who wished to know about the movement. He and his wife came in August of 1843 and were received by the Baptists. An inevitable separation quickly took place, however, and, when Mueller left six

---

35. See Ernest R. Sandeen, *The Roots of Fundamentalism: British and American Millenarianism 1800-1930* (Chicago: University of Chicago Press, 1970), pp. 3-80.

36. Neatby, *History*, p. 42.

37. Ibid., p. 271.

38. Ibid., p. 84.

39. See Turner, *Darby*, pp. 18-19.

months later, there were about twenty-five Brethren worshiping together.[40] According to *Whitaker's Almanac* (1935) there were then seven hundred assemblies in Germany.

The first to take Brethrenism out of Europe was Henry Groves, one of the early leaders. In 1833, Groves moved into India and succeeded in causing a split in the Church Missionary Society mission in Tinnevelly. His convert and follower, Aroclappen, was responsible for establishing Brethrenism in the north of Tinnerly.[41] Groves himself later fell into the Arian heresy, returned home, and died in 1856 in the home of his brother-in-law, George Mueller.[42]

---

40. Neatby, *History*, p. 97ff.
41. Ibid., p. 72.
42. Ibid., p. 220.

THREE

DISPENSATIONALISM IN THE U.S.A.

I n the United States, the theology of the Plymouth Brethren blos-
somed into Dispensationalism.[1] This theological movement gained
adherents from among Christians of every sort, some so remote from
Brethrenism as to be shocked upon learning the source of their doctrine. Dispensationalism has produced a large body of literature, a
great number of schools, and many Christian movements. Its adherents have constituted, if not the backbone, at least much of the
bony structure of American theological conservatism for the past hundred years.

Yet Dispensationalism is a theology which is treated with studied
ignorance by large sections of the theological world. A striking example is found in the *Twentieth Century Encyclopedia of Religious
Knowledge* which devotes one column to a discussion of "Dispensationalism," while giving seven columns to an explanation of
"Sufism."[2] Under the topic, "Theology, Twentieth Century Trends in,"
there is no mention of Dispensationalism. A number of reasons account for this apparent neglect. For one, Dispensationalism has tended
to develop its own schools, while other theologies have gained their

---

1. We acknowledge our indebtedness to the thesis of Talmadge Wilson, "A History
of Dispensationalism in the United States of America: The Nineteenth Century"
(Th.M. Thesis, Pittsburgh-Xenia Theological Seminary, 1956). Wilson wrote this for
me while a student at Pittsburgh Theological Seminary, and I have here revised,
modified, amplified, and up-dated his original account.

2. *The Twentieth Century Encyclopedia of Religious Knowledge*, s.v. "Sufism;"
"Theology, Twentieth Century Trends in."

first footholds in established seminaries. Also, the literature of the movement has been aimed primarily at lay people. It is often in pamphlet form and in not very profound language. Finally, the implications of Dispensationalism seem only recently to have made much of an impression on the theological world, particularly on the conservative wing in whose bed the dispensationalist has slept so comfortably for so long. Whatever the reasons, it is strange indeed that there should be such widespread neglect.

The Development of American Dispensationalism

We have already seen that John Nelson Darby made repeated visits abroad from 1862 to 1877. E. R. Sandeen has estimated that forty percent of that time was spent in America.[3] His first visit to the United States seems to have been in 1864. There can be no doubt that, wherever this forceful man went, many found his views persuasive. His influence was greatest among Presbyterians and Baptists. One of the centers of his labors was the city of St. Louis where the prominent Presbyterian pastor, Dr. James H. Brookes, was associated with him. Since Brookes may be thought of as the "father of American Dispensationalism," it is well that we should know something about this man.

James H. Brookes and Early Dispensationalism

James H. Brookes was born in 1830 in Pulaski, Tennessee. The child of a minister who died when James was three years old, his early life was lived with friends and relatives. He attended Miami University in Ohio and, while there, took theological work at the United Presbyterian Seminary in Oxford, Ohio. Later, he was graduated from Princeton Seminary and served a charge in Dayton, Ohio with great success. After four years there, he went to St. Louis in 1858. Here he was noted for starting "colony" churches from the "parent" church which he served. A severe throat ailment threatened his career, but he found relief in Paris.

The Civil War brought him hurrying back to be with his people. While a southerner, he was not a secessionist and, though earnest in prayer for peace, he could not bring himself to pray for the success of the southern army. This aroused the ire of his more patriotic congrega-

---

3. Ernest R. Sandeen, "Toward a Historical Interpretation of the Origins of Fundamentalism," *Church History* 36 (1967): 70.

tion, and Brookes moved to the pastorate of one of the colony churches that he had helped to found. This was the 16th and Walnut Avenue Presbyterian Church (which moved to Washington and Compton Avenues in 1879), where he was to remain until his death in 1897.

This was the man who met and worked with J. N. Darby. Beyond the bare fact of it, however, it is difficult to uncover evidence as to the real nature of their association. We are told that Brookes was an expert scholar in Hebrew, Greek, and Latin, and that he was a great lover of books (we are shown a picture of his library, its walls lined with books). Yet, when he writes a pamphlet entitled *How I Became a Premillennialist*, he tells us he became one by Bible study alone. We would like to take this statement at face value. It is difficult to do so, however, for such statements abound in dispensational literature. On the other hand, it is difficult to prove the source of Brookes' opinions. We may reasonably conjecture that he was familiar with the writings of the Brethren before welcoming Darby to close association.

This conjecture is at least not weakened by a circumstance connected with the publication of Brookes' book, *How to Be Saved*, in 1864. This book bears on the title page the author's name listed only as "J. H. B." This is a characteristic Brethren way of signing an author's name. While Allis calls attention to the reluctance of Brookes to credit Darby for influencing his views, many of Brookes' associates bore ample witness to the great influence which Brethren writers exercised.[4] It is difficult to escape the conclusion that Brookes came by his views under the considerable influence of Darby, however unaware he may have been of the force of this influence.[5]

Brookes became a most influential exponent of Dispensationalism by three chief means. The first of these was his own Bible study and his habit of gathering young proteges around him for such study. By far the best known of these students was C. I. Scofield. The second means was his literary work. He published many books and pamphlets and he edited *The Truth*, a Christian magazine, from 1874 until his death.[6]

---

4. Oswald T. Allis, *Prophecy and the Church: An Examination of the Claim of Dispensationalists that the Christian Church Is a Mystery* (Phillipsburg, N.J.: Presbyterian and Reformed, 1945), p. 13.

5. Biographical material is largely drawn from the work of his son-in-law, David Riddle Williams, *James Hall Brookes: A Memoir* (St. Louis: Presbyterian Board of Publication, 1897). See also Joseph H. Hall, "James Hall Brookes: New School, Old School, or No School," *Presbyterion* 14 (1988):35–54.

6. When Brooks died, *The Truth* merged with A. J. Gordon's magazine and became *Watchword and Truth*. On this transaction, Gaebelein comments, "*Watchword and*

The third means was his leadership in the Niagara Bible Conference and the various prophetic conferences of his day.

The importance of his public ministry notwithstanding, by far the greatest contribution made by Brookes to the dispensational cause was his personal influence on C. I. Scofield. In my own encounters with dispensationalists, in person or in their literature, almost all are intimately familiar with Scofield but relatively few seem to have read Darby directly. Even fewer are aware of Brookes. They tend to go from Scofield forward to contemporary Dispensationalism rather than backward to their roots elsewhere.

Before turning to Scofield, however, we must take stock of the historical factors which contributed to the success of Scofield and his cohorts. Ian Rennie draws a larger canvas on which he locates the crucial emergence of C. I. Scofield. The British historian aptly describes the American scene:

> The strident period of dispensationalism began with the new century. The non-dispensational leaders of premillennialism in America felt they could not honestly participate in a movement whose dominant theology contained implications to which they could not subscribe. Their secession brought an end to the Niagara Bible Conference and might have wrecked the movement; but instead it made the movement more homogeneous and ready to move forward when the right opportunity arose. This opportunity came with the revival of 1904–08 which was the last in that chain of movements of spiritual renewal which began with Wesley. In 1908, a presentation edition of W. E. Blackstone's, *Jesus is Coming*, a dispensational work first published a generation before, was sent to several hundred thousand ministers and Christian workers. Then in 1909, profiting from the same impetus, the Scofield Reference Bible was published. Its orthodoxy was unambiguous in a day of battle, and its eschatology more than ever, appeared to provide a valid interpretation of the current situation. Soon the badge of North American Evangelicalism was the Scofield Bible. It was revised in 1917, with the result that its distinctive teachings were even more cogent and forceful than ever, and just at the time that the British mandate of Palestine provided an apparent fulfillment of premillennial hope in the promised return of Jews to their native land.[7]

Truth did not continue in the prophetic witness of Drs. Brookes and Gordon, and so it came that *Our Hope* [Gaebelein's magazine which Brookes had warmly endorsed] was looked upon as the true and legitimate successor of *The Truth*." Arno C. Gaebelein, *Half a Century* (New York: Publication Office of *Our Hope*, 1930), p. 45f.

7. Ian S. Rennie, "Nineteenth-Century Roots," p. 48.

C. I. Scofield

Cyrus Ingerson Scofield was born in 1843. Like Brookes, he was reared in Tennessee. He served with distinction in the Confederate army and later determined to study law. He was admitted to the bar in the territory of Kansas, served in the Kansas House of Representatives and was, for two years, U.S. District Attorney for Kansas. Leaving this post, he went to St. Louis to take up private practice. He also began gaining a reputation as something of a dissolute person. In 1879, he was led to the Lord by a persistent friend named McPheeters and all his intensive nature was now brought to the service of God. He soon came under the influence of Brookes, and for many months he studied the Bible in the latter's home. Through the influence of Brookes, Scofield became involved in a Congregational church and before long he was asked to become pastor of a struggling Congregational church in Dallas, Texas. He was ordained to the ministry there and served as pastor from 1882–1895.

Bible study was an important part of his ministry, and soon he began to write. *Rightly Dividing the Word of Truth*, embodying many of the principles of his studies with Brookes, came off the press in 1885.[8] The lessons which were later to form the *Scofield Bible Correspondence Course* gradually began to take shape and were hammered out on the anvil of teaching experience with young men.[9] Later, these pamphlets were brought together in three bound volumes and the course is still available through the Moody Bible Institute, which took it from his shoulders in 1915.

Scofield began to make a name for himself in Bible conference work throughout much of America. He met Hudson Taylor on a number of occasions at the Niagara Bible Conference. This served to stir up within him a missionary imperative and later led to his leadership in the Central American Mission. W. Cameron Townsend, one of its early missionaries, later founded the Wycliffe Bible Translators. Scofield was called to the Moody Church in Northfield, Massachusetts as pastor in 1895. There he served as president of the Northfield Bible Training School from 1900–1903. Though he returned to his own church in Dallas in 1902, his service there was very limited from then until 1907 when he was made pastor emeritus.

---

8. C. I. Scofield, *Rightly Dividing the Word of Truth* (Philadelphia: Philadelphia School of the Bible, 1928; reprint ed.).

9. C. I. Scofield, *The Scofield Bible Correspondence Course*, 19th ed. (Chicago: Moody Colportage Association, 1905).

Between 1902 and 1909, he was largely engaged in work on the *Scofield Reference Bible*.[10] According to Arno C. Gaebelein, Scofield and he talked together around the first of August, 1902 concerning the production of such a work. This conversation occurred at the Sea Cliff Bible Conference, which had been largely financed by John T. Pirie, a Plymouth Brother, as a successor to the former Niagara conference. It was agreed that Gaebelein should speak to some friends to sound them out about financial support. He received a "considerable sum of money to assist in the project" pledged by Alwyn Ball, Jr., and John T. Pirie put up a similar amount. Others, among them John B. Buss of St. Louis, and Francis B. Fitch, who had published *The Scofield Bible Correspondence Course*, also contributed.[11] Francis B. Fitch, John T. Pirie, and Alwyn Ball, Jr. were all Plymouth Brethren and it was through them, in 1899, that Gaebelein himself

> became acquainted with the works of those able and godly men who were needed in the great spiritual movement of the Brethren in the early part of the nineteenth century, John Nelson Darby and others. I found in his writings, in the works of William Kelly, Mackintosh, F. Grant, Bellett and others the soul food I needed. I esteem these men next to the Apostles in their sound and spiritual teaching.[12]

Financial support being secured from these Plymouth Brethren, and receiving leave of absence from his Dallas Church, Scofield went abroad to gain more free time. In London, through the good offices of Mr. Scott of the religious publishers, Morgan and Scott, Scofield secured the Oxford University Press as the publisher. Then he went to Montreaux, Switzerland where almost at once he fell ill. After some time, he was able to resume the work in earnest. He returned to his Dallas church around 1905, but it soon became apparent that he must give up one or the other. He gave up the congregation.

Later he returned to Europe, staying at Oxford. While there, he worshiped with a group of Open Brethren. Another trip to Montreaux saw the completion of the work, which was first printed in 1909 and revised in 1917. About that year, Scofield left the Congregational church because of his concern about alleged modernism in that denomination, and he became a member of Texas Presbytery of the

---

10. C. G. Trumbull, *Life Story of C. I. Scofield* (New York: Oxford, 1920).

11. Arno C. Gaebelein, *The History of the Scofield Reference Bible* (New York: Loizeaux, 1943), p. 48ff.

12. Gaebelein, *Half a Century*, p. 83ff.

southern Presbyterian church. Scofield died in 1921, having lived to see his *Reference Bible* become an extraordinarily influential document in American evangelicalism.

The Theology of the Scofield Bible

There can be no doubt that Scofield believed that his ideas came from the Bible and that he held and propagated them as such. The Scofield Bible is, after all, only the King James version of the Bible with interpretive notes affixed.

On the other hand, Scofield did not start interpreting the Bible *de novo* without previous exposure to other interpretations. Rutgers observes that Plymouth Brethrenism was advocated by the saintly Malachi Taylor in the vicinity of New York shortly before or after the beginning of this century. "Scofield making acquaintance with it became so enthused and enamored of its charm, that he proposed to issue a Bible with appended notes and cross references in accordance with this scheme."[13] Clarence Bass asserts that Scofield "borrowed ideas, words, and phrases" from Darby, and Boettner detects the same influence.[14]

Hardly anyone questions that Scofield was profoundly influenced by Darby in the production of *The Scofield Reference Bible.* Charles Ryrie, however, while admitting this fact, attempts to qualify it in a way with which we will take issue. He writes:

> Although we cannot minimize the wide influence of Darby, the glib statement that dispensationalism originated with Darby, whose system was taken over and popularized by Scofield, is not historically accurate.[15]

How does Ryrie justify this charge of inaccuracy? He simply asserts that Scofield's system is more like that of Isaac Watts than Darby. We have already seen that Ryrie has egregiously misrepresented Isaac Watts' "Dispensationalism" (see chapter 1). Any resemblance between Scofield and Watts is purely superficial while that between Scofield and Darby is deep and systemic.

Some have maintained, not that Scofield did not derive from Darby, but that the Scofield Bible did not necessarily derive from Scofield. Some have urged differences among the very editors of *The Scofield*

---

13. Rutgers, *Premillennialism in America*, p. 173.
14. Bass, *Backgrounds*, p. 18; Loraine Boettner, *The Millennium* (Grand Rapids: Baker, 1958), p. 369f.
15. Ryrie, *Dispensationalism Today*, p. 76.

Reference Bible. Daniel Fuller, however, has laboriously shown that, though there was some independence and variation in the committee of sub-editors, Scofield himself shaped the views and was ultimately responsible for them.[16] Clarence Bass correctly argues that Scofield's "synthesis of Darby's principles forms the core of *continuing* dispensational hermeneutics."[17]

One sub-editor who clearly did have a marked influence on Scofield was Arno C. Gaebelein. Indeed, it appears that the Scofield Bible's prophetic teachings were mainly those of Gaebelein. Scofield wrote a foreword for Gaebelein's *The Harmony of the Prophetic Word* and requested and received from Gaebelein a number of analyses of prophetic books and interpretations of disputed prophecies. On September 2, 1905, Scofield wrote to Gaebelein:

> By all means follow your own views of prophetic analysis. I sit at your feet when it comes to prophecy, and congratulate in advance the future readers of my Bible on having in their hands a safe, clear, sane guide through what to most is a labyrinth.[18]

Gaebelein's views were in turn largely developed through three contacts. Around 1888, when he was a twenty-seven-year-old Methodist preacher, he had contact with Orthodox Jews and he began to adopt their hopes for a literal fulfillment of Messianic prophecies. This brought him into conflict with the "spiritualizing method" (quotation marks his) which he had previously followed.[19] Through the Niagara Bible Conference, he came to know James H. Brookes who, he said, "took me literally under his wings."[20] Finally, we have seen that, in

---

16. Daniel P. Fuller, "The Hermeneutics of Dispensationalism" (Th.D. dissertation, Northern Baptist Theological Seminary, 1957), p. 117ff.

17. Bass, *Backgrounds*, p. 150 (emphasis mine).

18. Gaebelein, *History*, p. 32.

19. In his autobiography, *Half A Century*, p. 20, Gaebelein makes this incredible statement about the traditional Christian view, which unfortunately, is characteristic of writers of the dispensational school. "Israel, that method teaches, is no longer the Israel of old, but it means the Church now. For the natural Israel no hope of a future restoration is left. All their glorious and unfulfilled promises find now their fulfillment in the Church of Jesus Christ." This certainly does make it hard on the Jews! When they might have had a glorious piece of real estate on the Mediterranean, all they end up with under this interpretation is Christ, of whom it was said that "it pleased the Father that in him should all fulness dwell" (Colossians 1:19). To add further irony, by no means all covenantalists deny a future for the Jews in Israel.

20. Ibid., p. 40.

1899, he became acquainted with the Brethren writers whom he ranked next to the Apostles.

Perhaps the clearest evidence of the continuing influence of Scofield's Darbyite Dispensationalism is seen in his most influential disciple, Lewis Sperry Chafer. Before we trace this influence, however, let us note the significant role of D. L. Moody in the dispensational heritage.

D. L. Moody and the Transmission of Dispensationalism

Moody is, of course, profoundly associated with the Northfield conferences which he founded in 1880. Ernest Sandeen calls attention to something he believes has been missed. "No historian of Moody's amazing career has noted, however, that his Northfield Conferences were virtually dominated by dispensationalists, particularly from 1880 through 1887 and again from 1894-1902."[21] Be that as it may, it is well known that Darby directly and indirectly influenced Moody's theological thinking (of which Darby did not have a high opinion).

Notwithstanding the importance of the Northfield conferences, there is no question that Moody's greatest dispensational influence has come down through the Bible institute that still bears his name. Ian Rennie tells this story more pungently and accurately than any other brief historical survey we have seen:

> Moody's Institute in Chicago, although not the first of such schools, became the prototype; and since Moody had imbibed a fair dose of dispensationalism in a rather typical unstructured form, and his colleague and successor R. A. Torrey in a more systematic way, it was natural that the burgeoning Bible school movement, with a few exceptions, should follow this line of thought. And as the Bible schools unintentionally became training centers for evangelical ministers as many of the theological seminaries opted for divergent views, Darby's prophetic teaching became more widely accepted than ever.[22]

Lewis Sperry Chafer and Dallas Seminary

Lewis Sperry Chafer (1871-1952) also had his ecclesiastical roots in the Reformed tradition. In 1900 he was ordained to the Congregational ministry in Buffalo. A few years later he joined the Presbyterian

---

21. Sandeen, "Origins," p. 76.
22. Rennie, "Nineteenth-Century Roots," p. 57.

Church, U.S.A. In that denomination he served a congregation in East Northfield while Scofield was in Northfield. Although Chafer moved to other pastorates and later gave himself to full-time Bible teaching, the contact with Scofield continued and, after the latter's urging, he established Dallas Theological Seminary in 1924.

Although a Presbyterian minister, Chafer had not undergone the usual Presbyterian seminary training. This fact led him naively to claim that "the very fact that I did not study a prescribed course in theology made it possible for me to approach the subject with an unprejudiced mind and to be concerned only with what the Bible teaches."[23] This leads his biographer, C. F. Lincoln, to conclude that "this independent research has resulted in a work which is unabridged, Calvinistic, premillennial, and dispensational."[24] Every claim except "Calvinistic" is indisputably true, though "premillennial" must be taken in the dispensational sense.

Chafer has, in the history of American Dispensationalism, a double distinction. First, he established and led Dispensationalism's most scholarly institution through the formative first thirty years of its existence.[25] Second, he produced the first full and definitive systematic theology of Dispensationalism. This massive eight-volume work is a full articulation of the standard Scofieldian variety of dispensational thought, constantly related to the Biblical texts and data on which it claims to rest. Its influence appears to have been great on all dispensationalist teachers since its first publication, though it is fading today.

All of Chafer's work and career was openly and obviously in the Scofieldian tradition. A few years before his death, Chafer, faithful to his mentor to the last, was to say of his greatest academic achievement, "It goes on record that the Dallas Theological Seminary uses, recommends, and defends the Scofield Bible."[26]

The major line of dispensational orthodoxy is clear and unbroken from Darby to Scofield to Chafer to Dallas.

---

23. C. F. Lincoln, "Biographical Sketch of the Author," in Lewis Sperry Chafer, *Systematic Theology*, 8 vols. (Dallas: Dallas Seminary Press, 1948), 8:5-6. A full-scale scholarly biography of Chafer is still lacking. See also Jeffrey Jon Richards, "The Eschatology of Lewis Sperry Chafer: His Contribution to a Systematization of Dispensational Premillennialism," (Ph.D. dissertation, Drew University, 1986).

24. Lincoln, "Biographical Sketch," p. 6.

25. See Rudolf A. Reafer, *A History of Dallas Theological Seminary* (Ph.D. dissertation, University of Texas at Austin, 1959), and John A. Witmer, " 'What Hath God Wrought' — Fifty Years of Dallas Theological Seminary," *Bibliotheca Sacra* 130 (1973):291-304.

26. Quoted in Jon Zens, *Dispensationalism*, p. 12.

Recent Developments in American Dispensationalism

The foregoing discussion should not suggest an absolute homogeneity of doctrine at Dallas and in Dispensationalism. Until recently, however, the differences have been peripheral and not touching the system itself. Nevertheless, even at Dallas there now appears to be a movement away from Scofield and Chafer, though the fact of any such movement has been challenged by the administration and the movement itself has been militantly challenged by Zane Hodges.

We mention a few instances of the tight dispensational conformity in Dallas Dispensationalism. For one thing, the doctrine of a pretribulational rapture of the church seems to be a litmus test of orthodoxy. To "outsiders," including classic premillennialists, this doctrine is not crucial, if it is believed at all. But not only is it vigorously maintained in Dallas Dispensationalism, but deviation from it causes a person to be suspect and institutions to shake and sometimes split. Second, professors at Dallas tend to be graduates of that institution. Very rarely is any chance taken with unknown and untried dispensationalists. This is one way of perpetuating an orthodoxy, and it is conspicuous at this academic "Jerusalem" of Dispensationalism. Third, there is the mandatory adherence to Dallas Dispensationalism required of students who would receive the Dallas degree.[27]

Now what appears to be a serious crisis at Dallas and elsewhere has arisen with the outspoken advocacy of traditional Dispensationalism by New Testament professor Zane Hodges. As we see the matter, Hodges is utterly loyal to Dallas Dispensationalism, but his militant advocacy has revealed slippage on the part of many, if not most, of his colleagues. Whether these colleagues are guilty of this slippage or not, they certainly are not shouting the traditional Dallas position from the rooftops in the way Hodges is prone to express his views.

In a later chapter, we will critique Hodges' *The Gospel Under Siege.*[28] It is sufficient to say here that what Hodges conceives of as the

---

27. I discussed this point several times with professors and students when I gave the Griffith-Thomas Lectures at Dallas in 1975. I received neither clear affirmation nor clear denials in response to my questions. I feel certain that this much can be accurately stated: students, no matter how competent, who basically oppose the dispensational system, would not be welcome to come or to stay at the seminary. Any who showed any serious departure from dispensational orthodoxy would be intensely investigated and *perhaps* not permitted to be graduated.

28. Zane Hodges, *The Gospel Under Siege: A Study of Faith and Works* (Dallas: Redencion Viva, 1981).

"gospel" is actually Antinomianism, and he is defending that anti-nomian "gospel" against the very general criticism it is today receiving from some of his fellow dispensationalists. Former Dallas professor S. Lewis Johnson has, by invitation, critiqued Hodges' book at Dallas Theological Seminary. Some on the faculty appear ill-at-ease with Hodges' position and are suggesting, albeit in somewhat muted tones, that it is "extreme." Some dispensationalists outside Dallas, including Johnson, the popular teacher at Believer's Chapel, and John MacArthur are not so muted. Old Testament scholar Bruce Waltke has left Dallas for Reformed theological institutions at Vancouver and Philadelphia. Others have gone elsewhere.

Whenever the present author has discussed the question of Anti-nomianism with various Dallas professors and others, I have usually been told that Hodges is the one. No doubt he is, but he is not alone. I will be demonstrating later in this volume that John Walvoord and Charles Ryrie are teaching (less polemically) the same doctrine. More importantly, what Hodges is maintaining *is* dispensational orthodoxy and those who are differing with his position (in and out of Dallas) are guilty of "declension" or departure from this orthodoxy.

Another dispensationalist who complains of the Dallas drift is W. C. Meloon. He maintains that Dallas has profoundly shifted its position and that this has been accomplished under cover of a ter-minological "camouflage" whereby the Dallas theologians now call the old dispensational orthodoxy *ultradispensational*, and claim the dis-pensational label for their new deviation.[29]

Obviously, a crisis is brewing. I believe it is a good thing, represen-ting the beginning of a possible return, on the part of many dispensa-tionalists, to true historic and Biblical orthodoxy. But, in all fairness, a departure must be admitted. Anti-antinomians cannot claim Darby, Mackintosh, Kelly, Tregelles, Pettingill, Arno Gaebelein, Scofield, and Chafer for fathers. The current "Lordship" controversy is a symptom of this crisis and will be discussed later in some detail.

If Hodges and others are now raising problems, Dispensationalism has been growing wholesale elsewhere. Hal Lindsey's *Late Great Planet Earth* was the non-fiction best seller of the seventies, if not of all time (apart from the Bible).[30] Many million copies have been printed even while formidable critics have lampooned Lindsey's inter-

---

29. W. C. Meloon, *We've Been Robbed! Or a Dispensationalist Looks at the Bap-tism of the Holy Spirit* (Plainfield, N.J.: Logos International, 1971), p. 15.

30. Hal Lindsey, *Late Great Planet Earth* (Grand Rapids: Zondervan, 1970).

pretation of Biblical terms such a *Meshech*, *Rosh*, and *Tubal* as referring to Moscow, Russia, and Tobolsk respectively.[31] Dyrness thinks "it
is no coincidence that the publication of Hal Lindsey's first book on
prophecy coincided with the greatest revival of astrology in three hundred years."[32] Jerry Falwell became a household name in the 1980s,
and his strong and influential pro-Israel stance is often, if not always,
supported by the dispensational theology which underlies it.[33] It was
popularly rumored that Menachem Begin, the prime minister of Israel,
would phone Falwell before President Reagan for help.

This remarkable popular success of Dispensationalism is balanced,
however, by an increasingly independent stance on the part of many
evangelical institutions toward dispensational orthodoxy. Not only has
dispensational fundamentalist and arch-separatist George Dollar[34]
been denouncing dispensational declensions everywhere, but less
stringent voices have raised questions about Wheaton and Gordon
Colleges, Eastern Baptist Seminary, and Baptists in general. For example, John Walvoord charges Gilbert Bilezikian with teaching amillennialism at Wheaton, and R. V. Clearwaters notes the conflict concerning
Dispensationalism in Baptist churches.[35]

The Institutions of American Dispensationalism

Although the conservative exodus from the mainline denominations
meant the loss of many educational institutions and denominational
organizations to liberalism, dispensationalists showed a remarkable
capacity to develop an alternative set of institutions to meet the growing needs of their movement. Indeed, the success of twentieth-century

---

31. See Cornelis Vanderwaal, *Hal Lindsey and Biblical Prophecy* (St. Catherines,
Ont.: Paideia, 1978); George C. Miladin, *Is This Really the End?* (Cherry Hill. N.J.:
Mack, 1972); Charles D. Provan, *The Church is Israel Now* (Vallecito, Cal.: Ross
House, 1987).

32. W. Dyrness, "The Age of Aquarius," in *Handbook of Biblical Prophecy*, ed.
Carl E. Armerding and W. Ward Gasque (Grand Rapids: Baker, 1977), p. 22.

33. Jerry Falwell, *Fundamentalist Phenomenon. The Resurgence of Conservative
Christianity* (New York: Doubleday, 1981).

34. George Dollar, *A History of Fundamentalism in America* (Greenville, S.C.: Bob
Jones University Press, 1973), pp. 26, 27, 231.

35. John F. Walvoord, "Postribulationism Today, Part II: The Rapture and the Day
of the Lord in 1 Thessalonians," *Bibliotheca Sacra*, 139 (1982):10; R. V. Clearwater,
Forty Years of History Looks Down Upon Conservative Baptists (Minneapolis: Central Baptist Press, n.d.).

American Dispensationalism was due, in part, to the vitality of dispensational schools, literature efforts, Bible conferences, and missions.

The Bible School Movement

In addition to the schools mentioned above such as Dallas Seminary and Wheaton College, another type of school has heretofore received little scholarly scrutiny — the Bible school. We need to consider this important factor in order to assess the larger movement properly.

The last half of the nineteenth and the first quarter of the twentieth centuries were periods of intense evangelistic activity by such leaders as Dwight L. Moody, J. Wilbur Chapman, Reuben A. Torrey, A. B. Simpson, and Billy Sunday. These were merely the greater lights of an evangelistic firmament which also included a multitude of lesser ones. The evangelistic campaigns which these men conducted produced a large number of people who felt the need for training in the Bible. A need for Christian lay workers, felt keenly in the conduct of the campaigns, became more widely recognized, and some means had to be found to provide Bible training for people who were in no position to undertake a standard theological course. As a result, Bible schools began attempting to fill the gap described. Brookes' work with a few men gathered around him for Bible study in his own home was rather typical of the humble beginnings of many of these schools. Often, evening classes were arranged to meet the needs of lay people employed during the day. If successful, these were expanded to day school status. Academic requirements, from the nature of the case, were traditionally minimized and emphasis lay on zeal, eagerness to learn, and spiritual qualifications.

The oldest of the modern Bible schools began in this fashion in 1882 with classes conducted in a New York theater under the leadership of A. B. Simpson, a former Presbyterian who was to found the Christian and Missionary Alliance church. Later, this developed into the Missionary Training Institute of Nyack, New York.

Not all of these schools were begun under such humble circumstances. McCormick money (Harvester) played a large part in the establishment of the Bible-Work Institute of the Chicago Evangelization Society in 1886. By 1899, this school was known as the Moody Bible Institute.[36] Stewart money (Union Oil) paved the way for the Bible Institute of Los Angeles to open under the presidency of R. A. Torrey in

---

36. William H. Smith, *D. L. Moody*, p. 76.

the second decade of this century.[37] LeTourneau money (earth-moving equipment) has backed the Toccoa Falls Institute in Georgia more recently. For most other schools, finances have been a chronic problem. Nevertheless, the need for such schools is still apparent as the Youth for Christ and Campus Crusade movements, the preaching of Billy Graham, and others have continued to give impetus to this need.[38]

The contributions of the Bible school movement to the spread of Dispensationalism in the United States have been enormous. While it should be pointed out that some of the evangelists, notably Moody and Simpson, did not allow their ministries to be taken up with concern for the second coming of Christ to the point of preoccupation, yet it must be admitted that all the more prominent evangelists leaned toward dispensational views of history and prophecy. Moody, as we have seen, had a somewhat unsatisfactory relationship with Darby. Darby held what Moody considered an extreme Calvinist position on the perversion of man's will and Darby later condemned Moody's work vigorously. W. G. Turner notes that "Mr. Moody even confessed his indebtedness to the writings of the Brethren for much help in understanding of the Word, but it was C. H. Mackintosh and Charles Stanley who had the greatest influence."[39]

While the evangelists may only have leaned in the direction of Dispensationalism, the serious study required by the presence of an inquiring student body soon brought the Bible schools to open avowal of a more fully developed Dispensationalism. An accrediting association was formed, of which Terrelle B. Crum was the secretary. Crum reported that the majority of Bible schools were then *dispensational*. This was true of both private and interdenominational schools, as well as denominationally controlled schools.

Of the forty-one schools listed in 1956 by the association as members or associates, fourteen were interdenominational. These schools, which were located in every region of the United States, included six of the eight largest and accounted for half of the student body of the forty-one schools. That student body amounted to over ten thousand students. When it is remembered that four-fifths of the Bible schools

---

37. Gaebelein, *Half a Century*, p. 207.

38. Information on the Bible School movement has largely been supplied by Terrelle Crum, dean of Providence-Barrington Bible College and secretary of the Accrediting Association of Bible Institutes and Bible Colleges, either through personal conversation, articles by him in the *Twentieth Century Encyclopedia of Religious Knowledge* or publications of the Association which he has kindly provided.

39. Turner, *Darby*, p. 21f.

were connected with the association, it will be seen how favorably this compares with the approximately twenty-two thousand students then enrolled in all the Protestant theological seminaries of the nation.[40]

The Bible schools have produced thousands of lay workers, missionaries, ministers, and Bible teachers, and have furnished thousands of wives for such Christian workers. In many cases, the students were given a more or less stereotyped course and were not exposed to literature of a different school of thought. The assumptions on which they operated were held with considerable naiveté. It should be emphasized that they are not the only students guilty of this, but they do share in this guilt to a large degree.

In this connection, we must say a word about other types of schools that have been headquarters for Dispensationalism. Liberal arts colleges such as Wheaton, founded around the turn of the century, and Bob Jones, founded in 1927, have undertaken a program of wider educational range. In theology, however, Bob Jones University has maintained a strict dispensational line up to the present. Wheaton College, while technically continuing to insist on faculty adherence to premillennialism, has clearly broadened its perspective in recent years.

Dallas Theological Seminary was founded in 1925 near the scene of C. I. Scofield's labors, and it still may be considered the flagship of dispensational seminaries. Quite a number of other dispensational seminaries have arisen, however, including Grace Theological Seminary, Western Conservative Baptist, and Capital Bible Seminary.

Dispensational Literature

We have already indicated that the literature of the movement is largely of the pamphlet type. Prominent in dispensational publishing were Paul and Timothy Loizeaux who came from England to Vinton, Iowa in 1876. Three years later, they moved to New York where they established the Bible Truth Depot, a most important source for Brethren and dispensational pamphlets and books.

Among other items of literature influential in the spread of American Dispensationalism, we mention only a few. *Jesus is Coming*, by W. E. Blackstone, had enormous impact in helping to popularize the movement.[41] First published in 1878, a presentation edition of several

---

40. Figures for the forty-one members or associations were derived from the official 1955–56 AABIBC listing. The figure for theological students is derived from an addition of the figures supplied by the *Twentieth Century Encyclopedia of Religious Knowledge*.
41. W. E. Blackstone, *Jesus Is Coming* (Chicago: Moody Bible Institute, n.d.).

hundred thousand copies was published in 1908, and in this fashion it came into the hands of thousands of Christian workers.

A great number of magazines devoted to these themes were regularly published. Especially influential were *The Truth*, edited by James H. Brookes, and the *Sunday School Times*, edited by C. G. Trumbull. In theological literature, *Bibliotheca Sacra*, the oldest theological quarterly in America which was taken over in 1933 from Pittsburgh-Xenia Seminary by Dallas Seminary, is outstanding as a dispensational guide.[42] This brief sketch will serve only to indicate the prodigious literary labors which have marked Dispensationalism.

The Bible Conference Movement

The Bible conference movement has also played an important role in the dissemination of dispensational theology. The Niagara Bible Conference was particularly significant. Begun in a small way by J. H. Brookes, Nathaniel West, W. J. Erdman, and J. M. Parsons near Chicago in 1875, the conference grew each year and changed locations until 1883 when it settled at Niagara-on-the-Lake, Ontario. The list of speakers at these conferences is a veritable catalog of outstanding American dispensationalists and premillennialists. Moorehead, Garrett, Gaebelein, Whittle, Needham, Gordon, and Pierson were prominent. That Brookes was a chief influence at the conference cannot be doubted, and it is significant that the conference dissolved two years after his death.

The manner of its dissolution is instructive. A controversy arose about the theory of the "two comings" of Christ, one *for* His saints, and one *with* His saints. Nathaniel West and others taught that this distinction originated with Edward Irving and bitterness, recriminations, and division followed. This type of controversy has not died out and is often seen to be the "Achilles heel" of Dispensationalism.

The Niagara Bible Conference gave impetus to many other such conferences built especially around the theme of the Second Coming. Out of the summer Bible conferences grew large national or regional "prophetic conferences." The first of these was in New York City in 1878 and attracted considerable interest even in the secular press. Again the leading spirit was James H. Brookes. Kromminga notes that the call for the conference was signed by thirty-one Presbyterians, ten

---

42. See G. C. Houghton, "Bibliotheca Sacra: Its Beginning in 1843." *Bibliotheca Sacra* 126 (1969):214–223.

United Presbyterians, twenty-two Baptists, ten Episcopalians, ten Congregationalists, and one Lutheran.[43] A similar conference was held in Moody's Farwell Hall in Chicago in 1886, where papers were read by many leading chiliasts. The representation was truly international and even included Franz Delitzsch of Leipzig and Frederic Godet of Switzerland. Allegheny in 1895, Boston in 1901, and Chicago in 1914 were scenes of additional prophetic conferences, and the practice was institutionalized at various Bible conference grounds around the country. More recently, volumes of prophetic conference addresses have been produced under the editorship of Charles Lee Feinberg—an indication of continuing interest in such matters.[44]

Dispensational Mission Efforts

American Dispensationalism has been very missions-minded. Scofield founded the Central American Mission, and the faith missions movement, which originated with Hudson Taylor's China Inland Mission, has been largely dominated by dispensationalists and has operated in accordance with dispensational principles. Operating in a very different manner from denominational mission agencies, faith missions have attracted a largely interdenominational and nondenominational constituency. In a large measure, interdenominational cooperation among members of a mission has been made feasible by the importance attached to agreement on eschatology.

Here at home, most leading evangelists have been teachers or followers of Dispensationalism. Earlier in this century, the radio broadcasts of dispensationalists such as D. G. Barnhouse, Charles E. Fuller, and M. R. DeHaan attracted a wide audience. Today, most of the noted "electronic" evangelists, including Rex Humbard, Jerry Falwell, Jim Bakker, Jimmy Swaggart, James Robison, and Billy Graham are dispensational.

A special concern has been missions among the Jews. This was the life work of Arno C. Gaebelein and many others have taken an interest in this work to the present day. Since the establishment of the modern state of Israel, a major factor in these endeavors has been the strong dispensational advocacy of Israel. This defense has stemmed in large

---

43. Kromminga, *Millennium*, p. 232.
44. See Charles Lee Feinberg, ed., *Prophetic Truth Unfolding* (Westwood, N.J.: Revell, 1968); *Prophecy in the Seventies* (Chicago: Moody, 1971); *Jesus the King is Coming* (Chicago: Moody, 1975).

measure from the dispensational insistence on the eternal claim of the Jewish people to the land of Palestine. It is curious, however, that dispensationalists ignore the clear teaching of the Old Testament to the effect that the occupancy of the land of Palestine was granted to the Jews on condition of covenantal obedience (see Deuteronomy 28:15–68). The return of the Jews to Palestine in unbelief hardly fulfills such a Biblical requirement.

Ultradispensationalism or "Bullingerism"

This movement, which many critics of Dispensationalism regard as the only consistent Dispensationalism, had its origins as a distinct movement in the work of Ethelbert W. Bullinger (1837–1913). Bullinger was, like Darby, an extraordinary man and, also like Darby, he came from a distinguished family and enjoyed a good education. Bullinger was a descendant of Heinrich Bullinger, the successor of Zwingli and a leader of the Swiss Reformation. An Anglican clergyman and a scholar of some note, Bullinger distinguished Israel and the church even more radically than Darby, maintaining that the origin of the church lies with the ministry of the Apostle Paul after the close of the book of Acts. Bullinger argued that the church was not to observe the sacraments of baptism and the Lord's Supper, and he advocated the theory of *soul sleep*—the notion that the soul passes out of conscious existence between death and the resurrection.

In America, the main exponent of the Bullinger views was J. C. O'Hair, pastor of the North Shore Church in Chicago and founder of Milwaukee Bible College. While disagreeing with Bullinger on such extremes as soul sleep and non-use of the Lord's Supper, O'Hair agreed on the abandonment of water baptism in this dispensation and he was tireless in attacking fundamentalists who disagreed with him. A self-taught man, he wrote nearly two hundred books and pamphlets, the style of which makes one wish he had been less diligent. Cornelius R. Stam has continued the tradition, and his literary output is both voluminous and cogent in its adherence to dispensational presuppositions.

Ultradispensationalism has been vigorously resisted by traditional Dispensationalism. Harry Ironside called Bullingerism "an absolutely Satanic perversion of the truth."[45] Then he affirms, "Let one point be

---

45. Harry Ironside, *Wrongly Dividing the Word of Truth* (New York: Loizeaux, n.d.), p. 11. The reader will note that while Ironside applies this title to Bullingerism, deemed extreme dispensationalism, I apply it to Dispensationalism in general.

absolutely clear: No one was ever saved in any dispensation on any other ground than the finished work of Christ."[46] While this statement is hardly consistent with Ironside's Dispensationalism, we may well rejoice that, when forced to choose between Christian orthodoxy and dispensational consistency, the specter of Bullingerism has caused traditionalists to reject Ultradispensationalism.

---

46. Ibid., p. 57.

DISPENSATIONALISM AND THE REFORMED CHURCHES

B rookes may have been the first Presbyterian convert to Dispensationalism, but he was not the last. Given the prominent role that Presbyterians played in the dispensational movement, it is necessary to pay close attention to this relationship.[1]

The Northern Presbyterian Church

The mainline northern Presbyterian alliance with Dispensationalism begins in the last quarter of the nineteenth century, especially with the Niagara Bible Conferences of 1883–1897 in which J. H. Brookes was a central figure. The nature of this alliance has been a matter of scholarly debate in recent years, however. According to Ernest Sandeen, it was the 1878 Premillennial Conference which "marks the beginning of a long period of dispensationalist cooperation with Princeton-oriented Calvinists. The unstable and incomplete synthesis which is known as Fundamentalism, at this point, first becomes visible to the historian."[2] This Sandeen account is insightful and instructive in one way but has so many misleading, if not inaccurate, details that the position has to be picked apart meticulously.

---

1. George M. Marsden, *Fundamentalism and American Culture: The Shaping of Twentieth Century Evangelicalism: 1870–1925* (New York: Oxford, 1980), p. 55f.
2. Sandeen, "Origins," pp. 72–73.

A large part of the problem stems from Sandeen's definition of fundamentalism as "an alliance between two newly formed theologies, dispensationalism and the Princeton Theology which, though not wholly compatible, managed to maintain a united front against modernism until 1918."[3] Sandeen's notion of an "alliance" of "two newly formed theologies" is highly problematic for a number of reasons. First, Princeton *theology* and dispensational *theology* were never in "alliance." They have generally been recognized as mutually exclusive by both sides of the discussion. Even Sandeen indulges in the understatements "not wholly compatible," "managed to maintain a united front," and "unstable and incomplete synthesis." Second, the "alliance" was between theologians of the two conflicting Christian theologies against a common anti-Christian enemy—modernism. Third, this "alliance" still exists. Contemporary Princeton theology men such as R. C. Sproul, Gleason Archer, Roger Nicole, and myself ally with dispensational theologians such as Charles Ryrie, John MacArthur, and Norman Geisler on the boards and programs of the recent International Council on Biblical Inerrancy. Dispensationalists and Princeton theology theologians are still fighting the common enemy of modernism plus tendencies in contemporary evangelicalism leading in that direction. Fourth, in the early days from 1878 to 1918, Dispensationalism (which is incompatible with the Princeton theology) was not always clearly distinguished from premillennialism (which is compatible). In any case, the alliance was on the basis of what the two theologies had in common against modernism.

Finally, the definition of the Princeton theology as a "new" nineteenth-century theology is mistaken. Dispensationalism has enough new features worked into a system of theology that it can accurately be called a nineteenth-century phenomenon. This is patently untrue of Princeton theology which clearly preserved the historic theology known as Augustinian Calvinism. Every doctrine in the *Institutes* of John Calvin reappears in the work of Archibald Alexander, Charles Hodge, and B. B. Warfield. Warfield is the greatest Calvinist theologian of the twentieth century, and Old Princeton is almost universally recognized as the American bastion of Calvinism.

Why does Sandeen think otherwise? Without explicitly denying my contentions above, he cites two "new" doctrines in Old Princeton. They are, in fact, not at all new. Even if they were new, however, a position holding to the whole Calvinistic system with two non-essential

---

3. Ibid., p. 67.

additions could not be called a "newly formed" nineteenth-century theology or said to be teaching "a unique theology." The two novelties Sandeen alleges are the doctrine of the inerrancy of Scripture and Biblical rationalism.

We critiqued Sandeen on the question of inerrancy in 1974.[4] There we commented on Sandeen's charge that Princeton championed inerrancy in a sense which seems to risk the *whole Christian faith* upon one proved error. This is so dreadful a misrepresentation that one wonders how anyone who knows anything about the Princeton theologians could write it.[5]

Whether Sandeen read this critique or not, his treatment of the matter in his later book, *The Roots of Fundamentalism*, is much more moderate.[6] Here he simply contends that the Princeton theology developed inerrancy and autographa arguments beyond the seventeenth-century position. No one denies *developments* in any definable school of thought. *Innovations* or *departures* are something else again.[7]

As far as the charge of rationalism is concerned, the same situation prevails. Here it is important to distinguish between "rationalism" (the belief that human reason is capable of attaining to all truth) and "rationality" (the commitment to the rational cognition and articulation of all truth including revelation). No one will deny that the Princetonians (every one of them utterly opposed to "rationalism") developed a more rational articulation of apologetics than is found in Calvin. That this again is a difference of degree and not kind is seen in the very title of a chapter in Calvin's *Institutes*: "So Far as Human Reason Goes, Sufficiently Firm Proofs Are At Hand To Establish the Credibility of Scripture."[8]

---

4. John H. Gerstner, "Warfield's Case for Biblical Inerrancy," in *God's Inerrant Word: An International Symposium on the Trustworthiness of Scripture*, ed. John W. Montgomery, (Minneapolis: Bethany Fellowship, 1974), pp. 115–142. Greg L. Bahnsen and Kenneth L. Gentry, Jr., *House Divided, The Break-up of Dispensational Theology* (Tyler, Tex.: Institute for Christian Economics, 1989). Jon Zens, "The Believer's Rule of Life: A Study of Two Extremes," *Baptist Reformation Review* 8 (Winter 1979): 5–19; See also his *Dispensationalism*.

5. See Gerstner, "Warfield's Case," p. 119.

6. Ernest R. Sandeen, *The Roots of Fundamentalism: British and American Millenarianism 1800–1930* (Chicago: University of Chicago Press, 1970).

7. For further discussion of this point see Gerstner, "Warfield's Case"; and "The Contributions of Charles Hodge, B. B. Warfield, and J. Gresham Machen to the Doctrine of Inspiration," in *Challenges to Inerrancy, A Theological Response*, ed. Gordon R. Lewis and Bruce A. Demarest (Chicago: Moody, 1984), pp. 347–381.

8. John Calvin, *Institutes of the Christian Religion*, 2 vols., ed. John T. McNeill, trans. Ford Lewis Battles (Philadelphia: Westminster Press, 1960), 1:81.

Brian Gerrish has pointed out the appeal to reason present in the thought of the Reformers (often thought by modern scholars, whom Sandeen echoes, to be absent), and E. Gilson has shown the same rationality to be present in Augustine.[9] Fideism (the notion that religious belief is utterly without rational foundation) is surely an academic disease widespread in the twentieth century, and it has a tendency to be read back into healthier centuries.

All of this notwithstanding, it cannot be denied that Dispensationalism did infiltrate Reformed ranks. The influential Presbyterian missionary and Western Seminary professor, Samuel Kellogg, was sympathetic with dispensationalists but, as even Sandeen admits, only at the premillennial level.[10] In more recent times, when Dispensationalism was clearly distinguished from premillennialism, some dispensationalists, such as the late Donald Grey Barnhouse, remained in the Presbyterian Church, U.S.A. and apparently never saw the discrepancy between Dispensationalism and the Reformed confessional standards they had pledged to uphold.

Wilbur Smith was another example of this contradiction in terms — a dispensational Presbyterian minister. For years he served a Presbyterian Church, U.S.A. congregation in Coatesville, Pennsylvania. Paul Johnson, present pastor of the Renton, Washington congregation of the Presbyterian Church, U.S.A., told me of an interesting episode in the lives of these two Presbyterian dispensationalists. (Note that Dispensationalism holds that the Lord's Prayer is not intended for the church.) Wilbur Smith was supplying the pulpit of Barnhouse's Tenth Presbyterian Church in Philadelphia. He concluded his pastoral prayer by inviting the congregation to join him in the Lord's Prayer. He found himself reciting that prayer all by himself without an echo from the congregation! Barnhouse had apparently taught his people a more consistent practice of Dispensationalism than Smith, a reviser of the Scofield Bible, was espousing.

There were other Presbyterians who, in the thirties, were holding this incompatible theology along with a professed adherence to Reformed confessions. T. Roland Phillips, Harold S. Laird, and Allan MacRae were only a few among them.

---

9. Brian Gerrish, *Grace and Reason: A Study in the Theology of Luther* (Oxford: Clarendon, 1962); Etienne Gilson, *The Christian Philosophy of Saint Augustine* (New York: Random House, 1960).
10. Sandeen, "Origins," p. 75.

By the mid-1930s, the *ad hoc* alliance of Princeton theology Presbyterians and dispensational Presbyterians was no longer able to stem the tide of modernism within the northern mainline church. A dispute over support for the denominational mission agency resulted in the dismissal of J. Gresham Machen and a number of other conservative leaders from the denomination. Machen and others formed what was then called the Presbyterian Church of America in 1936 and, initially at least, a number of dispensationalists were also a part of this new church. The difference between the two groups was immediately apparent and a second division was inevitable. As Jon Zens bluntly put the matter, "Pre-mils were welcome in the Church. Scofield-followers were not. There *is* a great difference between the two."[11]

When the Presbyterian separation of 1936 took place, Machen saw three problems facing the new group. One was the presence of Carl McIntire. The second was the influence of *The Scofield Reference Bible*, and the third problem was premillennialism. The problem with the Scofield Bible was that its interpretive notes were fundamentally inconsistent with the Westminster Confession. The problem posed by premillennialism was the tendency on the part of many to confuse it with Scofield Dispensationalism. The problem with McIntire was that he was the chief example of one who tended to confuse the two.[12] Machen, with the help of fellow Westminster Seminary professors John Murray and R. B. Kuiper,[13] was firm in his opposition to Arminianism and Dispensationalism, while not opposing premillennialism (as compatible with membership in the new denomination).

In 1937, the inevitable split occurred, and the Presbyterian Church of America (later called the Orthodox Presbyterian Church) and the more dispensational Bible Presbyterian Synod went their separate ways. The Bible Synod then actually revised the Westminster Confession of Faith to teach premillennialism (though not Dispensationalism). The Bible Synod suffered a further split in 1956 which resulted in the formation of what came to be known as the Evangelical Presbyterian Church. This group merged with the non-dispensational Reformed Presbyterian Church in North America, General Synod in 1965 to form the Reformed Presbyterian Church, Evangelical Synod (RPCES). It is interesting to note that Barnhouse's old church, now pastored by

---

11. Zens, *Dispensationalism*, p. 48.

12. J. Gresham Machen, "Editorial," *Presbyterian Guardian* (November 14, 1936), pp. 41–55.

13. John Murray, "Modern Dispensationalism," *Presbyterian Guardian* (May 19, 1936), pp. 77–79; R. B. Kuiper, "Why Separation Was Necessary," *Presbyterian Guardian* (Sept. 12, 1936), pp. 225–227.

Barnhouse admirer James M. Boice, joined the RPCES without difficulty (though the Scofield Bibles were removed from the pews of Tenth Church). The RPCES joined the new Presbyterian Church in America in 1982. Although it is difficult to be certain at this stage, it appears that the threat of Dispensationalism has been quietly defused in these more conservative Presbyterian denominations.

The United Presbyterian Church of North America

Dispensationalism also infiltrated the former United Presbyterian Church of North America (UPCNA). This Reformed body was formed in 1858 and exactly a century later united with the Presbyterian Church, U.S.A. to form the United Presbyterian Church in the United States of America (UPCUSA). One president of Xenia Theological Seminary of the UPCNA, W. G. Moorehead, was actually an editor of the original *Scofield Reference Bible* of 1909. So far as we can find, there was little or no protest on this manifest inconsistency though the UPCNA held to the Westminster Standards as its only creed at that time.

When I attended Pittsburgh-Xenia Theological Seminary (1936–1937), I never heard a single reference to Dispensationalism or *The Scofield Reference Bible* in any class. Dispensationalism was no issue on campus. Melvin Grove Kyle, the famous archeologist, had retired earlier, and Sandeen says of him that there is some "circumstantial evidence" that he was a dispensationalist.[14] That "evidence" seems to be that Kyle was one of the editors of the *Sunday School Times*. That would indeed be merely "circumstantial" because, as we have seen, Reformed thinkers and dispensationalists did cooperate against the common enemy of modernism then and now. Kyle's successor, James L. Kelso, certainly seemed unaware of the existence of Dispensationalism (though unfortunately he was not a Reformed theologian either, but tended to disparage theology *per se*).

The United Presbyterian Church of North America, until its union in 1958, seemed to be tolerant of Dispensationalism. Its motto was "The Truth of God—Forbearance in Love." The emphasis, without question, was on the *forbearance* and not the *truth*. At the time of this author's licensure in the UPCNA, the other candidate for licensure was a thorough dispensationalist. Neither he nor the presbytery seemed aware of, or concerned with, the discrepancy. When I was later

---

14. Sandeen, "Origins," p. 79, note 55.

nominated for the chair of church history at Pittsburgh-Xenia Theological Seminary, I was opposed in one of the presbyteries because I was an "Augustinian" until one of the presbyters asked what was wrong with having an "Augustinian" in an Augustinian seminary. In other words, the UPCNA tended to be apathetic to both Dispensationalism and Calvinism.

The Southern Presbyterian Church

It is not surprising that Dispensationalism encountered more opposition in the predominantly southern Presbyterian Church in the United States (PCUS). Dallas Theological Seminary was located in its domain, and students from that dispensationalist seminary poured into its ministry. In 1943, PCUS theologian James Bear wrote:

> The situation in our Church today is: Dispensationalism is being widely taught in our Church. The Dispensationalists seem undoubtedly to be right when they say their position is widely divergent doctrinally from that of the Church, even on such an important doctrine as the Covenant of Grace. Yet we have not heard of any move being made by the proponents of "Dispensational truth" to revise our *Confession of Faith* in accordance with the teaching of this "Dispensational truth" which they declare to be the teaching of the Word of God.[15]

Ultimately, this distress about Dispensationalism in the Presbyterian Church in the United States climaxed in the appointment of an ad interim committee (headed by Bear) to consider whether Dispensationalism was compatible with the church's subordinate standard, the Westminster Confession of Faith. The committee reported at the General Assembly of 1944, and the Assembly approved the report which stated that Dispensationalism was not compatible with the Westminster standards.[16]

The struggle with Dispensationalism, unfortunately, was not always clear and uncomplicated. The PCUS, for example, which clearly enough repudiated Dispensationalism in 1944, was not equally clear in

---

15. James E. Bear, "Dispensationalism and the Covenant of Grace," *Union Seminary Review* 49 (1938):307. See also Zens, *Dispensationalism*, p. 42.

16. Presbyterian Church in the United States, "Dispensationalism and the Confession of Faith," *Minutes of the 84th General Assembly* (May 25-30, 1944):123-127.

its own commitment to Reformed theology. Dispensationalism was clearly designated as error on the conservative side of the theological spectrum, but comparable care and skill was not devoted to noting the errors of the liberal left. As we have seen, theological conservatives in the northern Presbyterian churches were sympathetic with Dispensationalism because of its thorough conservatism. This was not so much the case in the PCUS, however, because of the strong and explicit stand which the PCUS took on confessional grounds against Dispensationalism.

The Presbyterian Church in America (PCA) was formed in 1973 by conservatives from the PCUS who were disturbed by the liberal trend of the southern church. This new group has largely echoed the PCUS rejection of Dispensationalism, and it has been much more diligent in its rejection of the modernist error than the denomination from which it emerged. The PCA and the RPCES merged in 1982, and, while Dispensationalism may still surface in this denomination, it seems to pose little threat at the present time.

The Dutch Reformed Churches

Dispensationalism has been considerably less evident in the two major Dutch-American Reformed denominations than in the Presbyterian churches. The ethnic character and confessional commitment of the Reformed Church in America (RCA) and, to an even greater extent, the Christian Reformed Church (CRC) have conspired to limit the appeal and spread of dispensational doctrines among these groups.

While the older Reformed Church in America has been somewhat more influenced by American religious trends than its sister denomination, its theologians were critical of Dispensationalism. The well-known Reformed church theologian, Albertus Pieters, pronounced *The Scofield Reference Bible* "one of the most dangerous books on the market."[17]

Within the Christian Reformed Church, dispensational doctrines were disseminated by Rev. Harry Bultema, but his contention that Israel and the church constitute two separate peoples of God was condemned by the CRC Synod of 1918 as incompatible with the Reformed confessions. The vigorous condemnation of Bultema within the CRC has resulted in a general suspicion within that denomination toward all

---

17. Albertus Pieters, *A Candid Examination of the Scofield Bible* (Grand Rapids: Douma Publications, 1938), p. 119. See also the trenchant criticism of Dispensationalism in his *The Ten Tribes in History and Prophecy* (Grand Rapids: Eerdmans, 1934), p. 24.

forms of premillennialism, whether dispensational or not. The only other premillennialist of note within this group was D. H. Kromminga, a professor at Calvin Seminary, whose rather muted advocacy of premillennialism aroused some suspicion within the denomination.[18]

The Problem of Premillennialism

The experience of the Presbyterian and the Dutch Reformed denominations in this country illustrates the difficulties involved in distinguishing historic premillennialism from dispensational premillennialism. Our historical survey has revealed the importance of making such a distinction however.

As we have seen, all dispensationalists are premillennialists, but by no means are all premillennialists dispensationalists. We noted that premillennialism was present, though not dominant, in the early church and that it virtually died out after Augustine for a thousand years. We also saw that the premillennialism which arose after the Reformation was of the non-dispensational or historic variety and that what can be meaningfully described as "dispensational" premillennialism was very much an innovation of the nineteenth century.

In America, we noted the conflict between historic premillennialists and dispensational premillennialists at the late nineteenth-century prophetic conferences and that Dispensationalism largely won the day. Since that time, Dispensationalism has professed to speak for premillennialism generally.

Moving into the twentieth century, we also see the vigorous resurgence of a self-consciously non-dispensational premillennialism associated with scholars such as George Eldon Ladd, Daniel Fuller, and J. Barton Payne. Fuller Seminary in particular, where Ladd taught for many years, became well known as a center of such thought. The effect of this was not lost on Fuller's founder, Dr. Charles E. Fuller, who is said to have admitted shortly before his death that he could find no Scripture to support the theory of a pretribulational Rapture, though he still believed in it anyway.

From the dispensational perspective, it is no historical accident that they are premillennialists or that many premillennialists are dispensationalists. For them, Dispensationalism is premillennialism in the

---

18. See James D. Bratt, *Dutch Calvinism in Modern America* (Grand Rapids: Eerdmans, 1984), pp. 95–98, 132–133.

purity of its expression. As a matter of fact, most dispensationalists maintain that a consistent premillenarian will logically be a dispensationalist. They do not deny that some premillenarians are not dispensationalists, but they deny that they are ever logical and consistent in that position.

For example, Dwight Pentecost goes so far as to say that "Scripture is unintelligible until one can distinguish clearly between God's program for his earthly people, Israel, and that for the Church."[19] That statement for Pentecost means that without pretribulational, premillennial Dispensationalism, the Scripture is "unintelligible." The church must be separated from Israel by the Rapture before the seven-year Tribulation. Even if a person were a traditional premillennialist, without this other element by means of which Israel is distinguished from the church, Scripture would remain a mystery and confusion would reign.[20]

There are many different responses to this claim of Dispensationalism that it is the consistent form of premillennialism. One inadequate response is a tendency of some non-premillennialists to agree with this dispensational allegation. For example, George Murray's *Millennial Studies* is a generally good eschatological analysis from a postmillennial viewpoint. Throughout, Murray opposes Dispensationalism, but unfortunately, he does not distinguish between it and premillennialism. Using the two terms interchangeably, he frequently makes statements which are true of Dispensationalism but not true of classical premillennialism.[21]

Loraine Boettner is more careful but, at the same time, he tends to equate premillennialism and Dispensationalism. He writes:

> While historical premillenarianism is a much less erroneous system than is that of Dispensationalism, it is only wishful thinking which assumes the two can be logically separated and kept in water-tight compartments. The two systems are basically the same and must stand or fall together. We believe that we have shown that the Scriptures not only fail to teach the premillenarian system, but that they definitely exclude it as a possible interpretation.[22]

---

19. Dwight Pentecost, *Things to Come* (Findlay, Ohio: Dunham, 1958), p. 529.

20. Ibid., p. 164f. This position that consistent premillennialism spells Dispensationalism is so common and constantly cited that further references in Scofield, Darby, Chafer, Walvoord, and Ryrie seem quite unnecessary.

21. George Lewis Murray, *Millennial Studies: A Search for Truth* (Grand Rapids, Baker, 1948).

22. Loraine Boettner, *The Millennium* (Grand Rapids: Baker, 1958), p. 375.

It is this latter statement that probably explains Boettner's earlier statement. Being convinced that premillennialism itself is unbiblical, he sees very little difference between that and the even more unbiblical Dispensationalism. Still, one might agree with Boettner that premillennialism is unbiblical but distinguish between the premillenarian system of doctrine and the dispensational system of doctrine. It may not be a "watertight" separation but it is a real one nevertheless.

The Dutch Calvinistic writers, being quite impatient with premillennialism as basically Judaistic and alien to the New Testament spirit, rather glibly identify it with Dispensationalism. Rutgers, Masselink, Berggraff, and a host of others following in the footsteps of Abraham Kuyper tend to make this mistake of confusing the two systems. Masselink, for example, writes:

> This is one of the saddest and most unscriptural defects in the whole premillennialist plan of the future [he is referring to bringing heaven down to earth in the millennium]. . . . We believe that when Christ comes again there will be a new heaven and a new earth. Creation will be restored and the curse will be removed. This is not the millennium of which the chiliast speaks, but this is the beginning of eternity on earth. Joyfully anticipating the renewing of all things, including the restoration of the whole creation of God, which shall accompany the complete consummation of the great purpose of redemption, the whole Christian Church looks forward to Christ's coming.[23]

A somewhat more adequate response to this dispensational claim of consistent premillennialism is found in writers such as G. E. Ladd. Ladd seems satisfied to stake his claim that premillennialism does not *necessarily* lead to Dispensationalism. We consider this a massive understatement, but it does at least maintain a significant difference between the two eschatologies. Ladd challenges the dispensational claim to antiquity, and he denies that pretribulationism even existed before the nineteenth century.[24] Ladd's position is similar to that of a number of early prophetic conference participants who tended to draw away from the dispensational movement when they sensed that it was going beyond their own conception of premillennialism. Nathaniel West, Henry Frost, and even Reuben A. Torrey are noticeable examples of this.[25]

---

23. Masselink, *Why a Thousand Years?*, p. 222.
24. George Eldon Ladd, *The Blessed Hope* (Grand Rapids: Eerdmans, 1956).
25. Lewis Sperry Chafer, *Major Bible Themes*, rev. John Walvoord, (Grand Rapids: Zondervan, 1974), p. 79ff.

Our historical survey will alert the reader to the fact that there is no historical support for (and considerable historical argument against) any identification of premillennialism and Dispensationalism. In light of this, dispensationalists should admit, at the very least, that the majority of historic premillennialists throughout history have been quite unaware of the alleged dissonance and confusion that dispensationalists claim to discern so clearly in the historic position. Now let me briefly indicate that there is no theological compatibility between these two traditions whatever.

The only fitting response to the dispensational claim of being premillennialism in full consistency is that, so far from that being the case, Dispensationalism is antithetically opposed to premillennialism properly understood. That is, these systems of thought, being properly understood for what they truly do teach, are in complete disharmony with one another.

The point here is that premillennialism is merely an eschatology while Dispensationalism is a theological system which includes "premillennialism." It is this which makes it impossible for a proper premillennialist to be a dispensationalist rather than inevitable that he will be. Premillennialists are persons who believe the Christian religion and entertain the notion that Christ is going to come at a later date and establish a thousand-year reign of some sort on this earth. That millennial doctrine may be true or false, but it will not make a person who in all other parts certainly holds to the Christian religion to deviate therefrom. Dispensationalism, however, in its eschatology and its entire system is in constant deviation from essential historical Christianity (as I will attempt to show in the doctrinal part of this book).

Anticipating the theological critique which will be undertaken later, let me simply note here two crucial areas in which Dispensationalism as a theological system diverges from orthodox Christianity. There is, first of all, the persistent Antinomianism which characterizes dispensational theology. This one feature alone, if demonstrated, vitiates any claim of Dispensationalism to Christianity. One simply cannot be antinomian *and* Christian in his theology. Antinomianism teaches that a person *may* be truly regenerate while in no way obedient to the commands of the law. That means that he may have "faith without works." According to the Bible, faith without works is "dead" (James 2:26). Even a dispensationalist will admit that, if his theological faith is a theologically dead faith, his is a theologically dead-in-the-water system of doctrine. He needs only to be convinced of this accusation.

Another dispensational departure from historic Christianity is evident in the separation of Israel and the church into two separate and distinct peoples of God—an earthly people with temporal rewards (Israel) and a spiritual people with heavenly rewards (the church). This notion is the crucial conviction behind the pretribulational Rapture theory.

We have already noted that this separation entails the rejection of the unity of the covenant of grace and the implicit denial, despite some dispensational protestations to the contrary, that Old Testament believers were saved by the grace that is in Jesus Christ. Thus, the giving of the Law to Moses on Mount Sinai is thought, by dispensationalists, to be a divine offer of a divine plan of salvation by works which Israel was ill-advised to accept. The Old Testament in its entirety is designated "legal ground" from which the dispensationalist is to flee.

That dispensationalists attempt to explain away the many scriptural passages which clearly teach or assume the essential unity of Israel and the church (see, for example, Romans 2:28–29, 4:11–17, 11:17–21, Galatians 3:7, Ephesians 2:11–16) is a continuing source of amazement to non-dispensationalists. The pretribulational Rapture theory, the utter novelty of which has already been noted, is so problematic because it is here that this alleged separation of Israel and the church comes to eschatological fruition. Here the theoretical Rapture becomes an actual historical rupture.

Consequently, I maintain that the dispensational claim that premillennialism rests on Dispensationalism, implies Dispensationalism, and comes to its perfect fruition in the dispensational eschatology is utterly mistaken. Premillennialism is an eschatology of persons holding to the Christian religion. Dispensationalism is a theology of persons holding to a deviation from the Christian religion. Just as truly as a proper premillennialist would resent being called a Jehovah's Witness because Jehovah's Witnesses also are premillennialists, or a Mormon because Mormons also are premillennialists, so also, a premillennialist should resent being called a dispensationalist because dispensationalists also are "premillennialists" (though I do not infer for a moment that Jehovah's Witnesses and Mormons are orthodox trinitarians at the heart as are *all* dispensationalists).

Dispensational Premillennialism
And the Trivialization of Eschatology

The dispensational penchant for endless distinction-making and the separation of things which ought not to be put asunder has lead to a host of quarrels over trivialities which, although sad because of the error they represent, are also comical. Charles Ryrie makes a rather amusing comment regarding the question of how many "Second Comings" there will be:

> Almost all agree that the rapture is to be distinguished from the second coming in the sense that the former is when Christ comes for his own people and the latter his coming with them in triumph and glory. But how far apart these two events are in time is the disputed question.[26]

He even goes on to say that amillennialists view the two events as simultaneously occurring and that they therefore admit no "time apart." This is surely a straining of a gnat swallowing a camel. This whole idea of a coming of Christ "for" His saints and a later coming "with" His saints is a dispensational novelty. Premillennialists *per se* do not entertain that, not to mention post- and amillennialists. Whether Christ comes before the Millennium (premillennialism) or after the Millennium (postmillennialism) or whether there is no separate Millennium (amillennialism), there is only one Second final Coming. When Christ comes, His saints among others are raised.

The differences among the dispensationalists, though extremely important in their own eyes, in the overall eschatological picture are trivial. Much ink has been spilled in debates over whether the Rapture will be silent or audible, whether it will be followed by seven years or by three and a-half years and so forth. For example, John Walvoord became annoyed with D. Meresco because Meresco refers to himself as a pretribulationist when he is, according to Walvoord, a "mid-tribulationist."[27]

Dispensationalists have also had trouble among themselves over the secrecy element in the Rapture. Certainly, the general position of Dispensationalism calls for a secret and quiet Rapture in which the saints alone see Jesus Christ and the world is left in ignorance. Lindsey, for example, rather floridly describes what he believes will happen:

> There I was driving down the freeway and all of a sudden the place went crazy . . . cars going in all directions . . . and not one of them

---

26. Charles Caldwell Ryrie, *Survey of Bible Doctrine* (Chicago: Moody, 1972), p. 167.

27. D. Meresco, *New Light on the Rapture* (New York: Bible Light, 1980); John Walvoord, review of Meresco in *Bibliotheca Sacra* 139 (1982), p. 76.

had a driver. I mean it was wild! I think we've got an invasion from outer space.[28]

All of this will happen because, as Lindsey believes, though the Second Coming is visible to all, "only the Christians see Him" at the Rapture.[29]

The audible or "noisy" rapturists, on the other hand, have been present in Dispensationalism from the very beginning. R. A. Torrey and others denied the secrecy doctrine, and one of the most famous of the Plymouth Brethren dispensationalists, William Pettingill, likewise gave up the notion of a secret Rapture. He writes,

> so it will not be silent, or secret, or unheard. I know that many teachers insist that all this will be hidden from the world and will be heard only by the redeemed, but the record does not so read.[30]

While proceeding further to chronicle the quarrels of dispensationalists would be tedious, it is evident that Dispensational eschatology is dying the death of a thousand trivializations. Such silliness should not, however, obscure the fact that, whatever differences dispensationalists may have among themselves about the details of the Rapture calendar, they agree unanimously on the Rapture as the final separation of Israel and the church. The unity of the church, even if it is ultimately healed according to some (inconsistent) dispensationalists, is nevertheless for some time, if not for eternity, destroyed.

We sympathize with the contentions of historic premillennialists Robert Gundry, Barton Payne, Dan Fuller, and others on behalf of posttribulationism. They generally believe that the seven years of tribulation can be purifying for the church of Jesus Christ. Fuller remarks that

> just as Scofield declared that the sufferings of the tribulation would function as a purifying chastisement for the Jewish remnant, so posttribulationism says that these judgments, which will be punitive for the world, will function as salutary chastisements for the believer.[31]

---

28. Lindsey, *Late Great Planet Earth*, pp. 124–125.
29. Ibid., p. 131.
30. William L. Pettingill, *Nearing the End* (Chicago: Van Kampen, 1948), p. 30.
31. Fuller, "Hermeneutics of Dispensationalism," p. 366. Cf. C. I. Scofield, ed., *The Scofield Reference Bible* (New York: Oxford University Press, 1917), p. 788.

Conclusion

In conclusion, history shows Dispensationalism to be a phenomenon of the last century. Its peculiar features were never developed into a system until John Nelson Darby. What gives Dispensationalism some aura of historicity is its premillennialism — which has admittedly been present in the church from the beginning. We have shown this historic premillennialism is not only to be distinguished from Dispensationalism, but is incompatible with it.

A pressing question today is whether Dispensationalism has changed in any significant ways in recent years. I think not. In the following pages I shall attempt to show the general character of Dispensationalism — its philosophy, hermeneutic, spurious Calvinism, and dubious evangelicalism. Along the way it will be seen that this has been its character yesterday and is so today.

PART II

PHILOSOPHY AND HERMENEUTICS

D ispensationalism is rather short on theory and long on practice. That is, it sees itself as a "Biblical theology" at heart and gets to the Bible as quickly as it can. In this sense, it is like Cocceius (see chapter 1), in the seventeenth century, who was moving away from scholastic Reformed theology via "Biblical theology," somewhat as Geerhardus Vos did in the early part of this century.[1] Consequently, it says relatively little regarding theological method, philosophy, natural theology, and other introductory matters which are, in traditional dogmatics, discussed under the rubric *prolegomena*. About hermeneutics, however, it says far more than necessary. That is, as we shall show later, it raises a virtual non-issue to a level of prime importance.

---

1. See Geerhardus Vos, *Biblical Theology* (Grand Rapids: Eerdmans, 1948); *Redemptive History and Biblical Interpretation: The Shorter Writings of Geerhardus Vos*, ed. Richard B. Gaffin, Jr. (Phillipsburg, N.J.: Presbyterian and Reformed, 1980). The influence of Vos is evident in Richard B. Gaffin, Jr., "Systematic Theology and Biblical Theology," *Westminster Theological Journal* 38 (1975–76):284–288.

F I V E

PHILOSOPHY AND APOLOGETICS

M ethodism has its personalism, Old Princeton its Realism, and Roman Catholicism its Thomism, but it would seem that Dispensationalism has no philosophy of its own. Indeed, Dispensationalism is almost anti-philosophical in that it tends to de-emphasize philosophy. It has always been sympathetic to apologetics, as we shall see a little later, but it has not been inclined to philosophize beyond the immediate needs for Biblical verification, and it is almost impatient in its desire to get to Holy Scripture.

John Nelson Darby, for example, was a masterfully knowledgeable man, with expertise in languages and an intimate familiarity with the content of the Bible. Nevertheless, his inclinations do not seem to have leaned in the philosophical direction, and he left no philosophical imprint on his followers.

The same has been true of the most eminent dispensationalists since Darby's time. One can hardly think of anyone who has been noted both as a philosopher and as a proponent of dispensational theology. A possible exception to this is Norman Geisler, who has taught theology at Trinity Evangelical Divinity School, Dallas Theological Seminary, and now at Liberty University. Geisler is noted, however, more for his wide knowledge and able critiques of various philosophical systems than for his own positive contributions to the fields of philosophy and theology.[1]

---

1. Norman L. Geisler, *Philosophy of Religion* (Grand Rapids: Zondervan, 1974). See also his *Christian Apologetics* (Grand Rapids: Baker, 1976).

A survey of *Bibliotheca Sacra*, the journal of Dallas Seminary, as well as the theses produced by Dallas students, reveals many competent exercises in Biblical and theological studies but relatively little concentrated attention to matters of philosophical importance. Indeed, it might well be argued that Dispensationalism in general has been largely content to depend on the theoretical labors of others, especially Reformed theologians, in the evangelical camp. For example, William Evans, in his popular dispensational theological textbook, expresses his debt to the theistic thinking of A. H. Strong and Francis Landey Patton.[2]

The origins of this dependence are evident in the early part of this century in the circumstances surrounding the publication of *The Fundamentals*, a cooperative effort of dispensational and non-dispensational conservatives.[3] Scholarly Princetonians and other conservative academicians joined with the less academic dispensationalists in their common cause to defend inerrancy and other fundamental doctrines of the Christian religion. Recognized dispensationalists, such as Philip Mauro and James M. Gray, were writing alongside Reformed theologians such as B. B. Warfield and James Orr. Thus, the more scholarly conservatives often handled the academic and intellectual problems for Dispensationalism when it was first becoming established in this country.

This rather strange partnership has continued to this day. For example, at the Congress on the Bible, held in San Diego on March 3–6, 1982, the same kind of alliance that produced *The Fundamentals* at the beginning of the century was again evident. There was the influential presence of old line conservatives such as James I. Packer, Francis Schaeffer, Gleason Archer, R. C. Sproul, and others. On the other hand, the Congress was undoubtedly dominated by dispensationalists such as Harold Hoehner, Norman Geisler, Charles Ryrie, John MacArthur, Ray Steadman, Bill Bright, and many others. It is apparent, however, that dispensational scholarship has made significant strides in recent decades. The scholarly imbalance, evident at the time of the publication of *The Fundamentals*, is not as much a factor today.

James M. Boice, the chairman of the International Council on Biblical Inerrancy and the Congress, is an interesting individual in this

---

2. William Evans, *Great Doctrines of the Bible* (Chicago: Bible Institute Colportage Association, 1912), p. 13f.

3. A. C. Dixon, Louis Meyer, Reuben A. Torrey, eds., *The Fundamentals: A Testimony to the Truth*, 12 vols. (Chicago, 1910–15).

context. He is the successor of one of the nation's most famous dispensationalists, the late Donald Grey Barnhouse, is a strong premillennialist, and at the same time is quite Reformed in his general theology. He seems to view Dispensationalism only as a methodology, and he may well become the transitional figure from traditional Dispensationalism to a sound Reformed theology.

Dispensational Epistemology

One might suppose that if Dispensationalism has no particular philosophy, it would be equally uninterested in epistemology. There can be no doubt, however, that Dispensationalism does have a tacit confidence in sense perception. While sophisticated philosophers try to argue and prove the fact of sense perception, virtually all dispensationalists confidently assume it without a great deal of discussion.

Dispensationalists also tend to place great stock in the laws of logic. While they believe in mystery and occasionally even use the word *paradox*, they generally "think straight." Some of them will bend their logic when they think it is in conflict with mystery, but apart from such a detour, they tend to follow a rather pedestrian line of logical thought.

The power of inductive logic is particularly attractive to dispensationalists. Alternative schools of thought are frequently dismissed with the charge that they impose an alien hypothesis on the data. Dispensational thought, on the other hand, is presented as an unbiased, empirical reading of the facts. This characteristic has prompted George Marsden to speak of the "Baconian ideal" of Dispensationalism, and he cites the following statement of A. T. Pierson as striking evidence:

> I like Biblical theology that does not start with the superficial Aristotelian method of reason, that does not begin with an hypothesis, and then warp the facts and the philosophy to fit the crook of our dogma, but a Baconian system, which first gathers the teachings of the word of God, and then seeks to deduce some general law upon which the facts can be arranged.[4]

This raises the question whether Dispensationalism is sympathetic to the Scottish Common Sense Realism of the Old Princeton theologians such as Charles Hodge and B. B. Warfield. Scottish Realism pro-

---

4. A. T. Pierson, quoted in Marsden, *Fundamentalism*, p. 56. See also pp. 43–71.

vided Old Princeton with the philosophical framework for its articulation of Calvinism, and this realistic school of thought prevailed generally in post-revolutionary America.

Scottish Realism, as it was articulated by the Scottish philosophers
Thomas Reid and Dugald Stewart, was a response to the unacceptable
eighteenth-century skepticism of David Hume and to the implausible
idealism of George Berkeley. Against Berkeley, who had argued that
the essence of a thing lies in its perception by mind and so had denied
the reality of material substance, and Hume, whose denial of general
ideas undercut the principles of causality, probability, and confidence
in moral reason, Scottish Realism proposed a new and compelling vin-
dication of the reliability of sense perception. Reid maintained that,
although there are no innate ideas, an analysis of the operation of the
human mind reveals an innate tendency to recognize ideas under the
stimulus of sense perception. These tendencies are the condition of
knowledge and, because these built-in tendencies are common to all
and correspond to objective reality, a person may have confidence in
the "common sense" appropriation of sensory perception.[5]

But how does Dispensationalism stand on all of this? It is virtually
impossible to know because dispensationalists, for the most part, have
avoided writing on that subject. We can only surmise that they were
sympathetic at least, to the realistic way of viewing the origin of ideas.
While the Princeton theologians were rigorously exact in their attention to a cogent articulation of realist epistemology, Dispensationalism, which arose during a period when Realism was taken for granted,
seems to have appropriated a generally realist stance without a great
deal of reflection. It tends to accept certain things which are defended
by Scottish Realism such as the reliability of sense perception, logical
laws, and the intuitions of the mind, without actually developing and
defending that system of thought.

Dispensational Apologetics

Many readers will be aware of the controversy in evangelical circles
over the methodology of apologetics. In recent years the so-called
"presuppositional" approach, which is associated with Cornelius Van
Til and Westminster Theological Seminary, has gained wide prominence.

---

5. For a complete and influential statement of the Scottish Common Sense epistemology, see James McCosh, *The Institutions of the Mind Inductively Investigated*
(New York: Robert Carter, 1866).

Van Til argued that one must presuppose God as a condition for rational belief in Him, and that the starting point for apologetic discussion must be the acknowledgement of God. I have argued extensively that Van Til's approach is not rational in that, by arguing that one must presuppose God as a condition for rational belief, Van Til assumes what he means to prove. In short, his reasoning is circular and his general stance fideistic,[6] although he and fellow presuppositionalists deny fideism rigorously and charge "evidentialism" with autonomy.

As an alternative to presuppositionalism, I have argued for the continuing viability of the "classical" approach to apologetics which is associated with the theologians of Old Princeton. I believe that presuppositionalism is not the historic position of the church and that valid, logically compelling reasons for the truth of Christianity can be advanced.[7]

Where does Dispensationalism fit into this? As we might surmise from the above discussion of dispensational epistemology, Dispensationalism tends to follow the historic or classical apologetic pattern, rather than presuppositionalism, but in a weakened form. By this, we mean that we find here the traditional arguments for the credibility of revelation but that they are usually somewhat less cogent than elsewhere encountered.

Dispensationalists are not disposed to conscious fideism. They wish to give reasons for their faith. Their "reasons," however, often leave much to be desired in tight argumentation. Frequently, they are so feeble that one suspects that the debater is resting his case on something other than the arguments he is offering.

Let us use Walvoord's revision of Chafer in *Major Bible Themes* as an example of a traditional apologetic rather inconclusively argued. Giving evidence for the supernatural inspiration of the Bible, Walvoord mentions, for example, the "influence" of the Bible. What is offered, however, is a mere assertion of the excellence of the influence with no effort to show why that requires divine inspiration, nor does Walvoord face any objections to the assertion.[8] Again he thinks that because the Bible's subject matter deals with man's past and future it must be supernatural![9] The fact that the Bible is candid in its description of man is supposed to prove that it came from God, Walvoord not noting that

---

6. See R. C. Sproul, John Gerstner, Arthur Lindsley, *Classical Apologetics* (Grand Rapids: Zondervan, 1984), pp. 212–338.

7. Ibid., pp. 3–179. Cf. also Gerstner, *The Rational Biblical Theology of Jonathan Edwards* in three volumes (Orlando: Ligonier Ministries, 1991) Vol. I, Chapter III.

8. Chafer and Walvoord, *Major Bible Themes*, p. 13.

9. Ibid., p. 14.

this argument would prove the inspiration of novelists such as Ernest Hemingway and Peter De Vries and Kantian philosophers.[10]

In the next chapter there is evident circularity of reasoning. Walvoord rightly argues that Christ affirmed the inspiration of the Bible. Therefore, he (Walvoord) unjustifiably concludes that the Bible is the Word of God. Our dispensational apologist does not notice that he has failed to prove that Christ is divine except on the assumption that the Bible is the Word of God.[11]

Miracles have been the staple of traditional apologetics. In this century the argument received its classic formulation in the first chapter of B. B. Warfield's *Counterfeit Miracles*.[12] The way dispensationalists use miracles in apologetics, however, it is a miracle that apologetics survives. Chafer may devote more than seventy pages of his *Systematic Theology* to the miracles of Christ, but he and other dispensationalists can demolish the arguments in one sentence, for as Hal Lindsey puts the matter bluntly: "Satan is a miracle-worker and he has been able to work miracles from the beginning."[13]

Evolution as a subject has always greatly concerned dispensationalists. While this theme is usually considered part of the realm of science, it nevertheless has important philosophical and apologetic implications. Dispensationalists, who are noted champions of creationism, have invariably opposed evolution on the ground of its opposition to the Biblical account of creation. Some dispensationalists, such as Norman Geisler who participated in the trial in Little Rock, Arkansas in February, 1982, have attacked the presuppositions of evolution as well as its anti-Biblical character, but most have been content to point out that almost all varieties of evolution have been at loggerheads with the first chapter of Genesis. In other words, Dispensationalism has, in the main, attacked evolution from Biblical rather than philosophical grounds and avoided any deep philosophical involvement in the debate with evolution.

As we noted above, dispensationalists have tended not to embrace presuppositionalism.[14] This is somewhat surprising because presuppo-

---

10. Ibid.

11. See Lewis Sperry Chafer, *Systematic Theology*, 8 vols. (Dallas: Dallas Seminary Press, 1975; reprint ed.), 1:75–77.

12. Benjamin B. Warfield, *Counterfeit Miracles* (Edinburgh: The Banner of Truth Trust, 1976; reprint ed.), pp. 3–31.

13. Lindsey, *The Late Great Planet Earth*, p. 95.

14. One dispensationalist who does make positive comments about presuppositionalism is John C. Whitcomb, Jr. See his "Contemporary Apologetics and the Christian Faith, Part III: Proof Texts for Semi-Rationalistic Apologetics," *Bibliotheca Sacra* 134 (1977):291–298.

sitionalists are in the vanguard of contemporary conservative apologetics. Also, presuppositionalists are invariably Calvinistic, and dispensational theology claims to be moderate Calvinism.

Nevertheless, a number of reasons can be advanced to explain the dispensational lack of interest in presuppositionalism. One reason for this has already been noted. Dispensationalists tend to be reflexively though naively realistic in their epistemology while presuppositionalists come out of the idealist tradition.

The second reason is that all presuppositionalists are thoroughgoing Calvinists and they do not think that Dispensationalism is an authentic form of Calvinism. The dispensationalists do not so much contest this point as ignore it. One gets the feeling that they do not really want to contest it. There is not much doubt that they do distrust presuppositionalism and, under the surface, are quite opposed to the Calvinism of the presuppositionalist. The extent of this dispensational opposition to Calvinism will be the subject of a later chapter of this book.

DISPENSATIONAL HERMENEUTICS

M any proponents and opponents regard the hermeneutics of
Dispensationalism as more basic than the theology itself. They
suppose that the mode of interpretation determines Dispensationalism
rather than Dispensationalism determining it. "The problem of Dispensationalism is its hermeneutical point of departure," said Daniel
Fuller. "It is a theological principle that militates against inductive
study and prevents it from seeing the unity in the Scriptures."[1]

Likewise, almost all dispensationalists maintain that their mode of
Biblical interpretation is more fundamental than their theology. They
view their theology as the result of the simple, literal reading of Scripture. A commitment to literal interpretation is seen as the hallmark of
one who "takes the Bible seriously," but they certainly reject the idea
that their theology provides the major impetus toward literalism.

In this chapter, I shall scrutinize Dispensationalism's view of the
Bible, its literal method of interpretation, and its handling of Biblical
quotations. I shall examine its way of "rightly dividing" Scripture, its
superficiality in so doing, and its inconsistencies. The interpretation of
prophecy comes in for special consideration, in particular as it raises
hermeneutical questions for the dispensationalist. What I call *spoof-
texting* is also part of Dispensationalism's interpretative style and will
receive scrutiny.

---

1. Daniel Fuller, *Gospel and Law: Contrast or Continuum? – The Hermeneutics of
Dispensationalism and Covenant Theology* (Grand Rapids: Eerdmans, 1980), p. 71.

Inspiration

With respect to the Bible, dispensationalists hold undeviatingly to plenary inspiration. They believe that the entire canonical Scriptures of Protestantism are entirely inspired. There is not much said on this subject largely because it is undisputed among them. Dispensationalism's commitment to the inspiration of Scriptures is well illustrated by the composition of the International Council on Biblical Inerrancy, many members of which were dispensationalists.

To note just one example of the viewpoint of Dispensationalism on the inspiration of the Bible, a viewpoint quite typical of the others, we cite their major theologian, John Nelson Darby. The Holy Scriptures, he says, are "inspired of God" and "authoritative."[2] The inscripturated Word is a "permanent guide."[3] The New Testament, as well as the Old, is inspired, he affirms, citing Peter's statement about "other scripture."[4] It is "not merely that truth is given in them by inspiration. . . . They are inspired."[5] As for the canon of Scripture, Darby says, "all is now complete, as Paul tells us that he was a minister of the assembly to complete the Word of God." "The subjects of revelation were then completed."[6]

Dispensationalists have tended to concentrate on popular Biblical exposition and not many have been particularly interested in questions of Biblical criticism. Exceptions to this include early dispensationalists E. W. Bullinger, who produced a Greek lexicon of the New Testament, and the outstanding New Testament scholar S. P. Tragelles. More recently, Allan MacRae has made his mark in the field of ancient Near East studies.

Literalism

Certainly dispensationalists claim to be literal in their method of interpreting the Bible. They pride themselves on this and claim a thorough faithfulness to Scripture. They generally think that other schools of

---

2. Darby, *Letters*, 1:187.
3. John Nelson Darby, *Synopsis of the Books of the Bible*, 3rd ed. rev., 5 vols. (London: G. Morrish, n.d.), 5:196.
4. Ibid., p. 197.
5. Ibid., p. 198.
6. Ibid., p. 199.

thought are not as faithful and that they fall into error primarily because of their adoption of a "spiritualizing" hermeneutic. While they will concede that many non-dispensational conservatives affirm the full authority and inerrancy of Scripture, dispensationalists also feel that not all are equally docile before Scripture. The non-dispensationalist tends, in his view, to be more sophisticated and less submissive while dispensationalists, to use the words of Isaiah, "tremble" more at God's Word (see Isaiah 66:5).

This conviction, in turn, can lead to a spiritual arrogance bordering on a feeling of infallibility. Thinking that they see the truth clearly (when others more learned do not because they do not follow the simple method of easy literalism), dispensationalists can feel superior with very little reason for doing so. By a certain naiveté they suppose that their method brings them into an immediate apprehension of Scripture as over against the "interpretations" of others.[7]

While we must recognize that the self-understanding of dispensationalists tends to highlight the *differences* between dispensational and non-dispensational Biblical interpretation (with the unfortunate psychological consequences noted above), and that dispensationalists *believe* that their theology flows from their literal hermeneutic rather than vice versa, a closer look at the matter reveals that dispensationalists are not as far removed from their non-dispensational conservative friends as they suppose.

In spite of all contentions that dispensationalists are the consistent literalists, they start out in their Biblical interpretation pretty much where everyone else does. They follow inductive, grammatical, historical method just as others do. Allan MacRae, for one, insists that the study of Scripture is like the study of any science—one gathers data, studies them, compares, finds their meaning, draws conclusions, and compares them with other data.[8] The great covenantalist Charles Hodge would not differ with this description.

What could be more conventional than Hal Lindsey's directions:

> When the plain sense of Scripture makes common sense, seek no other sense; therefore, take every word at its primary, ordinary,

---

7. See James Snowden, *Coming of the Lord*, pp. 205–219; Floyd Hamilton, *Basis of Millennial Faith* (Grand Rapids: Eerdmans, 1955), pp. 38, 39, has also commented on this.

8. Allan A. MacRae, "The Scientific Approach to the Old Testament—A Study of Amos 9," in *Truth For Today, Bibliotheca Sacra Reader*, pp. 111–122, edited by John F. Walvoord (Chicago: Moody Press, 1963), p. 10. Cf. Charles Hodge, *Systematic Theology*, 3 vols. (Grand Rapids: Eerdmans, 1981; reprint ed.), 1:9–16.

usual, literal meaning unless the facts of the immediate context, studied in the light of related passages and axiomatic and fundamental truths, indicate clearly otherwise.[9]

James Boice, one of the more scholarly so-called dispensationalists, advises us "to take a passage in the literal sense unless it is demonstrably poetic or unless it simply will not bear literal interpretation."[10]

We *all* agree that most literature, including the *Bible*, is usually meant to be understood according to the literal construction of the words which are used. Even in common speech with one another, we assume the other person is to be taken literally unless it is perfectly obvious that he is using a metaphor, or is allegorizing, or is in some other way alerting us to the fact that the usual meaning of words is not in play at the moment. Then, and then only, will we interpret other than literally. All interpreters do that.

The same is true with respect to the Bible. Most of what it says is to be construed, everybody admits, "literally." There are certain parts of it which everyone, including the dispensationalist, admits are not to be construed literally. There is not a dispensationalist living who believes that, when Christ said He was "the Vine," grapes were to be picked from Him.

Finally, there is a small area of Scripture, mainly in the area of prophecy, where there is lively debate as to whether one interprets literally or figuratively. The vast proportion of Scripture is admitted by both sides to be either obviously literal or obviously figurative. It is only in a relatively few disputed areas where we differ with one another. Only there does the question whether Scripture is to be taken literally or figuratively arise. We should not accuse the dispensationalists of being absolute literalists nor should they accuse non-dispensationalists of being absolute spiritualizers. We all are literalists up to a certain point. *At the point where we differ*, there is a *tendency* for the dispensationalists to be literalistic where the non-dispensationalist *tends* to interpret the Bible figuratively. But to say on the basis of that limited divergence of interpretation that the two schools represent fundamentally different approaches is not warranted.

Many on both sides think that this minor "hermeneutical" difference is a more foundational difference than the theological. We profoundly

9. Lindsey, *Late Great Planet Earth*, p. 40. See also Blackstone, *Jesus Is Coming*, p. 21.

10. James M. Boice, *The Last and Future World* (Grand Rapids: Zondervan, 1974), p. 26.

disagree for we believe that the dispensational literal hermeneutic is driven by an *a priori* commitment to dispensational theological distinctives. To demonstrate this, however, it is necessary to examine the dispensational interpretation of Biblical prophecy.

Prophecy

It is necessary to note, first of all, the utter impossibility of a consistently literal approach to the interpretation of prophecy. A few examples of this are sufficient to show that dispensationalists, despite insistent claims to the contrary, are not at all consistent in literal interpretation of prophecy.

Critics of dispensational exegesis have been quick to pounce on the many inconsistencies which are apparent. Miladin applies utter literalism to the dispensationalist conception of the future and asks:

> Is Russia really going to use chariots and horsemen and bows and arrows against the King of the South? According to Ezekiel 39:9-13, there will be seven years that the House of Israel will bury the Russian shields, bows, arrows, etc., and, at the same time, the great tribulation of dispensationalism is to be three and one-half years in duration. . . . every time Hal Lindsey assigns modern-day weaponry to Old Testament predictions, he is casting aside the literal canon of interpretation which is almost the "sine qua non" of the dispensational school.[11]

No one has better exposed the inconsistency of the dispensationalists on this literalistic principle as applied by them to history and prophecy than O. T. Allis. He points out that they tend to reverse the usual view and instead of reading history literally and prophecy figuratively, they spiritualize history and literalize prophecy.[12] *Israel* must mean Israel, *Canaan* must mean Canaan. On the other hand, Eve, Rebecca, and Zipporah may be viewed as spiritual types and *branch* is a symbol.[13]

> But if it be argued that the "stars" signify a heavenly seed and the "dust" an earthly seed, then the question arises, What is the difference between dust and sand? . . . Why is Israel of the days of Solomon

---

11. G. C. Miladin, *Is This Really The End?* (Cherry Hill, N.J.: Mack, 1972), pp. 11-12. See also George Murray, *Millennial Studies*, pp. 36-37.
12. Allis, *Prophecy and the Church*, p. 23.
13. Ibid., pp. 23, 24.

likened to the "sand" in I Kings 4:20 and to the "dust" in II Chron. 1:9 and why are the stars referred to in I Chron. 27:23 in David's census of earthly Israel? "Sun of Righteousness" (Mal. 4:2) and "morning star" (Rev. 22:16) are beautiful figures used of the coming of Christ.[14]

Some dispensationalists try to defend their inconsistent procedure. Thus, M. R. DeHaan explains what we could call the spiritualizing of Ezekiel's vision of the valley of the dry bones. Dispensationalists apply this vision to the revitalization of the Jews in the end-time period. "To be sure, the vision of the valley of dry bones is a figure, but it is a figure of a literal thing and this is certainly not the church, or the nations of the world."[15] We are not here concerned with the application of the dry bones, whether to the world, to the church, or to Israel. We merely observe that DeHaan is "spiritualizing" the bones and that he justifies this procedure (which he would condemn in others) by saying that "it is a figure of a literal thing."

Needless to say every "spiritualizer" teaches that the things spiritualized are real, or literal, things. If we say, for example, that the vision of the lamb and the wolf lying down together has a reference to ferocious and docile people dwelling together under the influence of Christ, we consider that a literal thing or a real thing to which the prophecy refers.

DeHaan is not the only literalist who has spiritualized some part of the Bible, though none has done it more ingeniously than he. Darby himself admits that the return of Christ referred to in John 14:18 is not visible and "literal" but an invisible coming through the Holy Spirit.[16] Kellogg, who was not a dispensationalist but a premillennialist who rested much of his case on literalism, admits that Zechariah's prophecy that all flesh shall come up every year to Jerusalem is necessarily figurative because of the practical impossibility of literal fulfillment.[17]

Of course, there is a real question what is meant by the word *literal*? While some of the illustrations given, by both sides, are literal enough to be absurd, one realizes that the literalist will have something to say by way of defense. Some speak of getting at the literal meaning of a figure of speech. Suddenly we realize that we are all literalists in that sense—the sense that behind every figure of speech there is something which can be expressed literally.

---

14. Ibid., p. 15.
15. Ibid., p. 34.
16. John Nelson Darby, *The Jews*, p. 70.
17. Darby, *Letters*, 1:100, 320.

The sheer impossibility of a consistently literal interpretation of Biblical prophecy, together with the manifest inconsistency of the dispensational attempt to put it into practice, demands an examination of the possibility that the dispensational self-understanding regarding the priority of hermeneutics, while no doubt sincere, is mistaken. If the usual distinction between dispensationalists and non-dispensationalists as literalists and spiritualizers is not a valid one, however, what is the issue here?

The question seems to resolve, at least initially, to a tendency on the part of dispensationalists to see division and separation in Scripture rather than unity. The tendency of the dispensationalist is to see in various periods diverse dispensations rather than a harmonious unfolding of one covenant in different dispensations. In other words, the difference here is not so much in the fundamental hermeneutical approach as in the application of a theological principle.

As the dispensationalist approaches prophecy, he does not differ from the non-dispensationalist conservative. They both believe they are addressing the Word of God, both have confidence in predictive prophecy, and both are endeavoring to understand what the Word of God means to convey. But there is a tendency at this point for the two interpretations to diverge drastically. On the one hand, there is a separation of one part of Scripture from another, on the other, an integration of the different parts of Scripture with one another.

The real point of divergence is that dispensationalists and non-dispensationalists have different conceptions of what constitutes a plausible interpretation. The question of what is plausible is, it should be noted, a theological rather than an interpretive question.

Let us take a Biblical example. Some of the most controverted words in history are Christ's "this is my body" at the institution of the Lord's Supper (Luke 22:19). There is no disagreement about the words *this*, *my*, or *body*. They are construed literally by all concerned. The debate concerns the interpretation of the word *is*. Some say *is* is to be taken literally; that is, it is understood to mean literal identity of body and bread, of blood and wine. Others say that *is* is to be taken non-literally or metaphorically; that is, to mean "represents." There is nothing in linguistics, *per se*, that will ever settle that question. There is no non-arbitrary way (nor can there be) of saying that the word cannot mean something other than its usual meaning.

At the Colloquy of Marburg (1529), Luther agreed with that as he defended his principle, "literal wherever possible." His opponents, likewise, agreed with him on that principle. But Luther thought it was necessary to take *is* literally. *"Hoc est corpus meum,"* Luther thundered. The Swiss theologians, Zwingli and Oecolampadius, found it palpably absurd that Christ could hold the bread in His hand (His body) and mean that that bread actually was His body. Both interpreters started as always with the literal meaning intending to accept it if possible. One found it necessary and possible in this case; the other found it absurd and impossible.

Is the situation with reference to literalism any different between dispensationalists and non-dispensationalists with regard to prophecy? We think not, but it is necessary to examine this matter more closely.

As we have seen, one of the major differences between the modern dispensational premillennialist and the classical premillennialist is that the latter applies much of prophecy to the church and the former excludes virtually all (they claim to exclude all). The classical premillennialist generally interprets the book of Revelation historically and so finds most of its fulfillment in the history of the church. The dispensationalist adopts the futurist interpretation and refers everything from chapter 4 onward to the unfulfilled future. In addition, a host of Old Testament prophecies, understood by non-dispensationalists to refer to the church, are thought by dispensationalists to speak of a millennial reign of Christ on earth.

A good example of this is the dispensational interpretation of Isaiah 11:6 which says that "the wolf will dwell with the lamb."[18] The question now becomes, how does it happen that dispensationalists have come to have the wolf and lamb actually lie down together while the non-dispensationalist sees a figure of speech? Is it a different hermeneutical principle when interpreting prophecy, as often thought? No, they both agree that Scripture should be interpreted literally if possible. Dispensationalists think this is possible and necessary in prophecy. Conservative non-dispensationalists agree that it is quite possible for God to cause wolves and lambs to lie down together but contend that this is not a plausible interpretation here. They note that this passage seems to be dealing with human beings and not animals, and that it seems to refer to the present age and not some future time. They would admit that if it were not referring to humans and was referring to an era still future it would conceivably and probably have a literal meaning. The dispensationalists would admit that if it referred to human beings in this dispensation it could conceivably and probably would have a figurative meaning.

---

18. Robert Saucy, "The Relationship of Dispensationalism to the Eternal Purpose of God," (Th.D. Thesis, Dallas Theological Seminary, 1961), p. 68. See also p. 152.

In other words, it is not the hermeneutic of literalism, even in prophecy, that makes the difference or even has any bearing on the interpretation. It is one's understanding of the context, local and general, of scriptural teaching that determines the literalizing or the spiritualizing. "Whatever can be shown to be in its literal sense inconsistent either with purity of life or correctness of doctrine must be taken figuratively,"[19] was Augustine's opinion.

Let us pursue this further. Dispensationalists would no doubt generally agree with what has so far been said. Whether we take wolves and lambs literally or not does indeed depend on that understanding of the immediate and general context of the Bible. It is precisely at this point that the dispensational theological system tends to push the hermeneutic in an extremely literal direction. The system will determine whether these are literal or figurative lambs and wolves. Both agree that one cannot tell from the words alone. Both agree, also, that these words should be construed literally if probable. The question is, is it plausible, given the total teaching of Scripture, to interpret this passage as referring to a literal fellowship of wolf and lamb in a literal millennial kingdom? It is not whether God is capable of achieving such a situation. Both sides agree on the doctrine of divine omnipotence. Rather, it is a matter of the compatibility of such an interpretation with the Biblical witness as a whole.

The dispensationalist should, of course, grant that other reasonable persons have a right and duty to consider any evidence against this millennial construction. We might ask, first of all, whether there is clear evidence elsewhere in Scripture that there is to be a thousand years of perfect peace and harmony of nature in this world under the Messiah? We think, in fact, that there is not only no clear evidence of a millennium in Scripture, but there is no evidence. We readily admit that many competent Christian scholars disagree with our opinion but the very disagreement over this matter indicates that the doctrine cannot be considered *clear* to all. The Second Coming is accepted by all Christians, but its relationship to a millennium cannot be assumed.

Second, is there clear evidence that this millennial era pertains to the creation in general? On this point even the premillennialists are not agreed. There are many *different* interpretations among them of the nature of the Millennium in this world. They are not even agreed on how it affects men, not to mention animals.

---

19. Augustine, *City of God*.

Third, is there evidence that, if there is to be such an era, the Old Testament prophets would *overlook* the thousands of years which, following the first coming of the Messiah, are to precede it? Here even the dispensational premillennialists are disagreed. Many believe that there is a total parenthesis between the First Coming of Christ and the Rapture, that the period of the church is not referred to at all by the Old Testament prophets. Some dispensationalists, on the other hand, see at least the union of the Jews and Gentiles at the First Coming in the formation of the church.

Fourth, is there any evidence that *Isaiah* does totally overlook this earlier messianic era? Isaiah is called, above all, the "evangelical prophet." No one denies that if there is any prophetic vision of the era of the First Coming, it is to be found in Isaiah. It is difficult to rule out the possibility that Isaiah refers to this present dispensation.

Fifth, if there is no evidence elsewhere, is there any evidence in this particular passage that Isaiah is here overlooking this earlier messianic era? Certainly there is nothing here that would rule out the *possibility* of a reference to the first coming of Christ.

Sixth, does the imagery of wolves and lambs lying down together militate against the millennial interpretation? Perhaps not, but assuming that the reference to wolves and lambs does rule out a metaphorical interpretation would of course be a *begging* of the very question we are trying to resolve.

Seventh, would not such imagery, construed figuratively, be especially *appropriate*? If figurative language is not incompatible with literalism, as we have shown, would not this manner of expression be especially appropriate? Not only would Jews and Gentiles, being one in Christ, be like wolves and lambs lying down together peaceably, but instances of personal reconciliation such as the zealot Simon being in the same apostolic band with Matthew the tax collector are aptly depicted by this imagery.

Eighth, in very fact, would it not be even *more appropriate* than a literal meaning of a literal millennial reign? The predicted Incarnation of Christ is agreed by all. The harmonizing influence of that First Advent is agreed by all. The appropriateness of the metaphor of wolves and lambs to the influence of the First Coming is agreed by all. The certainty of the Second Coming being followed by a millennium is not agreed by all Christians. The nature of the Second Coming's effects on nature is not even agreed upon by all dispensational premillennialists. *Therefore, a figurative interpretation of these passages might well be more appropriate than an interpretation involving a literal millennial reign.*

This exercise should indicate that the question of a literal or figurative interpretation of this prophecy is not really a matter of hermeneutics *per se*, but of the understanding of the larger context of Scripture that one brings to the interpretation of any passage. It will be evident that the dispensational answers to the above questions are founded, not on any allegedly neutral rules of interpretation, but on their own theological system.

A Typical Dispensational Interpreter

A striking example of the dispensational tendency to smuggle theological assumptions in under the guise of "literal interpretation" is found in the work of Charles Lee Feinberg, whose standing as a former Dallas Seminary professor, dean of Talbot Seminary, and reviser of *The New Scofield Reference Bible* certainly qualifies him as an exponent of mainstream Dispensationalism.

Especially interesting is his discussion of what he calls the "well-defined specific laws for the interpretation of prophecy." According to Feinberg, "For the true force of any prophecy the entire prophetic scheme must be kept in mind, as well as the inter-relationship and interplay between the parts in the plan."[20] Feinberg is talking about a whole program of revelation and an entire prophetic scheme at the very outset. We are supposed to determine how to interpret prophecy, and we are already confronted with an "entire prophetic scheme." If we begin with a whole scheme of prophecy, we must already know what the method of interpretation is. In other words, the dispensational theological scheme must be assumed if we are to interpret prophecy.

Another of Feinberg's principles of prophetic interpretation is more significant and highly controversial.

In interpreting prophecy which has not yet been fulfilled, those predictions which have been fulfilled are to form the pattern. The surest method to know how God will fulfill prophecy in the future is to ascertain how He has worked in the past.[21]

Here he is not proving his point. His point is that we must interpret *all* prophecy as *some* prophecies have been interpreted. What he is

---

20. Charles Lee Feinberg, "The Rebuilding of the Temple," in *Prophecy in the Making*, ed. C. F. H. Henry (Carol Stream, Ill.: Creation House, 1971), p. 92.
21. Ibid., p. 93.

supposed to be proving however, is not what God has done in the past but that that is a fixed principle to guide us in interpreting other prophecies relating to the future. This Feinberg does not address here or elsewhere though it is of the greatest importance. He merely asserts a conviction.

He next tells us that "a splendid passage to test this canon is Luke 1:31-33." Feinberg does not even quote the passage but he feels that it clearly shows that the manner of fulfillment for the Second Coming is to be deduced from the manner of the First. For the sake of further elucidation let me at least quote the verses:

> And, behold, thou shalt conceive in thy womb, and bring forth a son, and shalt call his name JESUS. He shall be great, and shall be called the Son of the Highest; and the Lord God shall give unto him the throne of his father David: and he shall reign over the house of Jacob for ever; and of his kingdom there shall be no end. (KJV)

On the face of it, this passage certainly has nothing to do with the fundamental principle that God will fulfill in the future in the manner in which He has in the past. The question is, what does Feinberg have in mind by citing it at all? Presumably, he feels that the immediate reference is to the birth of Jesus as the Son of the Highest and that the reference to His reigning "over the house of Jacob forever" and of His kingdom there being "no end" is to something future and temporally far removed from the Lukan birth narrative. The passage says no such thing. We know from Feinberg's general eschatological viewpoint that he hears it distinguishing between the literal birth of Christ and His literal return to establish the literal kingdom. Certainly that does not lie on the surface of the passage which is used as a paradigm for a hermeneutical principle.

On the basis of this non-foundation, Feinberg proceeds to conclude that "if the spiritualizers had their way consistently, then the second coming of Christ would have to be a spiritual coming instead of literal one."[22] After this stunning *non sequitur*, Feinberg goes on to argue, using Louis Berkhof as a foil, that "the literal fulfillment of prophecy in the past is an obstacle that the allegorizers strive to minimize."[23]

The quotation from Berkhof, which Feinberg finds so objectionable, is worth citing in full:

---

22. Ibid.
23. Ibid.

But we are told that all the prophecies fulfilled in the past, received a literal fulfillment; and that, therefore, the presumption is that all prophecies will be so fulfilled. However, though it was but natural that prophecies referring to the near future should be fulfilled in the exact form in which they were uttered, this is not to be expected a priori, nor is it likely in the case of prophecies pertaining to the distant future, to a new dispensation with greatly altered conditions.[24]

Berkhof is here proceeding in as rational a manner as Feinberg's is arbitrary. Berkhof simply observes what no one, including Feinberg, questions—that many prophecies in the foreview of the viewer were fulfilled literally. He suggests that it would not be reasonable to *assume* that the same would be true of things to be fulfilled at a much later date when the circumstances could be quite different. That seems eminently reasonable. God could fulfill things in a given historical sequence in ways which the people of the time the prophecy was made were conversant with. When one is dealing with periods far removed (where the situation may be quite inconceivable from the perspective of the circumstances in which the prophecy was made), it would not be at all natural to *assume* that the fulfillment would be in exactly the same terms as it was for those in the near future.

Feinberg concludes this paragraph with this statement following his quotation of Berkhof: "Prophecies like Psalm 22 and Isaiah 53 will not tolerate such handling."[25] He is attributing to Berkhof what Berkhof manifestly does not say. That is, Berkhof does not lay down a principle that must be observed in all prophetic interpretation. He simply notes that, *a priori*, we cannot necessarily anticipate literal fulfillment in all instances where the fulfillment is temporally far removed from the prophecy itself. In any event, we certainly cannot be *dogmatic* about it.

With regard to Psalm 22, a psalm which is usually thought to describe the sufferings of Christ on the cross, it is curious that Feinberg should cite it. While certain prophecies of this psalm were literally fulfilled, others manifestly were not. For example, Jesus did cry out "My God, my God, why hast thou forsaken me?" (22:1), and soldiers did cast lots for His clothing (22:18). Berkhof is not embarrassed by this since he had never asserted that it could *not* happen as literally described.

On the other hand, Christ was not a worm (22:6); many bulls, including the strong bulls of Bashan, did not beset Him round (22:12);

---

24. Louis Berkhof, quoted in ibid.
25. Ibid.

His heart was not literally melted in the midst of His bowels (22:14); it was not dogs who compassed Him (22:16); Christ was not afraid of the power of a dog and the lion's mouth (22:20-21); nor was He on the horns of a unicorn (22:21).

Feinberg goes on to accuse Berkhof and others of employing the method of allegorical interpretation, obviously assuming that allegorical and spiritual interpretation are one and the same. This is a debater's ploy rather than a substantive argument. As anyone who knows the slightest bit about the allegorical method of Origen and the school of Alexandria (with its concern with multiple and simultaneous "senses" and its undue preoccupation with the most minute details of the text) will recognize, there is very little resemblance between the two. The equating of allegorizing and spiritualizing is particularly unfortunate as it incriminates people who are not guilty and misrepresents this metaphorical form of interpretation.

Having stated these principles of prophetic interpretation and established none of them, Feinberg goes on to apply them to a most difficult prophetic passage—Ezekiel 40-48. While we are concerned with the dispensational theory of literal interpretation rather than the details of Feinberg's exegesis of this passage, we will examine certain of his arguments in some detail because they illustrate the tendentious nature of the hermeneutic here.

Two arguments advanced by Feinberg against the figurative interpretation of this passage merit more detailed refutation. Feinberg first of all argues that, were this passage to refer to the church, it would have no meaning for Ezekiel and his contemporaries.[26] This is a rather surprising remark inasmuch as it is generally acknowledged and explicitly stated in Scripture that the prophets did not always understand what they were prophesying. Even with respect to the Incarnation itself and details concerning it, they were mystified as we read in 1 Peter 1:10-12:

> As to this salvation, the prophets who prophesied of the grace that would come to you made careful search and inquiry, seeking to know what person or time the Spirit of Christ within them was indicating as He predicted the sufferings of Christ and the glories to follow. It was revealed to them that they were not serving themselves, but you, in these things which now have been announced to you through those who preach the Gospel to you by the Holy Spirit sent from heaven— things into which angels long to look. (NASB)

---

26. Ibid., pp. 95-96.

If prophets could be mystified about the "sufferings of Christ and the glories to follow," events which are central to the redemptive work of Christ, it would not be surprising that they could be baffled by minute measurements of a future temple. The one message which would have been unmistakable to every contemporary of Ezekiel, as well as the prophet himself, would be that a great day was coming for true Israel. That day would see a magnificent worship of God in a temple that transcended anything they had presently known.

The dispensational concern for prophetic intelligibility and clarity deserves further exploration, however. The argument that prophecy must be interpreted literally often has intuitive appeal for many people because the well-meaning Christian tends to believe that God gives His Word to enlighten us rather than to confuse. For example, Charles Ryrie writes:

> Based on the philosophy that God originated language for the purpose of communicating His message to man and that he intended man to understand that message, literal interpretation seeks to interpret that message plainly.[27]

We must point out, however, that although the central message of salvation through Jesus Christ is abundantly clear, it does not follow that all portions of Scripture are *equally* clear. Scripture teaches in very direct fashion that prophecy, in particular, is often mysterious. Notice these words of God to Aaron and Miriam when they had spoken against His designated leader Moses:

> Hear now My words: If there is a prophet among you, I the LORD shall make Myself known to him in a vision. I shall speak with him in a dream. Not so, with my servant Moses, He is faithful in all My household; with him I speak mouth to mouth, even openly, and not in dark sayings. (Numbers 12:6-8, NASB)

Here we see that the very nature of prophetic speech (Moses excepted) is that it is often enigmatic. It is, by scriptural definition, a matter of "dark sayings." The dispensational insistence here on literal interpretation and clarity flies in the face of the literal teaching of Scripture.

Another argument which Feinberg urges against the more traditional interpretation is that if Ezekiel's vision does apply to the church, then "since the Church has been in existence for centuries, it should be

---

27. Ryrie, *Dispensationalism Today*, p. 96.

enigma - puzzling

easy to interpret the figures and symbols."[28] Our response to this is that it is easy to see that this prophecy applies to the church but how each detail does is something else again. Although genuine allegorical interpretation is concerned with every detail of a text, a spiritual interpretation is not an allegorical interpretation. We do not know what every particular dimension may signify. Many passages in Scripture — and not only prophetic ones either — have been difficult for the church to understand and there is, as we have seen, a lack of unity even among dispensationalists over prophetic interpretation. In addition, Feinberg's argument assumes that all the minute details of a prophetic passage are equally significant — an assumption which he assumes rather than demonstrates. Thus we see that Feinberg has not given us one substantial argument against the spiritual or figurative interpretation.

When Feinberg turns to defend his own interpretation of the passage, we find that the arguments advanced in favor of his own are no more cogent that those advanced against the figurative. What has already been noted should, however, be sufficient to demonstrate the point that hermeneutics is not determinative of dispensational theology. Rather, the reverse is the case. It should also be evident that the dispensational insistence on literal interpretation of prophecy flies in the face of the scriptural witness to the nature of prophetic language.

Dispensational Divisions

A central proof-text of dispensational theology is 2 Timothy 2:15. Here the Apostle Paul exhorts Timothy: "Study to show thyself approved unto God, a workman that needeth not to be ashamed, rightly dividing the word of truth" (KJV). C. I. Scofield's first book had the final phrase of this verse as its title.[29]

From the beginnings of the movement, this verse has been interpreted by dispensationalists as meaning that the Bible is presented in various sharply divided parts, or "dispensations." Correct interpretation of the Bible involves the correct separation of these dispensations from one another.[30]

---

28. Feinberg, "Rebuilding," p. 96.
29. C. I. Scofield, *Rightly Dividing the Word of Truth* (Philadelphia: Philadelphia School of the Bible, 1928).
30. Ibid., see chapter 8.

In itself, this is not an erroneous opinion. Paul's word *oikonomia* means administration and implies a discerning or distinguishing of the differences in the various periods of Biblical revelation. The church has always so understood it through the ages. What, then, is peculiar about the dispensational understanding of the matter? It is not in seeing different stages of unfolding revelation but in the way those stages are understood. Unlike traditional interpreters, dispensationalists "divide" these sections sharply such that they virtually conflict with one another rather that unfold from one another. Biblical revelation is developmental, one stage unfolding naturally from another just as the blossom unfolds from the bud of a flower. For dispensationalists, however, these periods are sharply divided from one another rather than integrated with one another. They conflict rather than harmonize. Even the word *divide* is a sharper term than Paul's original requires but the dispensationalists have made it sharper still. It is a veritable scissor separation of one part from another.

Oswald Allis has noted this feature. As an Old Testament scholar with an intimate knowledge of a wide range of Biblical criticism, he was impressed by the analogy between Dispensationalism and radical Biblical criticism.[31] While Dispensationalists believe that the Bible is the Word of God and radical critics view it as a purely human product, both divide the Bible into sections which share little or no unity. The radical scholars would divide the Old Testament into different and conflicting documents with varying theologies. Dispensationalists did not go about their job in quite the same way but the unity of the Bible is just as surely lost. As we have seen in our survey of dispensational literalism, this particular theme is foundational to the whole theology.

Spoof-Texting

We mention, finally, another of the dispensationalists' devices (though they have no monopoly) which I call "spoof-texting." It is simply the cumulative effect of massive citation. The reader is so busy reading or listening to the volume of citations (each text carrying the solemn dignity of being the inerrant Word of God) that he has no time to ponder the meaning. He tends to assume they do teach what the dispensationalist says that they teach. John Nelson Darby himself may

---

31. Oswald Allis, "Modern Dispensationalism and the Doctrine of the Unity of the Scriptures," *The Evangelical Quarterly* 8 (1936): 22–25.

have been the pioneer: "I prefer quoting many passages than enlarging upon them."[32]

Bear has noticed this spoof-texting. Dispensationalists, he observes,

> are content to reiterate the catch-phrases which set forth their distinctive principles, supporting them by reference to Bible passages of which they do not stop to show the validity. They usually do not attempt in their books to follow out their principles to their logical conclusions, and one often wonders if many who call themselves "Dispensationalist" have ever actually faced the conclusion which must flow from the principles which they so confidently teach.[33]

Sandeen, on the other hand, throws out the baby with the wash. He simply indicts dispensationalists for holding the classic orthodox view of inerrancy from which he himself has departed. Dispensationalism, he argues, has "a frozen biblical text in which every word was supported by the same weight of divine authority."[34] Luther, too, had an inerrant Bible, one word of which would "slay" the devil. We should praise the dispensationalists for their virtues and censure them only for their faults.

The vice of "spoof-texting" is not to be confused, as Sandeen and others do, with the virtue of proper proof-texting. Luther is right that one little word (rightly interpreted) will destroy the devil, but a hundred words used only for cumulative effect have no effect on any argument. At the same time, however, those who would interpret God's Word have the duty to use it responsibly and not to trade casually on the authority of Scripture as a means of endowing dubious arguments with divine sanction.

Conclusion

In this chapter we have seen that the literal hermeneutic, upon which so much weight is placed by dispensationalists, is a very shaky affair indeed. Not only is it impossible to interpret Scripture in a consistently literal fashion, but the Bible itself clearly teaches that parts of Scrip-

---

32. John Nelson Darby, *The Collected Writings of J. N. Darby*, 34 vols., ed. William Kelly (London: G. Morrish, 1867–83): 11:363.
33. Bear, "Dispensationalism," pp. 289–290.
34. Sandeen, "Origins," p. 70.

ture, especially prophecy, are not intended to be taken in a consistently literal fashion.

Furthermore, we have seen that, far from determining dispensational theology, the dispensational literal hermeneutic (with all its inconsistencies), is in fact the direct result of that theology. It is appropriate that we now turn to an examination of dispensational theology.

PART III

THEOLOGY

There have been essentially only three theologies in the history of the church. One is usually called Augustinian, Calvinistic, or Reformed. The second is called Semi-Pelagian, Arminian, or (often) evangelical. The third is called Pelagian, Socinian, or liberal (modernist).

Only the first two (Calvinistic and Arminian) can qualify for the terms *Christian* or *Biblical*. Calvinism is consistent Christianity and Arminianism is inconsistent Christianity, while Pelagianism or liberalism (anti-supernaturalism) is not Christianity at all but a counterfeit that has fooled a significant portion of the church in the modern period.

The main Calvinistic branches are the Presbyterian, the Reformed, and the Anglican. The main Arminian branches are the Roman Catholic, Eastern Orthodox, Lutheran, and Methodist. The main liberal denomination is the Unitarian, though liberalism exists primarily as a parasite on the Calvinistic and Arminian churches.

Where can we locate Dispensationalism on this theological map? It is rarely denominationally organized, and it tends instead to exist as a theological party within denominations. As a theology, however, it belongs to the Arminian or evangelical branch, though it does not admit to Arminianism, and has a questionable right to the evangelical label. In this part I will endeavor to show that, theologically speaking, it is a spurious form of Calvinism and a dubious form of evangelicalism.

Here we face a situation similar to what we saw in the previous chapter. There we noted that the dispensationalist understanding of their literal hermeneutic differs markedly from the actual facts of the matter. Likewise, in this chapter we will see that, while Dispensationalism insistently claims to be Calvinistic, careful scrutiny reveals it to be Arminian.

SEVEN

SPURIOUS CALVINISM

S o far as we know, there never has been a study of the dispensational theological system as a whole. Various parts of the doctrine have been studied, many of them in detail. This is especially true of the eschatological part of the dispensational system. As a matter of fact, the dispensational doctrine of future things has been studied so extensively that many people think Dispensationalism is nothing but an eschatology. While there can be no doubt that the future looms large in the theology of Dispensationalism, it is by no means all that there is to this teaching. It has its own distinctives, of course, which will be duly emphasized, but it also holds to a generally recognized theological form. That form, as we shall see, is what is commonly called Arminianism. In its views of the creation of man, the Fall, the Atonement, soteriology, and eschatology, this system is a variation of the Arminian system.

Adherence to Calvinism is often measured according to the famous "Five Points" which were propounded by the Synod of Dordt in 1619. These five points, stated in response to Arminian error, include total depravity, unconditional election, limited Atonement, irresistible grace, and the perseverance of the saints (resulting in the well-known TULIP acronym). Of the five points, Dispensationalism is thought to maintain four—total depravity, unconditional election, irresistible grace, and the perseverance of the saints. It specifically rejects the doctrine of limited Atonement but generally professes to hold all the other doctrines of TULIP. Thus it would seem, at first glance, to be a Calvinistic system with one element in that system lacking. We will see, however, that the one anti-Calvinistic feature, which seems to be an exception to the rule, is actually indicative of a thoroughgoing departure from Calvinism.

Another strange thing about Dispensationalism is that it seems to
have had its strongest advocates in Calvinistic churches. It was born in
the mind of an Anglican rector (John Nelson Darby), was widely
popularized by a Congregationalist lawyer (C. I. Scofield), and had its
most thorough systematization by a United Presbyterian theologian
(Lewis Sperry Chafer). As we have seen, it has been widespread in
American Presbyterianism during this century. That too would tend to
confirm its reputation as a Calvinistic system. It certainly has appealed
most extensively to people who are in churches belonging to the Calvinistic heritage. However, though these persons who have championed
Dispensationalism often were found in Reformed or Calvinistic denominations, they were not notably Reformed or Calvinistic in their
own personal theological commitments—due, perhaps, to a preoccupation with eschatology rather than systematic theological concerns.[1]

Generally speaking, those who are knowledgeably Reformed and
Calvinistic in the aforementioned denominations have been quite
hostile to dispensational theology. They have never labored under the
impression that it was a genuinely Calvinistic system. Charles Hodge,
Princeton's most famous nineteenth-century Reformed theologian,
certainly looked askance at this theology. Southern Presbyterianism's
Robert Dabney had even more trenchant criticisms.[2] B. B. Warfield
was another major critic of the dispensational theology from a Reformed standpoint. His most concentrated criticism, which we will examine in more detail later, was an extensive book review of Chafer on
the dispensational doctrine of sanctification.[3]

Oswald T. Allis, of Princeton and later Westminster Seminary, was
a major opponent of Dispensationalism. His Old Testament studies, led
him to critique the divisive effect of dispensational Bible studies, and he
wrote what is still the most definitive exposé of the incompatibility of
dispensational and Reformed ecclesiology.[4] This consistent trend of incisive Reformed critique of Dispensationalism has continued into the
present, and it raises strong questions about the accuracy of dispensational claims to be Calvinistic.[5]

---

1. Many will cite the late great Donald Grey Barnhouse as a staunch Calvinistic dispensationalist. It is true that he held to dispensational doctrines and *some* distinctively
Calvinistic ones as well.

2. Charles Hodge, *Systematic Theology*, 3:861ff. Robert L. Dabney, *Discussions, by
Robert L. Dabney*, 3 vols., ed. C. R. Vaughn (Richmond: Presbyterian Committee of
Publication, 1890-92), 1:169-228.

3. B. B. Warfield, "Review of L. S. Chafer, *He That Is Spiritual*," *Princeton Theological Review* 17 (1919):322-327.

4. Oswald Allis, *Prophecy and the Church*.

5. See, e.g., Vern S. Poythress, *Understanding Dispensationalists* (Grand Rapids:
Zondervan, 1987).

Having made these general remarks about dispensational theology as being a species of Arminianism, I will now proceed in more detail to demonstrate these serious allegations. Before doing so, however, let us recall the seriousness of this matter. We believe with the great Baptist preacher, Charles Haddon Spurgeon, that Calvinism is just another name for Christianity. The denial of Calvinism is a very grave mistake.

Dispensational Total Depravity Is Not Total

Let us begin our exposition of the dispensational theology at this fundamental point of Calvinism. This basic doctrine maintains that man by the Fall became sinful in every aspect of his being. By the Fall he lost the moral image of God; that is, holiness or "original righteousness." Subsequently, man is motivated purely by self-interest and without any concern whatever for the divine interest. This means that he sins in thought, word, and deed. His understanding, his emotions, and his will are affected. Even his body is rendered liable to suffering and death.

When we come to the dispensationalist doctrine of man, we find an Arminian type of deviation from this teaching. It is, however, Arminian doctrine with some novelties added. The doctrine begins in a characteristically Arminian manner by denying that man can have a *created character*. Only his own volitions make him a good or bad person. Prior to acting he must be in a neutral condition, a state of moral indifference. The dispensationalists call this neutral state of Adam, as created and before moral actions are taken, the state or "dispensation of innocence."[6]

J. N. Darby, commenting on Genesis, makes no mention of righteousness and holiness as characterizing the newly created Adam. Only absence of evil distinguishes his character.[7] Again, "man, then, was tried in his innocence by the enemy."[8] In that statement we note that Adam was merely *innocent* and that his trial was fundamentally an enticement of the devil rather than ultimately a probation of God. After the Fall, man has a "totally different" kind of nature.

---

6. See *The Scofield Reference Bible*, p. 5. For a thorough refutation demonstrating the futility and unscripturalness of this notion see Jonathan Edwards, *Freedom of the Will*, ed. Paul Ramsey, *The Works of Jonathan Edwards* (New Haven: Yale University Press, 1957), 1:166, n. 3.

7. Darby, *Synopsis*, 1:10.

8. Darby, *Inspiration of the Bible*, p. 25.

On the other hand, the human nature of Christ is different from that of fallen or unfallen man. According to William Kelly, Christ "alone was born holy."⁹ So, as Wallace observes, Dispensationalism has three types of humanity—"innocent" Adam who was neither righteous nor evil, fallen humanity, and the righteous Jesus Christ.¹⁰ Over against all this, the answer to the tenth question of the Westminster Shorter Catechism affirms that "God created man, male and female, after His own image, in knowledge, righteousness, and holiness, with dominion over the creatures."

Another Arminian characteristic of Dispensationalism is seen in its view of the imputation of Adam's sin. According to Dispensationalism, Adam was in some sense a representative but, when he fell, his sin was not imputed to his descendants. Oddly enough, dispensationalists come over to an Arminian position again at this point, but for an entirely different reason. Wesleyan Arminians hold that God cannot properly hold a person responsible for repenting and believing the gospel unless he is morally able to do so. Consequently, they deny the doctrine of total inability by saying that Christ's death removed inability from all persons so that all are morally able to believe the gospel. This is maintained, despite considerable scriptural evidence to the contrary, because the justice of God is thought to require it. That is, Arminians insist that God is not just if He condemns man after the Fall without giving him a chance to be saved. This error puts God under obligation to sinners and makes the gospel a matter of justice due, rather than grace given.

Dispensationalists, on the other hand, reject the imputation of Adam's guilt outright. They do so by arguing that there was in Eden no law and, therefore, no imputation of a transgression of the law. The law, together with the covenant of works, was not established until Sinai. Though there is original sin and man is subjectively bound, he is not under the guilt of Adam's sin by imputation.¹¹

On the surface, contemporary Dispensationalism does seem to teach emphatically the doctrine of total depravity. This is so constantly reiterated by theologians of this school that it seems superfluous to bother with any quotations. One quote from Schuyler English will suffice:

---

9. William Kelly, *Christ Tempted and Sympathizing* (London: R. L. Allan, 1906), p. 6.

10. Wallace, *Plymouth Brethrenism*, p. 31f.

11. See Darby, *Letters*, 1:314; 2:164, 477, 501.

It is true that man may reform, that is, change his habits and even improve them. But at his best he is utterly bankrupt spiritually, that is, in God's reckoning.[12]

All of these theologians preach salvation by grace and they seem to recognize this state of sin from which no one can be rescued except through the atoning blood of Jesus Christ. As we shall see later, there is a sense in which Dispensationalism out-does traditional Calvinism on this doctrine. Calvinism teaches that this depravity is ultimately overcome by the redemption of Christ and man's nature is genuinely made righteous. When we consider the dispensational view of sanctification, we will notice that nothing really happens to this nature. It is allowed ultimately to die and be annihilated. This is, of course, a travesty of the Reformed doctrine, but it certainly seems to take the sinful nature so seriously that even God does nothing with it except ultimately to destroy it.

In spite of this, the dispensational view of the totally depraved man is one who is not totally depraved after all. It turns out that he is not totally disabled. According to the Reformed doctrine, total depravity makes man *morally* incapable of making a virtuous choice. While Dispensationalism seems to go along with this idea to a degree, this "totally depraved" man is nevertheless able to believe. We shall see that his faith precedes or is at least simultaneous with (and not based upon) his regeneration. As long as that doctrine is maintained, the nerve of total depravity is cut. If total depravity does anything, it renders man totally unable because he is indisposed to respond to the overtures of grace.[13] If the dispensationalist maintains, as he does, that man is *morally* able to respond to the gospel, then Dispensationalism does not believe that man is totally depraved after all.

Possibly the best way to illustrate this is by Dwight Pentecost's treatment of *depravity*.[14] Pentecost thinks this doctrine "says that man is as bad *off* as he can be. There is a vast difference between being

---

12. E. Schuyler English, *Things Surely Believed* (Neptune, N. J.: Loizeaux Brothers, 1956), p. 201. See also Chafer, *Systematic Theology*, 1:233–238; 4:402–403; 7:287–289.

13. See John Murray, "Irresistible Grace," in *Soli Deo Gloria*, ed. R. C. Sproul (Phillipsburg, N.J.: Presbyterian and Reformed, 1976), pp. 63–72. Note also the statement in the Westminster Confession of Faith VI, 4: "From this original corruption, whereby we are utterly indisposed, disabled, and made opposite to all good, and wholly inclined to all evil, do proceed all actual transgressions."

14. J. Dwight Pentecost, *Things Which Become Sound Doctrine* (Grand Rapids: Zondervan, 1970).

as *bad* as he can be, and being as bad *off* as he can be."[15] This is, as we shall see, a fatal concession.

According to Biblical doctrine, fallen man is as bad as he can be at the moment but not as bad as he can and will become. There is room for deprovement. Scripture says regarding man that "every intent of the thoughts of his heart was only evil continually" (Genesis 6:5, NASB). "There is none righteous, not even one. . . . There is none who does good" (Romans 3:10, 12, NASB).

Pentecost himself notes these passages without seeing their conflict with what he had written elsewhere.[16] He explains that depraved man is "under sin," "spiritually dead," "under condemnation," "under the power of Satan," and "lost." Still, to our amazement he concludes that this "is what it means to be depraved. Man is *not* as bad as he can be, but man is as bad off as he can be."[17] If being lost, under sin, condemnation, Satan, and being spiritually dead is not as bad as can be, I, for one, cannot think of what would be worse. Those in hell are no worse.

But Pentecost, like all dispensationalists, can think of what would be worse. What would make it worse would be for man *really* to be lost, under sin, condemned, Satan-bound, and spiritually dead. It is quite obvious that is not really the case because Pentecost thinks that this lost, condemned, enslaved, dead person is quite able to come, of himself, to Jesus Christ. Corpses live, the dead walk, and Satan's slaves can break his bonds because "that which accomplishes the new birth is [their, self-generated] *faith* in Jesus Christ."[18]

Pentecost was true to himself the first time. Depraved men are not "bad," they are only "bad off." If he reflected a little more on what he wrote he would realize that men are not even "bad off." They can spend their whole lives in sin with absolute impunity, because they can walk out free into the arms of Jesus at any moment that they *of themselves* choose to avoid the consequence of sin and inherit eternal life instead. Even after coming to Jesus they may continue to live ungodly lives, although Pentecost would counsel them not to do so.

Dispensationalism's "totally depraved" man turns out to be neither really "bad" nor "bad off." When we come to study the dispensational view of sanctification, we will learn that the "totally depraved" remain "totally depraved" *after* being "saved" and made heirs of eternal life.

---

15. Ibid., pp. 9, 10.
16. Ibid., pp. 10–18.
17. Ibid., p. 16 (emphasis mine).
18. Ibid., p. 37 (emphasis mine).

Dispensational Unconditional Election
Is Not Unconditional

Here we focus on the second of the five points of Calvinism — unconditional election. Dispensationalists profess to believe in unconditional election, and we are grateful for their approbation of the doctrine. Nevertheless, one can hardly believe a doctrine which he misunderstands.

If there is anything which is characteristically associated with Calvinism, it is the doctrine of predestination. Of course, Calvinism believes all the classic, fundamental tenets of the Christian religion. But that which distinguishes it in the popular, and even in the academic mind is its strong adherence to and affirmation of predestinating, unconditional election by an almighty, all-sovereign God. If a dispensationalist wants to be known as essentially Calvinistic, he cannot give any uncertain sound on this doctrine. The very best thing that can be said for the dispensationalist at this point is that his sound is very uncertain.

Let us see what dispensationalists mean by their affirmation of unconditional election. Darby, commenting on Romans 8:29, translates the Greek "whom he foreknew he predestinated to be conformed" and then goes on to say, "No trouble with 'foreknew.' "[19] The thought is that if predestination may be viewed as dependent on foreknowledge, the offense of the Reformed doctrine is removed.[20]

This line of interpretation continues in the Scofield Bible. The reference note on 1 Peter 1:2 says that "election is according to the foreknowledge of God (1 Pet. 1.2), and wholly of grace, apart from human merit."[21] So we see what is meant by unconditional election. It is unconditional *justification* that dispensationalists are talking about. One can see by this statement that the Scofield editors view God as foreseeing that the sinner will repent. Because God foresees this repentance and belief of the sinner, He, without any meritorious condition on the sinner's part, chooses him to everlasting life. That is to say, He

---

19. Darby, *Letters*, 1:476.

20. Note that "foreknew" in Romans 8:29, according to Reformed theologians, is one of many instances of the Biblical use of "know" as own, acknowledge, or love. See, e.g., Romans 11:2; Deuteronomy 33:9; Psalm 1:6; Jeremiah 1:5; Matthew 1:23; 25:12; 2 Timothy 2:19. It is inconsistent with this text, this context, and general Bible teaching to interpret "foreknew" as mere "had prior knowledge of the certain futurition of events."

21. *Scofield Reference Bible*, p. 1311.

elects the sinner without the sinner having *any condition of virtue* which recommends him for election. This is unconditional salvation, not unconditional election.

It is quite true that God elects the sinner without that sinner having met any condition of virtue, but this is not what "unconditional election" means. That doctrine teaches that God from all eternity elects the sinner without dependence on that sinner's "foreseen faith." The election is *un*conditional. If God chooses or elects a person, foreseeing his repentance and faith, that is not an *un*conditional election. God does not forsee any faith in the depraved sinner except as He Himself bestows it on those He *un*conditionally elects.

Reformed theologians have traditionally spoken of a logical order of the eternal divine decrees as a means of clarifying this issue. The decree of God to elect or choose some for eternal life (while at the same time decreeing to pass over others) is carefully recognized as logically prior to God's foreknowledge of the elect person's exercise of faith. In addition to their intrinsic importance, the decrees of God are important here as a test of the allegedly Calvinistic character of the dispensational theology. The Arminian theologian, Steele, whose *Antinomianism Revived* claims to trace the Antinomianism of the Brethren to their Calvinism, nevertheless admits a significant absence from Brethrenism of a hallmark of Calvinism—sovereign decrees. "Nothing is said of sovereign decrees and of unconditional election."[22] Steele should have suspected the basic Arminian character of this system from this silence on the decrees.

Let us see how Dispensationalism's stance on election relates to the dispensational position on total depravity. The dispensationalist is convinced, as we have seen, that he believes in total depravity. We ask the simple question—how could a person possibly believe that men are dead in trespasses and sins, that they hate God, that they are utterly indisposed to Christ, that they are totally depraved, and that they are morally unable to incline toward any virtue, and then say in the next breath that God foresees these persons as believing and that God elects on the ground of that foreseen faith? Men are either "dead" in sin or they are not. If they are "dead" then, of course, spiritual corpses do not give birth to spiritual effects. They would have to be, as all sound Calvinists say, unconditionally elected to repentance, faith, and the salvation which Christ specifically purchased for them and brings to them by first making them come alive.

What are we to make of the dispensational talk of unconditional election together with the apparent denial of it? There seems to be, on

---

22. Daniel Steele, *Antinomianism Revived*, 3rd ed. (Chicago: Christian Witness, 1899), p. 94.

the part of dispensationalists, a genuine desire to honor the predestinating, electing grace of God. There are so many passages in the Bible which affirm this truth, and dispensationalists are so avowedly Biblical, that it is almost inevitable that they would affirm predestination. On the other hand, the Biblical meaning of the doctrine makes the dispensationalist uncomfortable. He cannot formally deny the doctrine because the words are in Scripture. On the other hand, he cannot accept the substance of it because it is incompatible with his theology.

How does the dispensationalist handle the problem? A number of strategies may be discerned. Some dispensationalists handle it by simply avoiding the matter. That is, they give lip service to divine sovereignty and human freedom, constantly reminding us that both are taught in the Bible, that both must be honored. How they can be in harmony with one another is a mystery. All that is true and wholesome but it does not say what the doctrine actually is. A predestination of some corpses to life and foreordination of some corpses to remain dead is what is meant by the Bible doctrine but dispensationalists refuse to accept that.[23]

The Biblical view of the matter is all very plain, but it is not very palatable doctrine. Dispensationalists, as well as many others, shrink from having to say God lets many persons perish and chooses to save only some of the multitude. That is plainly what God and unconditional election say. While they will not deny the doctrine outright, neither will dispensationalists affirm it.

When dispensationalists feel it necessary to give a more disciplined answer to these questions, the results are usually neither Calvinistic nor coherent. C. H. Mackintosh, the popular Plymouth Brethren teacher says: "The grand truth of *election* is fully established; the repulsive error of *reprobation*, sedulously avoided."[24] He goes on to explain that this is because the wicked damn themselves and the elect are saved by God. By that remark, he attempts to clear God of any involvement (not merely any guilt) in reprobation. According to true Calvinism, men do damn themselves and God is not the author of their sin. But Calvinism does not stop there and neither can Mackintosh if men are "totally depraved." If they are, when God elects to save some of them, He chooses *not* to save the others. He therefore decrees to leave them to their own wickedness by which they damn themselves. God as truly

---

23. Chafer and Walvoord, *Major Bible Themes* (Grand Rapids: Zondervan), p. 233.

24. C. H. Mackintosh, *Works*, p. 606.

reprobates some wicked as He elects to save others; He permissively reprobates and positively elects.

How does L. S. Chafer interpret this doctrine which he ostensibly favors? Chafer attempts to combine Scofield's position that foreknowledge is prior to election with the assertion that such an election really is, after all, unconditional. He views free-will as self-determination and, as such, it cannot be foreknown, being in its nature unknowable before it occurs. Somehow, however, God is supposed to foreknow it. Foreknowing the sinner's free-will choice of Christ, God (it is supposed) elects him. Chafer claims that this election is not grounded on the sinner's faith because it is an *eternal* knowledge of that faith—a curious argument indeed.[25]

Harry Ironside is often the most orthodox exponent of unorthodox Dispensationalism. This is true with reference to this doctrine also. His erroneous view of free agency makes it easy for him to affirm a true, unconditional election. He says that though man was created a "free agent" he is not such now. In fact, he is a captive and slave of the devil and cannot, as such, possibly choose Christ. Erroneously supposing the sinner no longer has true choice at all, Ironside concludes that God must bestow true choice on man because he (Ironside) thinks that God has to restore any power of choice at all. Having said that, he falls back into the opposite error and views regenerated man as the "captive of Christ," in the sense of still having no true choice.[26]

Ironside does not seem to understand that free agency means that a person of himself chooses what seems "good" to him (however good or evil it may be in itself). That is all there is to free agency, and no human being ever loses it in heaven, this world, or hell. Though a person freely chooses evil only (because he finds only evil "good"), he is a *free* agent. He is thus a free captive of Satan and, if converted, afterward becomes a free captive of Christ. In the first state Satan seems good to him and he willingly (freely) follows him. In the second state, Christ seems good to him and he willingly (freely) follows Him.

What does Charles Ryrie have to say on this crucial Biblical doctrine? First, I note his failure to understand the specific meaning of election. He defines election as "God's unconditional and free *temporal* choice of those individuals whom He would save."[27] Election is an

---

25. Chafer, *Systematic Theology*, 1:231.
26. H. A. Ironside, *Eternal Security of Believers* (New York: Loizeaux, 1934), p. 25.
27. Charles Caldwell Ryrie, ed., *The Ryrie Study Bible* (Chicago: Moody, 1978), p. 1948 (emphasis mine).

eternal determining decree and the very words *temporal* and *would* suggest something hypothetical or an expression of mere desire. Especially is that true in the discussion of this doctrine where even some recognized and genuine Calvinistic theologians say that God truly desires what He does not decree. Furthermore, the use of the term *temporal choice* as an equivalent of an *eternal* decree defies comprehension.

Elsewhere, Ryrie seems to take refuge in the notion of corporate election. The Biblical doctrine has to do with the choice of individuals as well as groups, but Ryrie speaks only of God's election of classes of people. That is, the doctrine speaks of God's choice of individuals such as Jacob, but Ryrie speaks only of His choice of a specific class of individuals; namely, believers in general. God, according to Ryrie, does not choose specific individuals to salvation but believers in general to salvation.

Under the topic of election and predestination in his *Ryrie Study Bible*, Ryrie has comments on seven verses (Mark 13:20; Romans 8:29; 10:14, 15: 11:7; Ephesians 1:5; 1 Thessalonians 1:4). The most clear and explicit statement is the comment on Ephesians 1:5 which reads, "God has determined beforehand that those who believe in Christ will be adopted into his family."[28] This involves a choice on God's part and faith on man's part. Thus Ryrie makes election an eternal divine choice *of believers* to be members of God's family. This is not only not a definition of election (which is a decree to bring sinners to believe in Christ), but it is something of an insult to the intelligence of God. How so? Because it presents God as decreeing that those who are in Christ should be considered in Christ.

In Norman Geisler, the implicit Arminianism of Dispensationalism has become explicit. This former Dallas Seminary professor, now at Lynchburg, very clearly makes the divine purposes in salvation entirely dependent upon human choice. Geisler writes, "God would save all men if He could. God will achieve the greatest number in heaven He possibly can."[29] The limitation on the divine will is human will. God will save as many as God can "without violating their free choice." Divine election is clearly dependent on the human sinner's "free choice." No Arminian has ever been more specific in his denial of Calvinistic doctrine than this self-designated dispensational Calvinist. Geisler not only denies the fourth point, "irresistible grace," but unconditional election as well because, emphatically, he makes divine election the result of fallen man's "free will."

Incidentally, the Bible, according to the Reformed understanding,

---

28. Ibid.
29. Norman L. Geisler, "God, Evil and Dispensations," in *Walvoord, A Tribute*, ed. Donald K. Campbell (Chicago: Moody, 1982), p. 102.

does not teach any divine "violence" to the will of man. *Violence means compulsion and coercion which Calvinists do not believe any more than do Arminians.* Dr. Geisler does not seem to grasp that fact.

So the first two of the five points go by the board in dispensational theology. It has neither a true doctrine of total depravity nor a true doctrine of unconditional election. It is at least conscious of its deviation from the doctrine of limited Atonement, and we hope we have succeeded in making it aware of its rejection of the first two points also.

Dispensational Denial of Limited Atonement Destroys the Possibility of Calvinism

We come now to a point—the design of Christ's atoning work—where dispensationalists frankly acknowledge their departure from Calvinistic orthodoxy. Reformed theologians have historically argued that, because Christ's death and resurrection accomplish salvation (rather than merely make salvation possible) and because God has purposed from all eternity to save the elect, Christ died with the intention of saving the elect. The term *limited Atonement* has been applied to this doctrine. Because this term can be misinterpreted as limiting the *value* of Christ's atoning work, some have preferred to speak of a "specific" or "definite" Atonement.

Before we address the issue of the extent of the atonement of Christ, we will first take a brief account of the dispensational view of the person of Christ—His deity and humanity which bears on this doctrine.

The Person of Christ

The major question concerning the christology of the Dispensationalist is not whether they believe in the deity of Christ, but whether they have a sound conception of His humanity. Darby clearly refers John 1:1 to Jesus thereby affirming His deity and equality with the Father.[30] Elsewhere he says, "The great truth of the divinity of Jesus, that he is God is written all through scripture with a sunbeam, but written to faith."[31] Chafer seems injudicious perhaps in using the word *emanation* for the relation of the Son and Father, but he is clear in his belief that Christ was independently, and not derivatively, divine.[32]

---

30. Darby, *Letters*, 3:103.
31. Ibid., 1:28, 29; See also 3:103, 266.
32. Lewis Sperry Chafer, *The Ephesian Letter Doctrinally Considered* (Findlay, Ohio: Dunham, 1935), p. 28.

With regard to the reality of Christ's humanity, Darby emphatically states, "His was a true and real human body and soul, flesh and blood, like mine as far as humanity is concerned, sin excepted."[33] On the other hand, he makes some statements which raise questions as to the extent to which Christ actually was fully human. Commenting on Hebrews 4:15, which reads that Christ "was in all points tempted like as we are, yet without sin" (KJV). Darby remarks that "*choris harmartias* means 'sin apart' namely: He was not tempted by sin as we are."[34] But, if Christ had a true human nature just like ours, why would He not be tempted just as we are? To deny this fact would seem to question whether He did indeed have such a nature as ours. This is what the Monophysite heresy did indeed question and deny.

C. H. Mackintosh makes some statements which raise similar questions. For example, he writes that the "first Adam even in his un-fallen condition, was 'of the earth' but the second Man was, as to his manhood, 'the Lord from heaven.' "[35] While this certainly seems to stress unduly the difference between Christ's humanity and the rest of humanity, it would seem that Dispensationalism in general wants to affirm fully the reality of the Incarnation. In their desire to stress the full deity of Christ they sometimes appear to do less than full justice to his humanity but this seems due more to a lack of theological care and precision than to heterodoxy.

The Work of Christ

Moving from the person to the work of Christ, we find a striking divergence from the Reformed tradition at the point of the three offices of Christ.[36] While Reformed theologians have seen Christ functioning in His offices of Prophet, Priest, and King simultaneously, Darby, with his penchant for historical division and separation, viewed these offices as successive rather than simultaneous. Christ was a prophet while on earth, a priest in heaven, and a king in the kingdom yet to come.[37] The reason for Darby's and later dispensationalists' denial of Christ's exercise of His priestly and kingly office during His Humiliation is no doubt related to their eschatological doctrine of the kingdom as strictly future.

---

33. Darby, *Letters*, 1:279.
34. Ibid., p. 469.
35. Charles Henry Mackintosh, *Notes on the Book of Leviticus* (Neptune, N.J.: Loizeaux, 1965), p. 35.
36. See, e.g., the Westminster Shorter Catechism, quest. 23.
37. Darby, *Synopsis*, 4:518.

The Atonement

With regard to the Atonement, dispensationalists believe that, since man is not totally depraved and is conditionally elected, Christ died to save all men. Here all dispensationalists are explicitly anti-Calvinistic. Lewis Sperry Chafer admits this with something approaching humility, almost contrition. He is firm and certain of his position but, at the same time, he recognizes that his departure from Calvinistic orthodoxy requires explanation and justification. This he endeavors to give in what I feel is perhaps his most competent theological effort.

Chafer not only denies that the Bible teaches limited Atonement but insists that the Bible teaches the opposite—a universal design of the Atonement. Furthermore, he argues that the notion of a universal Atonement is not incompatible with the general Calvinistic system of doctrine. Let us examine Chafer's argument for the consistency of unlimited Atonement with the Calvinistic system of doctrine.

In his view the question is simply this: is there any inconsistency between God making "all men savable" by the Atonement and actually saving only the elect by effectual calling? Chafer maintains that God does exactly that. He makes all men "savable" by the Atonement and actually saves only the elect by calling them. Or, the Son makes all men savable and the Holy Spirit actually saves only the elect.

Viewed in isolation, this construction of the matter is conceivable, but in the Calvinistic context it is quite incongruous. In fact, it is the Arminian who says precisely that and, though wrong, he is at least consistent with his system of doctrine. The inconsistency at work here is not difficult to demonstrate. In the Reformed view, the totally depraved are simply not savable apart from effectual calling. They are dead and no external act (such as Christ's death on the cross) is going to help corpses. Christ could die a thousand deaths. All would be of no avail to dead people.

A significant problem facing Chafer's position is that the Atonement does not even make all people "savable." If Chafer were to say that Christ's death purchased the Holy Spirit by whose effectual calling these corpses are made alive, the Calvinist would agree completely. However, an unlimited Atonement did not, according to Chafer, secure the Holy Spirit for everyone salvifically. So, according to Chafer himself, the universal Atonement does not in fact make all men savable, by their own faith, the faith not forthcoming as a result of the *Atonement* alone.

What is it that drives Chafer and other dispensationalists to this desperate theological strategy? The answer is clear—they suppose that, on traditional Calvinistic grounds, there is no foundation for the offer of the gospel. "How," they ask, "can we invite men to receive Jesus when we cannot say that Christ died for them?" With this evangelistic concern all Calvinists deeply sympathize while assuring dispensationalists that their anxiety is unnecessary.

First, all Calvinists and even dispensationalists recognize the principle that inability does not limit responsibility. Chafer acknowledges that the unregenerate cannot believe but holds them responsible and worthy of eternal condemnation for not believing nonetheless. He refers to "spiritual death from which they are impotent to take even one step in the direction of their own salvation."[38] Yet he considers them guilty sinners notwithstanding.

Second, the evangelical call itself is only to the regenerate. Unfortunately, this point is often poorly explicated by authentic Calvinists. That is, the evangelical call is not to unregenerate people to come into the kingdom but to regenerate, for without regeneration no one will enter the kingdom (see John 3:3). The call is to whomever will (the regenerate), and not to whomever will not (the unregenerate). The call is to those who labor and are heavy laden (see Matthew 11:28), and not to those who are proud in their self-righteousness. The call is to sinners and not to the righteous (see Matthew 9:13). The offer and promise are to the penitent and not to the impenitent (see Acts 11:18). The only ones who do become regenerate are the elect (see John 6:44). So the call is always to the regenerate and never to the unregenerate. It is not even to the elect while unregenerate but only to the elect when regenerate. The elect are the ones for whom Christ died and who are regenerated at the appointed time when they hear Christ calling by the gospel.

Chafer is afraid that we may be calling the unsavable non-elect. So he tries to make them the savable non-elect so that the evangelist may be justified in calling them. But calling the elect when non-savable is as unjustified as calling the non-savable non-elect. Unjustified calling is never authorized or required by the Scriptures. The only Biblical call, properly understood, is to the regenerate.

But, the objection comes, are we not commanded to call all men everywhere to repentance? Indeed we are (see Acts 17:30). It is the duty of all human beings who ever lived or shall live to repent and believe the gospel. It is their duty to believe and be saved. The sin of unbelief

---

38. Lewis Sperry Chafer, "For Whom Did Christ Die?" *Bibliotheca Sacra*, 137 (1980): 310, 311.

is the ultimate condemnation. They are not, however, invited to come
to Christ as impenitent, unbelieving, unwilling, unconvicted sinners.
Rather, they are to come as penitent sinners, believing in the atoning
death of Christ.

The calling is as limited and specific as the design of the Atonement.
It is extended to the whole world of believers—to all of them and to no
one else. Christ died for His sheep and not for those who are not His
sheep. His sheep (and they alone) hear His voice calling them by name.
Those choose Him whom He has first chosen. "How blessed is the one
Thou dost choose, and bring near to Thee" (Psalm 65:4, NASB).

The traditional Reformed distinction between the internal and external call can be a source of confusion.[39] There are not two different
calls. They are one and the same call. The internal spiritual call is to
the regenerate. The external audible call is to the regenerate. This one
call to the regenerate is heard by the ears of many unregenerate. But
what they hear is not a call to them but to the regenerate. "I did not
come to call the righteous, but sinners" (Mark 2:17, NASB). Christ is not
calling those who fancy themselves righteous but those who know
themselves to be sinners (the regenerate elect).

Let me illustrate. A church meeting is in progress. The service is in-
terrupted by a call that a car with a specified license plate has its lights
on. Everybody in the room hears that call. All but one hearing that call
knows it does *not* refer to him/her. The one owning that car knows
that "universal" call is a call to him specifically and not for the others,
though they all hear it as a call to Him.

In other words, many unregenerates hear this one call to the many
regenerates and know that the call is heard by themselves, but not addressed to them. They would be insulted if it were. They are the "righteous," not sinners. They know what the call is and definitely know
that it is not addressed to those who consider themselves as not need-
ing it at all.

Chafer's concern for the evangelistic call of the gospel was as mis-
placed as his solution to the non-problem was disastrous. We move now
to his exegetical arguments for the theory of a universal Atonement.

Chafer does attempt to address the challenge posed to his position
by the numerous Biblical texts which clearly delimit the saving work of
Christ to the elect. Citing passages such as John 10:15; 17:2, 6, 9, 20,
24; Romans 4:25; and Ephesians 1:11, Chafer contends that, while
Christ did die for the elect, this does not imply that Christ did *not* die

---

39. Even the excellent Puritan, Joseph Alleine, has misunderstood this point. See
his *Alarm to the Unconverted* (London: Banner of Truth Trust, 1957; reprint ed.).

for the non-elect also.[40] "He may easily have died for all men with a view to securing His elect."[41] Chafer would apparently have us believe that Christ died to save those He had no intention of saving while aiming at saving those He intended to save.

As we have seen, according to Chafer's view, Christ did not, strictly speaking, die to save all men. In fact, He did not die to save anyone. He died only to make all men "savable."

In reality, concrete intentionality seems to be entirely lacking in Chafer's view of the Atonement. This is really "hypothetical redemptionism" with a vengeance. Chafer's view compares unfavorably even with traditional Amyraldianism. Seventeenth-century theologian Moises Amyraut (from which the name Amyraldianism derives) argued that, in the logical order of divine decrees, the decree to redeem through the death of Christ was logically prior to the decree to choose the elect. Thus, the decree to redeem was at that point not specific to the elect. For Chafer, however, the Atonement is altogether hypothetical to the point of effectual calling, whereas in traditional Amyraldianism it was hypothetical until foreseen as futile and then it became a limited Atonement from start to finish.

In summary, the logic of Chafer's view amounts to this:

1. Christ died to make all men savable.
2. Dead men cannot be made savable without being made alive.
3. Therefore, Christ died for the salvation of no man.
4. So far from Christ's having "died for all men with a view to securing His elect," He has not even died for the elect, not to mention the non-elect.

We must conclude that Chafer's view of the design of the Atonement is explicitly Arminian and not Calvinism in any form.

Other Dispensational Views

Let us consider what more recent dispensationalists have to say on this subject. Charles Ryrie, for example, maintains that the unlimited Atonement view does not spell frustration for God. "Christ is not defeated in having died for all even though all are not ultimately saved because personal faith is as necessary for salvation as the death of Christ."[42]

---

40. Chafer, *Systematic Theology*, 3:196–199, 201, 242f, 321–322, 5:203f, 248f.
41. Ibid., 3:322.
42. Ryrie, *Ryrie Study Bible*, p. 1949.

Can Ryrie mean that, since Christ knew that salvation was by faith and that unless all people had faith in His death they would not be saved, He consciously ran the risk of not saving all He intended to save? He was not defeated because He knew the possibility of defeat? By contrast, Chafer's view, though quite wrong, is at least coherent. Not only is Ryrie's conclusion wrong, but his route to it is inconceivable. In that he differs from his mentor.

Another dispensationalist, William Evans, states the matter this way: "The atonement is limited only by men's unbelief."[43] Yet if men's unbelief limited the efficacy of the Atonement, no one would ever have been saved by the Atonement. All men are dead in sin and unbelieving by nature. Therefore, if unbelief could limit the Atonement, it would be limited by all and none would have benefited from it.

It is the Atonement which overcomes unbelief and not unbelief which overcomes the Atonement. It was by the Atonement that forgiveness of sins, including unbelief, and the purchase of the Holy Spirit was secured. By that Spirit unbelief was overcome; that is, in those for whom the Atonement was offered and the purchase made.

Unbelief continues in those for whom the Atonement was not made. Can it be said that because of their unbelief the Atonement was limited in its effect? It is true that, so long as they remain unbelieving, men cannot be saved by the Atonement of Jesus Christ. It could also be said that as soon as any man believed he was saved by the Atonement of Jesus Christ. Could it not, therefore, be said that unbelief limited the Atonement? But, as we have seen, it is the limited design and application of the Atonement that limits the unbelief and not the unbelief that limits the Atonement.

Robert Lightner also goes beyond Chafer in his view that Christ actually obtained "redemption and forgiveness for all men." Christ "died for all men and for every man, so that *He has obtained for them all* by His death on the cross redemption and forgiveness."[44] This dispensational theologian should realize the shocking character of that statement. The reader is inevitably going to hear him say that all men are forgiven and redeemed—that all are in fact saved. This is exactly what he says but apparently not what he means to say. He will add that men must exercise faith to make this redemption and forgiveness theirs (though Christ has already "obtained" it for them, not merely made it available to them).[45]

---

43. Evans, *Great Doctrines*, p. 79.

44. Robert P. Lightner, "For Whom Did Christ Die?," in *Walvoord, A Tribute*, ed. Donald K. Campbell (Chicago: Moody, 1982), p. 160 (emphasis mine).

45. Ibid., p. 163.

He finds Biblical analogy for this contradictory pattern of thought in the Old Testament where "The blood of the Passover lamb became efficacious only when applied to the doorpost."[46] That is what Moses says about the Passover lamb, but it is not what Lightner says about the Passover Lamb of God. According to Lightner, unlike Moses, that blood of Christ "has obtained for them all" "redemption and forgiveness."

Lightner may protest that what he meant by "obtained redemption" was not redemption obtained but redemption made obtainable. Without Christ's blood redemption was not possible for anyone. Christ's blood made redemption possible for everyone. Of course, if we can say this, Lightner is equally capable of saying it. No one considers "obtained" and "made obtainable" equivalent expressions.

Lightner defends unlimited Atonement with a number of arguments. First, he contends that by "unbiased exegesis, . . . no Scripture says Christ died only for the elect."[47] On the contrary, we maintain that all texts dealing with this subject, properly understood, teach that Christ died only for the elect. For example, Christ says that He laid down his life for His sheep (John 10:11, 15). Lightner will immediately and correctly observe that even those texts do not say that Christ laid down his life *only* for his sheep. Lightner is correct if he means that, according to technical logic, this is a definite but not an exclusive statement. It says that Christ did die for His sheep, but it does not explicitly deny that He died for those not His sheep.

But, will it not also be granted that the context implies that Christ did not die for those who are not His sheep? Note, first of all, that Christ contrasts His sheep with those who are not His sheep. So His sheep and non-sheep are both before His mind when He says that He died for His sheep (John 10:1-18). Surely, therefore, He is *suggesting* that His death for His sheep is not for His non-sheep. Furthermore, His sheep are those who hear His voice and come to Him. The non-sheep do not hear His voice. So it is His sheep for whom He died and whom He calls. Therefore, He is plainly (albeit in a round-about logical way) *inferring* that He died *only* for His sheep.

Consider 2 Corinthians 5, an alleged proof text for a universal Atonement, and note that it too teaches that Christ died only for the elect. In verses 14-15 we read "that if one died for all, then were all dead: And that he died for all, that they which live should not henceforth live unto themselves." So, those for whom Christ died are those

---

46. Ibid.
47. Ibid., p. 165.

who live for Christ. Those who become alive in Christ are the elect
of God. Therefore, according to 2 Corinthians 5:14–15, Christ died for
the elect and only the elect (the alive) and not for the non-elect (those
who do not come alive). In verse 19 we read that "God was in Christ
reconciling the world to Himself, not counting their tresspasses against
them." Those to whom sins are not reckoned are the justified elect
(Romans 8:33, 34). So God is in Christ reconciling the *elect in the world*.

Next to John 3:16, 1 John 2:2 is the text most often cited in support
of unlimited Atonement.

> He Himself is the propitiation for our sins; and not for our sins only,
> but also for those of the whole world. (NASB)

First, Christ is here said to be a propitiation for our sins. Clearly "our"
refers to believers. This is universally granted. Then it is claimed that
the following statement just as clearly extends that propitiation to
everyone ("for those [the sins] of the whole world"). However, this
cannot refer to everyone in the world but only those for whom propitiation has been made in the whole world. Why so? Because, if God
was propitiated and no longer angry but actually at peace with the
world, there would be no more divine wrath upon it now or ever. John
3:36 clearly states that God's wrath is upon all who do not believe
(obey) even now. A wrathful God is not a propitiated God. So the
apostle is speaking not of all men in all the world but of the believers in
all the world.

The same could easily be shown for the other so-called proof texts
for unlimited Atonement. But let us conclude by considering more
fully the passage considered by many to be the strongest bulwark of
unlimited Atonement – John 3:16.

> For God so loved the world, that He gave His only begotten Son,
> that whoever believes in Him should not perish, but have eternal life.
> (NASB)

We first consider the very common misunderstanding of John 3:16.
It is supposed to teach that God so loved everyone in the world that He
gave His only Son to provide them an opportunity to be saved by
faith. What is wrong with this interpretation? First, such a "love" on
God's part, so far from being love, would be the refinement of cruelty.
As we have already seen, offering a gift of life to a spiritual corpse, a
brilliant sunset to a blind man, and a reward to a legless cripple if only
he will come and get it, are horrible mockeries. The reason the dispen-

sationalists do not see this is because, though they profess to believe in total depravity, they are in fact Arminian.

Second, the verse clearly states for whom this love gift was given. "He gave His only begotten Son, that whoever *believes* in Him should not perish." John 3:16 says more clearly than probably any verse in Scripture that the Atonement was made *for believers only.* God so loved the world that He gave His Son that *believers* should have eternal life.

Third, since even Arminians admit that believers are the elect, even Arminians should see that John 3:16 has in the plainest possible language said that God gave His only Son that the elect (whoever believes) "should not perish but have everlasting life."

Reformed Views of the Atonement

There has been an attempt, especially in modern times, to maintain that limited Atonement was not a doctrine taught by John Calvin himself.[48] If this *were* the case, it would not prove that the doctrine is untrue but that Calvin was not sound on that doctrine.

However, the doctrine cannot be denied in John Calvin. Granted that he said relatively little explicitly on this subject. Even if he were totally silent this would not prove that he did not believe and teach the doctrine. No one suggests for a moment that he attacked the doctrine or says anything in opposition to it. The greatest charge is that he did not say very much in support of it.

Even if Calvin had been silent on limited Atonement, his system of doctrine is not. A system of doctrine speaks louder than explicit statements in that system. When Lightner and others say that it is "highly debatable" whether Calvin believed this truth, they can only be referring to the relative paucity of explicit statement.[49] But even had Calvin made no affirmation of this doctrine at all, the logic of his theological position is utterly undebatable. It is rather interesting to observe, in passing, that this point would have been recognized immediately by Calvin scholars at the turn of the century but has to be proven in our day. The reason for this is that seventy-five or more years ago Calvin was caricatured as a logical machine. Today he is made out to be something of a mystic. While scholars at the turn of the century had to be

---

48. See R. T. Kendall, *Calvin and English Calvinism to 1649* (New York: Oxford, 1979); and the reply by Paul Helm, *Calvin and the Calvinists: A Reply to R. T. Kendall's Calvin and English Calvinism to 1649* (Edinburgh: The Banner of Truth Trust, 1982).

49. Lightner, "For Whom Did Christ Die," p. 159.

shown that he was not opposed to experience, scholars today have to be shown that he was not opposed to logic.

If we may give John Calvin credit for believing in rational thought, it will be a simple matter to show that he believed in the limited Atonement. No one has ever disputed the doctrine of particular election in Calvin. Nor has anyone ever questioned the fact that, for John Calvin, Jesus Christ is the only way of salvation. *What other conclusion could he have in his mind except that the Savior of men came to save those whom His Father had chosen to be saved?* A doctrine of universal Atonement simply has no place in Calvin's thought. This may even explain why Calvin says so little about the subject of limited Atonement. It is so self-evident in his system that the great Genevan probably felt he had more urgent duties than belaboring the obvious.

Some discomfort with the doctrine of limited Atonement is evident on the part of even otherwise *solid Reformed* theologians. One way of minimizing this discomfort has been the assertion that the Atonement is "sufficient for all but efficient only for the elect." R. B. Kuiper, for instance, says that Christ intended the Atonement to be sufficient for the world.[50] Indeed, if God intended an Atonement at all He would intend it to be infinitely sufficient (as Anselm's *Cur Deus Homo* demonstrated definitively a millennium ago).[51] Christ could not make less than an infinite Atonement. So if anyone says that the meaning of unlimited Atonement is a divine intention to make it sufficient for the world he is giving a "shattering glimpse of the obvious." Such a strategy, however, will not satisfy those who maintain a meaningful, though erroneous, doctrine of universal *design* of the Atonement, an Atonement not only sufficient for the salvation of everyone, but designed to save everyone.

Along similar lines, some solid Reformed theologians argue that Christ's death was infinite so that His ministers could offer it to everyone. Thus Buswell's statement that "Christ died so that the offer might be presented to you."[52] By *you* Buswell apparently means "everyone." This statement, while it is not untrue, is inaccurate in this context. We have already seen that the offer is not made to everyone but to the con-

50. R. B. Kuiper, *For Whom Did Christ Die? A Study of the Divine Design of the Atonement* (Grand Rapids: Eerdmans, 1969), p. 37.

51. Anselm of Canterbury, "Cur Deus Homo," in *Basic Writings of St. Anselm*, translated by S. W. Deane (La Salle, Ill.: Open Court, 1962).

52. James Oliver Buswell, *A Systematic Theology of the Christian Religion*, 2 vols. (Grand Rapids: Zondervan, 1962), 2:555. A somewhat similar argument is made by Donald A. Dunkerly, "For Whom Did Christ Die?" in *The Presbyterian Journal* (May 12, 1982):9–10.

scious sinner. Strictly speaking, it would not have to be infinite in extent (the number of sinners never could be infinite), but only infinite in relation to the depth of guilt (which would be necessary if only one sinner were saved).

The point we are making here is almost trivial. Its only justification is that this is an area where some well-meaning *genuine* Reformed theologians are trying to stress the unlimited character of the Atonement in order to agree, where possible, with their opponents (dispensationalists and Arminians in general). The intention is noble but the statements tend to be innocuous at best. More often, such statements are inaccurate and misleading.

We must also sadly admit that the majority of Reformed theologians today seriously err concerning the nature of the love of God for reprobates. We mention this here only because this defect in contemporary Reformed theology makes it all the easier for the dispensationalists to continue in their abyssmal error.

Most Reformed theologians also include, as a by-product of the Atonement, the well-meant offer of the gospel by which all men can be saved. Some Reformed theologians take a further step still and say that God even intends that they should be saved by this Atonement which nevertheless was made only for the elect. For example, John Murray and Ned Stonehouse write:

> Our Lord . . . says expressly that he willed the bestowal of his saving and protecting grace upon those whom neither the Father nor he decreed thus to save and protect.[53]

One may sadly say that Westminster Theological Seminary stands for this misunderstanding of the Reformed doctrine since not only John Murray and Ned Stonehouse but also Cornelius Van Til, R. B. Kuiper, John Frame, and, so far as we know, all of the faculty, have favored it. The Christian Reformed Church had already in 1920 taken this sad step away from Reformed orthodoxy and has been declining ever since. The Presbyterian Church, U.S.A. had even earlier, though somewhat ambiguously, departed and the present mainline Presbyterian church affirms that "The risen Christ is the savior for all men."[54]

The Presbyterian Church in the United States (now part of the Presbyterian Church, U.S.A.) is not far behind, and the separatist

---

53. John Murray and Ned Stonehouse, *The Free Offer of the Gospel* (Phillipsburg, N.J.: Presbyterian and Reformed, 1979), p. 26.

54. *The Confession of 1967,* in *The Book of Confessions* (New York: Office of the General Assembly, 1983), 9–10.

Presbyterians such as the Orthodox Presbyterian Church and the
Presbyterian Church in America are following in this train. Only the
Protestant Reformed Church seems willing to hold to the whole coun-
sel of God on this doctrine.

Serious as this error is, it does not constitute a radical break with
the Reformed tradition, though it does lay a foundation for it. For example, Murray and Stonehouse insist that, though God truly desires
the salvation of the reprobate, He does not decree that. Rather, He
decrees the opposite. They recognize theirs as a very *dangerous* position
and appeal to great mystery:

> We have found that God himself expresses an ardent desire for the
> fulfillment of certain things which he has not decreed in his in-
> scrutable counsel to come to pass. This means that there is a will to
> the realization of what he has not decretively willed, *a pleasure to-
> wards that which he has not been pleased to decree.* This is indeed
> mysterious, and why he has not brought to pass in the exercise of his
> omnipotent power and grace, what is his ardent pleasure lies hidden
> in the sovereign counsel of his will.[55]

However this is not "mystery" but bald contradiction, as these two
fine Reformed theologians well realized. How does one account for
Homer(s) nodding? The answer is simple—the exegesis *seemed* to demand it. The two authors "tremble at God's Word" and God's Word
seemed to them clearly to say that God desired what God did not
desire. We certainly agree that if God says that He desired what He did
not desire we would have to agree with God. Since we know that God
does not desire what God does not desire, for this is evident on every
page of Scripture, as well as in the logical nature of God and man, we
know this exegesis is in error, must be in error, cannot but be in error.

But where is its error? It must be that Murray and Stonehouse are
taking God literally where He desires to be taken anthropomorphically.
Almost everything said about God or by God in Scripture is an anthro-
pomorphism. The "everlasting arms," His "riding on the clouds," the
"eyes" and "ears" of the Lord—there are literally hundreds of such
metaphorical, anthropomorphic expressions describing God. This is,
of course, admitted by all. On the other hand, it is rightly contended,
God is also described *literally* as loving, rejoicing, happy, thinking,
and so forth. Can we say that when God is described in physical or
finite terms the expressions are metaphorical, but when He is described

_____

55. Murray and Stonehouse, *Free Offer*, p. 26 (emphasis mine).

ontologically or psychologically the expressions are literal? No, for sometimes that is the case and sometimes not. When God is described psychologically as suffering, frustrated, or grieved, Murray, Stonehouse, and all sound theologians would deny these to be literally true. They know that, in the early church, patripassionism (the teaching that the Father suffers) was a heresy.[56]

The question facing us here is whether God could "desire" that which He does not bring to pass. There is no question at all that He can desire certain things, and these things which He desires He possesses and enjoys in Himself eternally. Otherwise, He would not be the *ever*-blessed God. The Godhead desires each Person in the Godhead and enjoys each eternally. The Godhead also desires to create, and He (though He creates in time) by creating enjoys so doing eternally. Otherwise He would be eternally bereft of a joy He presently possesses and would have increased in joy if He later possessed it—both of which notions are impossible. He would thereby have changed (which is also impossible) and would have grown in the wisdom of a new experience (which is blasphemous to imagine).

If God's very blessedness means the oneness of His desire and His experience, is not our question (whether He could desire what He does not desire) rhetorical? Not only would He otherwise be bereft of some blessedness which would reduce Him to finitude, but He would be possessed of some frustration which would not only bereave Him of some blessedness, but would manifestly destroy all blessedness. This is clearly the case because His blessedness would be mixed with infinite regret. Our God would be the ever-miserable, ever-blessed God. His torment in the eternal damnation of sinners would be as exquisite as it is everlasting. He would actually suffer infinitely more than the wicked. Indeed, He would Himself be wicked because He would have sinfully desired what His omniscience would have told Him He could never have.

But why continue to torture ourselves? God, if He could be frustrated in His desires, simply would not be God. When, therefore, we read of God's "desiring" what He does not bring to pass, let us not "grieve" His Spirit by taking this literally, but recognize therein an anthropomorphic expression.

Genuinely Reformed theologians such as John Murray, Ned Stonehouse, Jay Adams, R. B. Kuiper, and many others, as well as all dis-

---

56. Thomas Aquinas has an excellent discussion of what experiences are and are not literally possible for the deity. See his *Basic Writings of Saint Thomas Aquinas*, 2 vols., ed. Anton C. Pegis (New York: Random House, 1945), 1:70–73.

pensationalists, have difficulty offering a limited Atonement unlimitedly. But what is the problem? The evangelist says, as ever, "Whoever will, let him come." "Believe on the Lord Jesus Christ and thou shalt be saved." There never was any other offer of the gospel and there never need be any other. Surely, the limited Atonement in no way limits *that* offer, and that is the only offer there ever was or will be.

Suppose an unconverted hearer asks, "Did Christ die for me?" The only true answer is: "I do not know. But, this I do know—if you will believe on Him, His blood will wash away your sins." That will satisfy anyone who wants to come to Christ. Suppose the inquirer then asks: "But may I come now?" The Christian will respond, "Of course." The inquirer may then inquire, "But *can* I come?" Our reply is: "What is stopping you?" In response the inquirer says, "I am. I do not find it in my heart." The Christian answers, "Whose fault is that? Do you think that God has put unbelief in your heart? Whose unbelief is it?" The inquirer may persist further and ask, "Is it not His fault for not giving me faith?" The Christian must answer, "I was not aware that God was indebted to you. If He is, salvation is not by grace but by law and justice." End of dialogue.

Before we leave the dispensationalists and their denial of the specific design of the Atonement, let us try to locate the source of their disaffection for this Biblical doctrine. God is thought by Arminians to love all sinners and send His Son to die for all of them, even though they disbelieve His Son and hate His gospel. If that is the attitude of the God who changes not, why would He come to hate them forever in hell for what He loves them in this world? If God loves men now it must be *God* who repents when He comes to hate them after their death. Since we know that "God is not a man . . . that he should repent" (Numbers 23:19, KJV), one of two things must be true—either God must hate reprobate sinners now or God must love reprobate sinners forever. It is inconceivable that an unchanging God loves impenitent sinners now and hates these same impenitent sinners after their death.

The problem here is a confusion of the "love of benevolence" with the "love of complacency." Ethicists speak of the distinction between a love of complacency, based on the excellency of another moral being, and a love of benevolence, which consists in doing some good for another being whether that being is excellent and deserving of that good or not. We know of no Reformed theologian who is aware of this distinction and who believes in a divine love of complacency for reprobates. On the other hand, almost all Reformed theologians recognize a divine love of benevolence even for reprobates in this world. This love of benevolence is usually called "common grace" (non-saving benefits for all mankind such as the sunshine and rain of Matthew 5:45).[57]

God "so loved" (benevolently) the world of the sinful elect whom He hated displacently as sinful. He so loved them that He gave His only Son, that the elect (those who believe in Him) should not perish but have eternal life. Those who believe have this eternal life by having Christ remove their sin so that they become the truly excellent in Christ and objects of God's complacent love. The non-elect, though in this life they enjoy God's benevolent love of common grace (sunshine and rain), were never the objects of His salvific benevolent love (intention to bestow eternal life), in this life or the next (where even the benevolent love of common grace is withdrawn in divine wrath because of their sinful, impenitent unbelief, for which they alone are responsible). The fact that "God is love" does not excuse sloppy thinking on our part regarding the nature of that love.

Dispensational Irresistible Grace Is Not Irresistible

In some ways, "irresistible grace" is the most telltale evidence of the presence or absence of Calvinism. Total depravity is often affirmed without being total (because it lacks inability). Unconditional election is commonly confused with unconditional salvation. Even limited Atonement is sometimes affirmed by non-Calvinists who confuse limited efficiency with limited design. Perseverance is constantly confused with an antinomian "eternal security." Irresistible grace, monergistic regeneration, new creation—these are very difficult to acknowledge if one has the notion that he is the ultimate initiator of saving faith and repentance. Difficult as it is to confuse Arminianism and Calvinism here, Dispensationalism has succeeded quite well.

We will show by several considerations that Dispensationalism does not teach this cardinal Reformed doctrine. First, irresistible grace is implicitly denied by the explicit denial of limited Atonement. Second, Dispensationalism denies that irresistible grace is taught in the

---

57. There are a few Reformed theologians, such as Herman Hoeksema and David Engelsma, who deny that this is divinely intended as any favor or grace at all. It only hardens the reprobate. Since this is what happens, it must have been so intended by God in His providence. It is therefore a mere fattening of the sheep for slaughter and the very opposite of grace, common or otherwise.

Old Testament. Third, it has no Reformed doctrine of regeneration even in its understanding of New Testament theology. We will conclude by considering various attempted dispensational defenses.

Irresistible Grace and the Atonement

First, having shown in the preceding section that Dispensationalism's opposition to limited Atonement is futile and worse, we now proceed to see what follows from this dispensational denial. Let us suppose that God had intended His Son's Atonement for the salvation of all men. What is the result according to dispensational theology? The answer is obvious—nothing. Man is dead and he remains dead to Christ's death. In this case, the death of Christ is not the death of death because Christ died not to save anyone but to make everyone savable. Nevertheless this sinner, if he is dead (as total depravity teaches), cannot benefit from anything outside him. The death of Christ is outside him—on his behalf and able to save him but accomplishing nothing within where it matters.

Of course, the dispensationalist teaches that the blood of Christ is offered to all. All whom? All corpses. It would be just as useful if the Atonement was not intended for any, or not made at all. It is no wonder that dispensationalists, in many cases, sense they are at a dead end and shift their doctrinal course. Their corpses show signs of life *before* they come to life in regeneration.

Irresistible Grace in the Old Testament

Second, according to Dispensationalism's consensus, the Old Testament people of God were not regenerated. To be a member of the New Testament people of God, one must be born of the Spirit. No matter how outwardly moral a person is, he is not saved and a member of the true church of Jesus Christ unless he is a new creature. By contrast, the Old Testament saint was not a born-again Christian. For example, Lewis Sperry Chafer contends, "individual regeneration, so far as the testimony of Scripture in general, is a New Testament provision."[58] Chafer says of Nicodemus that he was a perfected Jew under the Old Testament law although he was not born again. He was a genuine member of the Old Testament people of God though he, at that time, had not entered the company of the New Testament people of God.

---

58. Chafer, *Systematic Theology*, 6:36.

Dispensationalists see Paul, prior to his conversion, after the same model. Before his conversion, this Jew was as "touching the righteousness which is in the law, blameless" (Philippians 3:6, KJV). The dispensationalist takes this to mean that he met the Old Testament requirements. In that dispensation he too was a "perfected Jew." Only when he was born again did he become a member of the church of Jesus Christ.

By contrast, the covenantal view of the people of God sees in both dispensations the same people of God. All are members of the church. All are born again and all are saved by the one mediator between God and man—the man, Christ Jesus. The same church of Jesus Christ comprises both. One is not an unregenerate, earthly people and the other a regenerate, heavenly people. They are both the people of God, born of His Spirit, created anew by the Lord Jesus Christ.

The church, say Chafer and Walvoord, is "the body of Christ, . . . called out of the world and joined together with a living union in Christ. This concept is not found in the Old Testament."[59] That is to say, the body of Christ did not exist in the Old Testament. A dispensationalist will say that all Old Testament saints are saved by Jesus Christ, though none are in living communion with Jesus Christ.

According to dispensationalists, there are three categories of people—the Jew, the Gentile, and the church of God. The Jews, or Israel, are the descendants of Abraham and Jacob (Israel) who have the earthly promises. Even Abraham is said to have "spiritual" as well as temporal blessings but not regeneration, adoption, and "living union in Christ." He was the "channel" of such blessing. These Jews are now scattered in the whole world and later will be gathered together. The church consists of those Jews and Gentiles who have been born again and are members of Jesus Christ. The Gentiles are the rest of mankind who never had any kind of acceptable relationship to God.

In other words, dispensationalists see three soteriological categories where the Bible sees only two—the people of God and those who are not the people of God. There are those who are born again and those who are not. There are those who are saved and those who are not saved. There are those who are in Christ and those who are not in Christ. But, what God has joined together (the Old and New Testament church), dispensationalists have rent asunder. The church is not only separated in this world, but often (with Chafer and others) even in the world to come.

---

59. Chafer and Walvoord, *Major Bible Themes*, p. 234.

Abraham himself shows that the dispensational division between Israel and the church is erroneous. In the New Testament, those who are in living union with Jesus Christ are the seed of Abraham. Christ himself says to the Jews, "If you are Abraham's children, do the deeds of Abraham. . . . Your father Abraham rejoiced to see My day; and he saw it, and was glad" (John 8:39, 56, NASB). According to our Lord, these unbelieving lineal descendants of Abraham were not really the seed or children of Abraham at all, since they did not come to living union with Jesus Christ. Those who have a living union with Jesus Christ are the true Israelites. So, we see that not all lineal descendants of Abraham were necessarily the children of Abraham, but only those lineal descendants of Abraham (as well as Gentiles) who came to Jesus Christ. The true children or descendants of Abraham and the Christian church are one and the same.

In Romans 4, Paul says the same thing—the children of faith are the children of Abraham. He himself was an Israelite, but he did not become a true child of Abraham until he became a believer in union with Jesus Christ. As such, he and all believers are in union with the people of God in all dispensations who are the true children of Abraham.

Christ is much more visible in the New Testament of course. Living union is much more apparent there, but there is no denying, even by the dispensationalists, that Christ is the eternal Son of God and was very active in the Old Testament. Even the salvation of the Israelites rested ultimately on faith in Jesus Christ.

Dispensationalists cannot have it both ways. If the Old Testament people of God had no union with Christ, they were not saved by Him. If they were saved by Christ, dispensationalists have to admit that the Israel of the Old Testament and the Church of the New are one and the same body of people, all of them in union with Jesus Christ and, as such, the true sons of Abraham. God has joined the people of God in all dispensations in Jesus Christ. Dispensationalists have divided them.

It is rather sad to see some dispensationalists on the very border of the Promised Land who, nevertheless, hesitate to cross over. For example, J. C. Woodring, Jr., writes:

> The godly lives of men like Moses, Joshua, Samuel, David, and the prophets, for instance, would be unthinkable as a product of the old fallen nature alone or as the attainment of legal works. Yet, on the other hand, it would be no contribution to true Biblical study to build a comprehensive doctrine based on speculation when Scripture is silent.[60]

---

60. H. C. Woodring, Jr., "Grace Under the Mosaic Covenant" (Th.D. dissertation, Dallas Theological Seminary, 1956), p. 314.

Can this be called silence when the Scripture says, on the one hand, that "except a man be born again, he cannot see the kingdom of God" (John 3:3, KJV), and then, on the other hand, gives instances of many Old Testament persons who have obviously entered into the kingdom of the Spirit? Can there be any doubt that the Scripture is teaching that those persons who have entered the kingdom of God have been born of the Spirit of God? If the Scripture says that only those who are born of the Spirit of God do enter the kingdom of God, then it unavoidably follows that "men like Moses, Joshua, Samuel, David, and the prophets" were regenerate. Here again, we notice a characteristic dispensational hermeneutical hesitation to affirm an undoubted implication of Holy Scripture. What Scripture implies, it teaches as truly as what it explicitly states.[61]

Before we leave this matter of regeneration in the Old Testament, let us notice an interesting difference among some leading dispensationalists on this matter. Dwight Pentecost says, "the fact of new birth had not been revealed in the Old Testament."[62] On the other hand, his mentors, Chafer and Walvoord, write that "an Old Testament saint who was truly born again was just as saved as a believer in the present age."[63] This is apparently a puzzling detail in dispensational thought. It is never quite clear how Old Testament saints can be "saved" without being regenerated.[64]

Irresistible Grace in the New Testament

Third, Dispensationalism has no sound doctrine of irresistible grace, even in its understanding of the New Testament dispensation. Regeneration, according to this theology, is the implantation of a new, sinless self into the soul. It is not, strictly speaking, a regeneration at all; that is, it is not a rebirth of the old nature or a quickening of the sinner himself. It is the introduction of a new self altogether, a distinct psychological entity. According to the Reformed view, regeneration is the

---

61. As the Westminster Confession of Faith (1:6) puts it, "The whole counsel of God concerning all things necessary for His own glory, man's salvation, faith, and life, is either expressly set down in Scripture, or by good and necessary consequence may be deduced from Scripture."

62. Dwight Pentecost, *The Words and Works of Jesus Christ* (Grand Rapids: Zondervan, 1981), p. 126.

63. Chafer and Walvoord, *Major Bible Themes*, p. 234.

64. See John H. Gerstner, *Steps to Salvation* (Philadelphia: Westminster, 1959), p. 126.

divine implantation of a new principle of behavior which transforms a person though it does not eradicate the sinful principle known as original sin. Not so with the dispensationalist. He makes this experience not a regeneration of the old soul, but a new generation of a different soul.

L. S. Chafer is most explicit. He refers to regeneration as a "structural change":

> This is a change so radical and so complete that there is thus achieved a passage from one order of believing into another. Eventually in this great change the Adamic nature will be dismissed and the ego as a separate entity will represent little else than the stupendous fact of being a son of God.[65]

What is so startling about this dispensational doctrine is its unmistakable pantheism. Such a charge may be indignantly resented and rejected by dispensationalists but it cannot, however, be legitimately denied. Dispensationalism's doctrine is not Christ *in* you, but Christ *as* you.

Before considering Dispensationalism's view of irresistible grace, we need to examine its conception of the nature of faith and its relation to repentance. Dispensationalists contend that, while repentance is required in the kingdom age, only faith is required in this dispensation of grace. Chafer argues, "The one and only requirement on the human side which the Kingdom gospel imposes is repentance; while the only requirement in the gospel of the grace of God is faith or believing."[66] He maintains that repentance occurs in the "kingdom portions" of the synoptic gospels but not in the gospel of John which deals with this dispensation and, he thinks it is not in the New Testament epistles.

This position is too obviously incorrect to require refutation. (The reader may consult Acts 17:30; Romans 2; and 2 Corinthians 7:10.) It is interesting, however, to note the dispensational view of the nature of saving faith. Steele remarks that "after a faithful and patient reading, extending through ten years, I can find in these writings no better notion of faith than a bare intellectual assent to the fact that Jesus put away sin once and forever on the cross."[67] That this endorsement of a rather nominal type of faith is really true to the whole dispensational movement will become clear as we later discuss the Antinomianism of the movement.

65. Chafer, *Systematic Theology*, 6:106.
66. Lewis Sperry Chafer, *Bibliotheca Sacra*, Vol. 93, No. 7, p. 336.
67. Steele, *Antinomianism Revived*, p. 100.

Curiously, we sometimes find an ultra-Calvinistic doctrine of inability among dispensationalists. An interesting anecdote illustrates this. D. L. Moody once invited J. N. Darby to Farwell Hall, where they had a conversation. Moody said that Darby maintained that man does not will to be saved. Darby confirmed this opinion and proved it, supposedly, by appealing to John 1:13 ("who were born not of blood, nor of the will of the flesh, nor of the will of man, but of God" [NASB]). Moody countered with the observation that Christ had said, "Ye will not come to me, that ye might have life" (John 5:40, KJV). He also cited the "whosoever will" passages (see Mark 8:34). At this, Darby shut the Bible and refused to go on with the discussion. From that time on, he warned against Moody as a teacher.[68]

Darby believed that a man must be born again before he could be saved. He believed that this new birth resulted in the impartation of an entirely new nature, a separate ego, a part of the divine nature. This new nature, he taught, did believe in Christ, while the old nature, which was of the flesh and evil, always continued as such. Had he held a Calvinistic doctrine, he would have told Moody that the sinner really does will to believe, though only in consequence of his having been given a new ruling disposition (not a new ego, or psychological entity) in regeneration.

Irresistible Grace in Contemporary Dispensationalism

We now focus more precisely on the dispensational view of irresistible grace. To do so, let us notice the position of the most famous dispensationalist — Billy Graham. Graham writes that the "new birth is something that God does for man *when man is willing to yield* to God."[69] Again, "Any person who is willing to trust Jesus Christ as his personal Savior and Lord can receive the new birth now."[70] Significantly, he also says that a "person cannot turn to God to repent or even to believe without God's help. God must do the turning."[71] One can see from this that Graham is Arminian and not Pelagian. This could also be said of most dispensationalists. That is, divine "help" is needed, but not divine regeneration. A man cannot believe without help, but he cannot be regenerated without believing. This is precisely the evangelical Arminian order — divine help, then human faith, followed by regeneration.

68. Ironside, *Historical Sketch*, p. 81f.

69. Billy Graham, *How To Be Born Again* (Waco, Tex.: Word, 1977), p. 150 (emphasis mine).

70. Ibid., p. 152.

71. Ibid., p. 157.

Graham even uses the term *dead man* to refer to the unregenerate sinner, but it is immediately clear that life remains in this corpse. "A dead man can do nothing; therefore we need God's *help* even in our repenting."[72] That statement, in its first part, sounds like John Calvin. Before the sentence is over, however, one realizes that this "nothing" that the "dead man" can do turns out to be quite a great deal. That is, he can even repent. Of course, he needs God's "help." The very fact that Graham talks about *help* rather than *new life* shows that he does not really believe that this man is a spiritual corpse. As we have said before, the dispensationalist confuses himself. He strongly insists on the new birth but he does not realize that he does *not* believe that the born-again person was *dead* before life was bestowed on him.

Graham goes on to make his Arminian thinking quite clear. Whatever the necessary "help" is, it is not regeneration. "The Holy Spirit will do everything possible to disturb you, draw you, love you—but finally it is your personal decision. . . . Make it happen now."[73] Billy Graham is not a professional theologian, but the professional theologians whom he follows are just as explicit. "It is entirely a supernatural act of God *in response to the faith of man*," say Chafer and Walvoord.[74]

Some dispensational theologians can occasionally sound as if they conceive regeneration to be the basis of faith. John Walvoord, for example, writes, "The fact that we need a work of grace before we can believe should make us recognize all the more the inability of the natural man, and should make men cast themselves on God for the work which he alone can do."[75] One can see, however, in this statement that the dispensationalist takes back with one hand what he has given with the other. It seems as if Walvoord recognizes that regeneration must precede faith. Nevertheless, he concludes that very sentence by saying that these unregenerate men should "cast themselves" on God for the work which He alone can do. That is, man needs to be regenerated in order to exercise faith. But what Walvoord infers by casting oneself on God for the work of regeneration is precisely the exercise of faith. So, he is seeming to say at the beginning of the sentence that regeneration must precede faith, but makes it clear before the sentence is over that the faith, or casting of oneself on God, must precede, or form the basis of regeneration.

---

72. Ibid., p. 158 (emphasis mine).
73. Ibid., p. 168.
74. Chafer and Walvoord, *Major Bible Themes*, p. 99 (emphasis mine).
75. John F. Walvoord, *The Holy Spirit* (Grand Rapids: Zondervan, 1981), p. 122.

So, dispensational corpses come alive. This is the classical theological case of *vigor mortis*. The dead live of themselves. The dead spontaneously generate their own life. Out of nothing living something comes alive. Dispensationalists may be too embarrassed to admit, or perhaps even realize, that they teach such doctrine. They themselves will call this absurd and accuse the interpreter of grossly misrepresenting dispensational doctrine. Of course, the dispensationalist will say, "God brings the sinner alive." The sinner does not bring himself alive. Christ effectually called dead Lazarus and then, and only then, new life came into him and then, and only then, did he emerge from the tomb. Many dispensationalists say this again and again, never realizing that it is a contradiction of their whole system.

A. W. Tozer, a dispensationalist himself, nevertheless seemed to sense something profoundly wrong in this area of dispensational thought. While he did not put his finger on the precise point, he seemed to feel deeply that the fundamentalist's or dispensationalist's confidence in man's ability to understand and turn to God of himself was destroying the evangelical heart of that system. He is saying this in a roundabout way but the perceptive reader can see that he is aware vaguely of the problem with which we are dealing here:

> Among Conservatives we find persons who are Bible-taught but not Spirit-taught. They concede truth to be something which they can grasp with the mind. If a man holds to the fundamentals of the Christian faith he is thought to possess divine truth, but it does not follow. There is no truth apart from the Spirit. The most brilliant intellect may be imbecilic when confronted with the mysteries of God. For a man to understand revealed truth requires an act of God equal to the original act which inspired the text.[76]

A couple of pages later comes this statement: "Philosophical rationalism is honest enough to reject the Bible flatly. Theological rationalism rejects it while pretending to accept it and, in so doing, puts out its own eyes."[77] Then Tozer comes to this conclusion:

> From this mortal error Fundamentalism is slowly dying. We have forgotten that the essence of spiritual truth cannot come to the one

---

76. A. W. Tozer, *Divine Conquest* (Harrisburg, Pa.: Christian Publications, 1940), p. 79.

77. Ibid., p. 81.

who knows the external shallow truth *unless there is first a miraculous operation of the Spirit within the heart.*[78]

Because of the dispensational view of nominal faith and the dispensational denial of irresistible grace, Tozer senses that if a person can produce faith of himself before regeneration, then that person is able to understand the gospel savingly and really to convert himself. Such a person, capable of turning to God, is not a totally depraved person. He has it within his power to turn or not to turn to God. Tozer mistakenly calls this *theological rationalism* but, at the same time, there is no doubt that he has placed his finger on an important issue. The very fact that he was himself a dispensationalist makes his awareness here all the more poignant and telling.

When I once asked Dwight Pentecost how theologians who profess to be Calvinists could teach that faith preceded regeneration, he answered that they did not. Then, I cited Article VII of the Dallas Seminary catalogue which states, "We believe that the new birth of the believer comes only through faith in Christ." I will never forget his expostulation: "Is that in the catalogue?" Pentecost went on to say that L. S. Chafer, the founder of Dallas Seminary, when he was alive was constantly saying, "The baby does not cry before it is born." That is, a child of God does not exercise spiritual life, such as faith, until he is born again. That certainly sounds Calvinistic, but as we have seen, the dispensational theological system teaches otherwise. If Dispensationalism taught that the new life must precede every sign of a new life, such as faith, its Calvinism at this point would be unquestionable.

When I have pressed this point with dispensationalists, I usually get this answer. They sense the gravity of my charge and the basis for it, but nevertheless do not admit it. Their explanation is that these two events (regeneration and faith) are simultaneous. They seem to be aware that this is pure Arminianism and they will not plead guilty. Their contention is, therefore, that this is not a case of the priority of faith to regeneration, but the simultaneity of faith with regeneration.

Even though this is so, it does not solve their problems. It may make them sound slightly less Arminian, but it does not make them non-Arminian. Granted that faith and regeneration are simultaneous, the real issue is not the time element but the relationship. The question is whether faith is *based* on regeneration or regeneration is *based* on faith. That is, is it *because* a person is regenerated that he believes, or is

---

78. Ibid., p. 79.

it *because* he believes that he is regenerated? There can be no question that the dispensationalists are saying that it is because a person believes that he is regenerated simultaneously. Consequently, it is obvious and indisputable that, according to the dispensationalists, man produces faith out of himself while he is still a spiritual corpse. According to dispensationalists, including Lewis Sperry Chafer, it is because a baby cries that it is a baby—not because it is a baby that it cries.

We do not forget that dispensationalists also say that man will not believe without divine help. Here again, their Arminianism is very much in evidence. The Arminian says the same thing. The evangelical Arminian, at least, maintains that a person who is a sinner cannot believe without the help of the Holy Spirit. That help stops short of regeneration in classic Arminian thought and that help stops short of regeneration in classic dispensational thought. Whatever the help of the Spirit may be, it is not regeneration that leads to the person's faith. That faith is produced by this sinner with the help of God. Both Dispensationalism and Arminianism are *synergistic* soteriologies. God and man work together and contribute their share. If there is any difference between Dispensationalism and Arminianism at this point, it is merely that Dispensationalism *thinks* it is Calvinistic—a case of mistaken identity.

Thus, there can be no doubt that Dispensationalism, old and new, does maintain the necessity of regeneration and equally clearly maintains that there is a necessity for unregenerate faith prior to regeneration. We know that the dispensationalist insists on the necessity of the new birth. We never said anything other than that. But he also says that man's faith is what brings the new birth. And if he says that, it means that person who exercises faith is not dead in trespasses and sins. He is able to save himself by throwing himself upon the saving grace of Jesus Christ. That some dispensationalists will claim that we have misrepresented their theological system merely shows that they have failed to understand their own system.

This then is the dispensational caricature of the fourth Calvinistic point—irresistible grace. This Reformed doctrine teaches that the elect person, while totally depraved, is efficaciously regenerated by the monergistic activity of the Holy Spirit, and is, in that sense, irresistibly drawn to Christ. Being dead, he is made alive and comes forth believing. Like Lazarus, when the power of Christ's word brings life to him who is dead in trespasses and sins, he responds to the call "Come forth." According to this dispensational travesty of the doctrine, Lazarus comes out under his own steam. It is not the regenerating, life-giving word of Christ that leads to his birth. It is this dead man's faith which brings him to life so that he responds to Christ.

Dispensational Perseverance of the Saints
Is the Preservation of the Sinner

We can touch on this doctrine lightly here because the root of the dispensational travesty of perseverance—Antinomianism—constitutes a major concern of this volume and will be discussed at length later. Here, we simply note that, in lieu of the doctrine of the perseverance of the saints (that the new life bestowed by irresistible grace is lived out the rest of the regenerate person's life), the dispensationalist substitutes the doctrine of the eternal security of the believer (that the new life bestowed by regeneration in response to faith may or *may not* be lived out without affecting the "security of the believer"). In other words, a true believer may not persevere in holiness. Reformed theology teaches that such a failure would prove that the person is not a true believer at all and that only those who persevere to the end will be saved.

As an unusually frank example of dispensational thought on this matter, we cite the popular work by J. F. Strombeck entitled *So Great Salvation*. Says this dispensational writer in what amounts to a dispensational classic:

> There is much, indeed very much, confused thinking between the old order under the Mosaic law as distinguished from God's order under grace. Under law, because of the fact that the standing before God depends upon what God did, it was possible to lose one's standing, and the blessings that went with it, and in the place of being blessed, one became cursed. Under that condition, the motive to conduct became one of fear of punishment. That motive to a very large extent underlies human conduct. It is a controlling motive in most lives. . . . The motive to true Christian conduct [by contrast] is love.[79]

We note that in this entire chapter, which is entitled "Salvation and Man's Conduct," there is nothing but what a man ought to do, nothing about "must" or "has to" and no corrective to Antinomianism. There is no obligation to good conduct except love, which is considered incompatible with obligation.

This notion of eternal security has its roots in a particular understanding of sanctification. Strombeck, whose Antinomianism is perhaps more obvious than most dispensational writers (except for Zane

---

79. J. F. Strombeck, *So Great Salvation* (Moline, Ill.: Strombeck Agency, 1940), p. 139ff.

Hodges), presents a lucid statement of this view of sanctification which is often merely implicit in other dispensational writers:

> With the new birth there is also a new nature. It is the *nature of God*, the One by Whom life is given. As the life of one born of the flesh is mortal, because Adam became mortal, so the life of one born of God is eternal because *God's life* is eternal.[80]

There, in plain speech, is the dispensational view of sanctification. It teaches the implantation and perseverance of the divine nature ("nature of God," "God's life"). Such a nature is eternal, indestructible, and incapable of sin. That being the new nature of the Christian, he is presumably the same—eternal, indestructible, sinless. This is, as we noted above, Christian pantheism—the perseverance of God, not of the regenerated sinner.

We find Strombeck equally candid and lucid about the old nature which he repeatedly says is not really affected by regeneration but is left alone ultimately to be destroyed. The "old nature" (that is, the sinner who is supposed to be saved) simply dies—it is not saved at all.

> But how about the old sinful nature of those who are saved? What becomes of that? It still lives on in the individual as long as that person lives in the present mortal body. When at death, the spirit of the saved departs from his body the old nature dies.[81]

Strombeck goes on to indicate that this old nature is the source of continuing sin:

> It is because the old sinful nature survives that those who have been saved can and do commit sin. This happens when, in the conflict between the carnal and spiritual, the carnal gains the upper hand.[82]

In other words, the sinful nature produces nothing but sinful acts just as truly as the sinless new nature produces nothing but sinless acts. Here the dispensational propensity to divide and separate has resulted in an anthropology which can only be characterized as bizarre. Such an anthropology is utterly lacking in a principle of the unity of the human person. From this perspective, Strombeck could just as easily

---

80. Ibid., p. 79 (emphasis mine).
81. Ibid., p. 79.
82. Ibid., p. 81.

have said that there cannot really be any strife between the old nature and the new nature. They are separate from one another, going their separate ways. They are contrary to each other, of course; but they are really, in this type of thinking, separate and apart from each other rather than engaged in direct combat with each other. They agree to disagree.

His concluding point in this discussion confirms our feeling that he does not sense the depth of his deviation from Scripture here. He says,

> Salvation, then, includes something vastly more than a restoration of man to the original perfect condition in which he was when created. It includes the new eternal life having a divine nature.[83]

Strombeck here says that salvation is a restoration of man to the original perfect condition in which he was created. But, according to his own view of things, it is "vastly more than" that because it is the implantation of the divine nature. In point of fact, this "restoration" is vastly less than "a restoration of man to the original perfect condition." That old nature is not made over again. It is simply ultimately displaced by the new nature which is utterly divine.

The relationship of this view of sanctification to the Antinomianism which afflicts Dispensationalism is evident in Strombeck's *Disciplined by Grace*. He writes, "While the believer's standing is no way conditioned upon his state there is, however, a close relationship between the two."[84] What he means by this traditional dispensational language is that, when a person believes, he is justified and that *standing* before God is no way conditioned upon his actual behavior (his *state*). Strombeck is plainly teaching that justification is without necessary works. The faith which justifies, or brings a person into this perfect standing, may be utterly devoid of good works because his standing is in *"no way* conditioned upon his state."

He goes on to say that this "standing must be perfect in every detail. This excludes all possibility of any fallible human contribution."[85] We note that Strombeck says "fallible human contribution." What he infers is a fallible contribution and not *human* contribution. We remember that this "contribution," to which he refers, is a product of the new nature, which is not the old human nature changed but actually the newly implanted divine nature in him. Strictly speaking then, it

---

83. Ibid., p. 4.
84. J. F. Strombeck, *Disciplined by Grace* (Chicago: Moody, 1946), p. 74ff.
85. Ibid., p. 75.

is not only not fallible, it is not even human. In our forthcoming analysis of the dispensational view of sanctification, we will hear dispensationalists continually calling this new nature, "human." Nevertheless, they are thinking always and expounding constantly in terms of it being the *divine* nature and, therefore, infallible.

Strombeck is interesting also in his comment on 1 Corinthians 3:15:

> All these (wood, hay, stubble) represent human accomplishment; things done in self-will, by human power, for self-gratification and for acceptance by men. . . . To God all are the same, without value, only to be consumed by His fire.[86]

Again our writer is utterly consistent with his misapprehension. There are, in the converted person, presumably two natures — an old nature which is altogether evil and which produces only wood, hay, and stubble; and a new nature which, being altogether divine, of course produces nothing but gold, silver, and precious stones. In other words, the genuinely human nature produces nothing but useless works which will be consumed by fire. God, dwelling in the "saint," produces nothing but absolutely excellent, divinely approved works. This Corinthian passage, as misinterpreted by dispensationalists, shows clearly that what they are thinking of is the works of man versus the works of God and not works of the sinful man contrasted with the works of the converted man.

Strombeck has so interpreted the new nature as a divine nature that, to be consistent with that apprehension of the situation, he cannot have anything necessary, however remotely, for this implementation of the divine nature. What he never seems to sense is that it is blasphemy even to suggest that the saint is actually divine.

Given this view of the matter, it is not surprising that dispensationalists view the condition of the "carnal Christian" as a regular, if not normal, state of affairs. Strombeck, with his characteristic candor, says, "For many believers, this may be all their earthly life. . . . How many believers are not like Lot?"[87] He frankly says that many of these persons, who are converted and indwelt by the Holy Spirit and the new divine nature, may yet live like Lot (that is, slandering Lot, in "rejection of God's Lordship over his life") throughout their lives. Nevertheless, as Christians they are saved for they have the foundation which is Jesus Christ.

---

86. Ibid., p. 137.
87. Ibid., pp. 137–138.

This is the typical dispensational misconception of the Reformed doctrine of the perseverance of the saints. As one can see, it is the doctrine of the preservation of the unchanged sinner through life only to be destroyed eternally at death. What perseveres is not the "saint." The "saint" (a changed sinner) never existed to persevere, or not to persevere. What perseveres is the *divine* nature, which had nothing to do with the sinner (except to dwell alongside him) and was never in any need of persevering grace.

We simply cannot leave this brief discussion of the dispensational caricature of the "perseverance of the saints" without a rather sad footnote. John Walvoord feels himself so thoroughly the champion of Reformed orthodoxy against Arminian heresy on this doctrine that he alludes to and attempts to refute no less than eighty-five texts traditionally used by Arminians against this doctrine.[88] Much of what he writes is sound critique of the Arminian misinterpretations. We regret that the wholesome attack he makes against Arminianism is in defense, not of the orthodox doctrine, but of a travesty of it worse than the Arminian doctrine itself.

In summary of this whole section on Dispensationalism's spurious Calvinism, we present Dispensationalism's defection from Calvinism in a tabular form showing graphically that it is at no point Calvinistic.

---

88. Chafer and Walvoord, *Major Bible Themes*, p. 220ff.

CALVINISM	DISPENSATIONALISM

Total Depravity

Man is totally sinful in his *fallen moral nature* which affects all aspects of his inalienable human nature (thought, feeling, and will).

Man is sinful in all aspects of his personality but morally able of himself to receive the gospel offer.

Unconditional Election

While all men are totally indisposed to God, God the Father mercifully elects a multitude to eternal life apart from any condition in themselves.

All men being sinful, God elects to eternal life those whom He foreknows will believe.

Limited Atonement

The Atonement of the Son was designed for the salvation of those whom the Father had unconditionally elected.

The Atonement was designed to save every sinful creature.

Irresistible Grace

The Holy Spirit regenerates those whom the Father chose and for whom the Son died, faith following simultaneously.

Fallen man of himself chooses to believe in Christ, regeneration by God following simultaneously.

Perseverance of the Saints

The Spirit of God continues to work faith in the regenerate and they therein persevere in good works, always struggling against the remnants of their original sin whose guilt is pardoned but whose power is decreasingly felt until destroyed at death.

The "regenerate" new nature, being divine, can never sin or perish, while the old nature is unaffected by it and continues to operate sinfully, as before regeneration, until destroyed at death.

EIGHT

DUBIOUS EVANGELICALISM: THE DISPENSATIONAL UNDERSTANDING OF "DISPENSATION" DENIES THE GOSPEL

W e turn now from the serious to the grave. Dispensationalism has been shown to be nothing less than a travesty on Calvinism. So far from being a moderate form of the Reformed Faith, it is modified beyond recognition. Instead of four-point Calvinism, Dispensationalism is five-point Arminianism. This is extremely serious, but the charge we now make, that dispensationalism is dubious Christianity, is grave indeed. We must sadly accuse dispensationalists (of all varieties) of teaching, always implicitly and sometimes explicitly, that there is more than one way of salvation and, in the process of developing that theology, excluding the one and only way even from this dispensation of grace.

It bears repeating that, when I refer to Dispensationalism, I am not simply referring to any theology in which the word *dispensation* may appear in a favorable light. Dispensationalists seem to have a penchant for including anybody and everybody in their theology who happens ever to have used the word, *dispensation*. We have already noted an egregious example of this in Ehlert's *Bibliography of Dispensationalism*.[1]

---

1. Ehlert, "Bibliography."

Though Ehlert's work may be the most glaring example of this abuse of the term *dispensation*, it certainly has no monopoly on that practice.

It is very frustrating, of course, when there is disagreement about the very meaning of terms. One must not, however, become weary in well-doing. If we have constantly to be reminding Calvinists what Calvinism teaches and dispensationalists what Dispensationalism teaches in order to show people who are going by those names whether they do or do not belong to those traditions, we are just going to have to take the necessary time. If the Lord we serve is the Truth, then we cannot be too painstaking in search for the truth in every area with which we have to do.

What is indisputably, absolutely, and uncompromisingly essential to the Christian religion is its doctrine of salvation. A theologian may depart from the Reformed system and travel at his own peril. To depart from the essential salvation pattern is inevitably to depart from Christianity. Consequently, the doctrine which we now consider is of the essence. If Dispensationalism has actually departed from the only way of salvation which the Christian religion teaches, then we must say it has departed from Christianity. No matter how many other important truths it proclaims, it cannot be called Christian if it empties Christianity of its essential message. We define a cult as a religion which claims to be Christian while emptying Christianity of that which is essential to it. If Dispensationalism does this, then Dispensationalism is a cult and not a branch of the Christian church. It is as serious as that. It is impossible to exaggerate the gravity of the situation.

What then does Dispensationalism teach about the people of God and salvation? Let me say happily at the outset that all dispensationalists whom I have ever heard or read maintain with vigor and emphasis that they believe the divine Jesus Christ is the only Savior in *all* dispensations. The cross of Christ is the way of justification for *everyone* from Adam to the last saint who will ever be saved. Lewis Sperry Chafer wrote "that God has assigned different human requirements in various ages as the terms upon which He himself saves on the ground of the death of Christ, is a truth of Scripture revelation."[2] Later, in his *Systematic Theology*, he stated still more explicitly:

> That the one who is saved will not perish, but is in present possession of eternal life, that he is united to Christ to share His peace and glory, and that he shall, when he sees his Savior, be like Him, could

2. Chafer, "Inventing Heretics Through Misunderstanding," *Bibliotheca Sacra*, 102 (1945):2.

never be accurately appraised by men. Over against this truth that, regardless of His infinite love which would bless the creatures of his hand, the moral restraint on God which sin imposes could not be removed even by a sovereign decree; it was necessary, in the light of this holy character and government, that the price of redemption should be required at the hand of the offender or at the hand of a substitute who would die in the offender's place. By the death of Christ for sinners, the moral restraint is removed and the love of God is free to act in behalf of those who will receive his grace and blessing.[3]

The first statement of Dr. Chafer explicitly affirms that salvation always rests on the work of Christ; and the second implicitly says the same thing by stating that no other possibility existed. John Feinberg argues that "earlier Dispensationalism never held multiple ways of salvation. However, various unguarded statements from dispensational works made it appear that multiple ways of salvation were advocated."[4]

Dispensationalists, whatever they may say about "dispensations," are also insistent in their claims that they entertain no other method of salvation in any dispensation than by grace. Speaking of the experiences of Israel under the dispensation of the law (the most suspect of all dispensations), Darby says, "But all is grace; God acts in grace, and is glorified where man fails; man too is with God, for redemption brings us to God (Exodus 19:4)."[5]

So, we gladly bear our dispensational friends witness that they emphatically affirm their adherence to the essential Christian way of salvation. However, we must sadly say that whatever their intentions may be, they do not carry them out in their theology of "dispensations." However frequently they affirm their loyalty to the indispensable way of salvation in the blood of Jesus Christ, their system of doctrine relentlessly militates against this.

Of course, dispensationalists have heard the criticisms voiced in this chapter many times before. Clarence Bass wrote that "these assertions of a single principle of salvation simply contradict the basic ideas of the system."[6] In spite of their denials, Daniel Fuller charges Dispensationalism with teaching different systems of salvation and making

---

3. Chafer, *Systematic Theology*, pp. 51–52. Walvoord, *Major Bible Themes*, p. 135, concurs, "All dispensations contain a gracious element."
4. John S. Feinberg, "Systems of Discontinuity," in *Continuity and Discontinuity*, ed. John S. Feinberg (Westchester, Ill.: Crossway, 1988), p. 337, note 28.
5. Cited by Ironside in his *Historical Sketch*.
6. Bass, *Backgrounds*, p. 35.

the cross "an after-thought."[7] Probably the ablest critique ever written of the heart of dispensational theology remains Oswald Allis' *Prophecy and the Church*. The sheer persistence of this line of criticism by competent and well-meaning Christian theologians says a great deal about the dispensational lack of success at rebuttal.

In the following sections I will examine dispensational statements which have prompted the charges that the school teaches more than one way of salvation as well as some dispensational attempts to refute the charge. We shall see that for the most part dispensationalists are satisfied to deny without refuting.

The "Scofield Problem"

Scofield sparked strong criticism of Dispensationalism with a seemingly unambiguous statement in a *Scofield Reference Bible* note to the effect that salvific grace is a *New Testament* phenomenon. Scofield went on to say that legal obedience to the law was the condition of salvation in the Old Testament while faith in Christ is the condition in the New Testament:

> As a dispensation, grace begins with the death and resurrection of Christ. . . . The point of testing is no longer legal obedience as the condition of salvation, but acceptance or rejection of Christ, with good works as the fruit of salvation.[8]

This view is consistent with Scofield's definition of a dispensation as "a period of time during which man is tested in respect of obedience to some specific revelation of the will of God."[9]

Dispensationalists have adopted a number of strategies in dealing with the scandal caused by this passage. One tactic has been simply to assert that Scofield did not really mean what he said. For example, Barndollar defends Scofield, but without really spelling out an argument.

> Dr. C. I. Scofield, for example, made a very unfortunate statement as follows: "The point of testing is no longer legal obedience as the condition of salvation, but acceptance or rejection of Christ." There are those who pick up this statement and say: "See, Scofield teaches

---

7. Fuller, *Gospel and Law*, p. 144. See also pp. 29, 35, 38, 188.
8. *Scofield Reference Bible*, p. 1115.
9. Ibid., p. 5.

more than one way of salvation." As an isolated statement this is unfortunate, for it really is an isolated statement, because if one will study carefully all that Scofield has to say on this subject, it becomes apparent that he made a slip of the pen. His real teaching is his over-all teaching as found in his note on Romans 1:16 where he says that salvation is by Grace through Faith. Therefore, critic's charge is not substantiated.[10]

Here, we have another example of the dispensational repudiation without refutation. Barndollar appeals to another "isolated statement" without exegeting either and without demonstrating which more adequately reflects the teaching of the system as a whole.

To look at the Scofield statement more closely, we notice that a covenant theologian could have made it in reference to the Mosaic *ceremonial law*. Observing such law (when it was in effect) was indeed "the condition of salvation, or rejection of Christ." It was not the *meritorious ground* but it was the *sine qua non*. The statement thus understood was unobjectionable and true. To deny it would be antinomian. Barndollar's criticism is instructive, showing something characteristic of dispensationalists. He and they do not understand either what the law does or does not accomplish. Not understanding what it does *not* do, they fall into legalism in the Old Testament. Not understanding what it *does* do, they fall into Antinomianism in the New Testament.

Yet, Scofield undoubtedly did not intend the statement in the Reformed and proper sense because (as we shall see when we discuss his Antinomianism) he did see the law dispensation as providing "legal ground" for acceptance with God in sharp contrast with the evangelical way of that dispensation of grace. So, Scofield's view of the dispensation of the law really was — as charged — another way of earning acceptance with God; that is, another way of salvation. The Jews did not succeed in that way, according to Scofield, but that was their fault and not any deficiency in the law.

Another dispensational tactic of dealing with the "Scofield problem" here posed is to modify the definition of a *dispensation*. Thus, for Chafer, a *dispensation* is a "specific, divine economy, a commitment from God to man of a responsibility to discharge what God has appointed him."[11] Ryrie also is very cautious: "A dispensation is a distinguishable economy in the outworking of God's purpose."[12]

---

10. W. W. Barndollar, *The Validity of Dispensationalism*, pp. 6–7.
11. Lewis Sperry Chafer, cited by Charles Caldwell Ryrie, in *Walvoord, A Tribute*.
12. Ibid., p. 2.

Perhaps the most obvious example of this approach is found in the *New Scofield Reference Bible* of 1967. Essentially the same definition as Scofield gave in 1909 is repeated but, since the intervening fifty years had raised many questions, the later commentators elaborate on the original definition.[13] Thus, it is now indicated that there are three important concepts implied in the definition: a new divine revelation, the nature of man's stewardship with respect to it, and a certain time period for it. We note in passing that virtually all three of these are qualified to virtual extinction. It is not really a new deposit because the dispensationalists remind us that these truths overlap. For example, conscience existed before the dispensation of conscience and after it. The third point, the time period, is seen as merely approximate. A particular quality is only "dominant" in the given period.

Most importantly, there is no real stewardship here because nothing is accomplished by keeping the commandments and nothing is lost by failing to do so. This is evident in the new definition of a "dispensation."

> The purpose of each dispensation, then, is to place man under a specific rule of conduct, but such stewardship is not a condition of salvation. In every past dispensation unregenerate man has failed, and he has failed in this present dispensation and will in the future. But salvation has been and will continue to be available to him by God's grace through faith.[14]

In terms of purpose, therefore, the existence of the dispensations is a downright absurdity. A person in a given dispensation would not be saved (this statement says) if he kept the deposit of truth, nor would he be lost if he did not. He may be damned if he did, or he may be saved if he did not. His conduct in a dispensation has nothing to do with his salvation, according to this view of things.

According to this revisionist Dispensationalism, the purpose of these dispensations is apparently not salvific. What is it? That question is not answered in this note. It is "not a condition of salvation." Salvation is available "by God's grace through faith," quite apart from the "specific rule of conduct." The newer Dispensationalism is one grand charade, its dispensations signifying nothing. While Scofield said too much, his successors, in their desire to avoid the scandal of the "Scofield problem," have qualified the term *dispensation* to the point of extinction.

---

13. *New Scofield Reference Bible*, p. 3.
14. Ibid.

The Negative Purpose of a Dispensation

Some dispensationalists give a negative answer to our question. According to this view, the purpose of a dispensation is to show that man cannot keep the requirements of God. The note cited above says that in "every past dispensation unregenerate man has failed." It does not say that it was the purpose of these dispensations to show that man would fail in them but other dispensationalists do express that idea. For example, A. T. Eade writes:

> Thus, human history, as studied dispensationally, ends in continuous judgement. Truly we have learned the lesson of the ages, that men's hearts are "only evil continually"; that unregenerated human nature is not changed from Eden to Gog and Magog—but thanks be unto God ". . . as many as received Him, to them gave He the power to become the sons of God, even to them that believe on His name."[15]

Chafer and Walvoord find the same purpose, negatively speaking, in the dispensations. "Throughout eternity no one can raise a question as to whether God could have given man another chance to attain salvation or holiness by his own ability."[16] We notice that these two authors have added something to Eade's statement—something that Scofield had articulated earlier. That is the very significant point that these dispensations are implicitly different ways of salvation. Notice the statement that man's failure was a failure "to attain salvation or holiness by his own ability." Presumably, if man had succeeded rather than failed in these different dispensations he would have attained salvation "by his own ability." There were theoretically various other ways of salvation, at least six of them, but man failed in each one. Had he succeeded in any one, he presumably would have saved himself by bringing himself onto "the ground of the death of Christ" which he had done "by his own ability."

Chafer and Walvoord constantly reassert the statement that there is only one way of salvation in all dispensations. What they mean, however, is that there is only one *successful* way of salvation; namely, through Christ. There are other ways of salvation, but man has never succeeded in those other ways. Yet, as we have shown, failure to do so is also failure to bring oneself onto "the ground of the death of Christ."

---

15. A. T. Eade, *The Expanded Panorama Bible Study Course* (Westwood, N.J.: Revell, 1961), p. 185.
16. Chafer and Walvoord, *Major Bible Themes*, p. 136.

How are we to evaluate this dispensational proposal regarding the purpose of the dispensations? Our answer is that dispensationalists have, in their desire to avoid the scandal of heresy, been driven by the nature of their theological system into absurdity. According to Dispensationalism, man is a fallen sinner. He is supposed to be totally depraved. He comes into the world under condemnation—the heir of Adam's guilt. What are the dispensations supposed to do for these dead sinners? They are supposed to show that these dead sinners will fail when they try to save themselves by the particular dispensation's provisions. The question, of course, is how can dead people possibly save themselves? How can they "do this and live" when they are already dead to begin with?

Suppose the dispensationalist counters this objection by saying, "Granted that we believe men are dead in trespasses and sins; we also believe that they do not admit that. It would serve a useful purpose to convince a dead man that he is dead. That is precisely what the dispensations do a half-dozen different ways. Is that not what evangelism is all about?"

Our first answer to this is a simple one: dispensationalists do not speak this way. We have put this objection into their mouths, but it sounds strange coming out of those mouths. That is to say, if they thought the strategy of God in providing these different dispensations was simply or mainly to convince sinners that they were sinners, then the dispensationalists would be saying so frequently. After all, this question of the purpose of the dispensations is a fundamental point. According to this argument, the dispensations present merely hypothetical ways of salvation, but as we shall see in coming chapters, dispensationalists do not see the dispensation of law, for example, as merely hypothetical in its offer of salvation.

The more substantive reply (which does grow out of this first observation) is that there is nothing new in the dispensations so far as tests of salvation are concerned. Consider the seven dispensations for a moment. The first is the dispensation of innocence in which man was not a fallen sinner and therefore is not relevant. The second is the age of conscience, but conscience was a part of the natural and human endowment. The same can be said about the dispensation of government. As soon as you have two human beings, which in fact you did have at the beginning of the human race, you have a need for human government and this provides no special salvific test. The dispensation of promise, according to the dispensationalists, is unconditional and so, if there is any testing at all, it is about the land and not salvation.

Moving on to the dispensation of law, we are informed in Romans 2:14–16 that it is written on the hearts of men. All men have the light of the knowledge of God and a conscience which tells them they have an obligation to follow that light. There is a difference of degree in the Mosaic law, but not a difference of kind. So there is nothing essentially new in principle in the dispensation of the law. We also observe that the dispensation of the kingdom is essentially nothing but a reenactment of the dispensation of the law.

Coming back to the sixth dispensation (grace), we have something which, according to dispensationalists, has existed as a possibility from the very moment that Adam first sinned. Salvation in all dispensations, according to the dispensationalists, is by the grace of God in Jesus Christ. So, surely there is nothing unique in the sixth dispensation. The promise has been there from the very beginning. The only difference would be a difference of degree. So, we conclude that nothing is proven by these dispensations, according to the dispensationalists' account of them, except something which is already proven in the very nature of fallen human beings.

Our third objection is that, upon closer examination, the dispensations are incapable of proving what the dispensationalists claim they prove. They are supposed to prove that man cannot be saved by any other way than the blood of Jesus Christ. They do not prove that at all. All that they do prove, if we assume the dispensational viewpoint, is that man never has previously achieved salvation any other way than by the blood of Jesus Christ. Such an argument says nothing conclusive about future possibilities. Anything short of the failure of all possible occasions would not prove the impossibility of success. In the light of this, the quote from Chafer and Walvoord cited above could be amended to read, "Throughout eternity anyone can always raise a question as to whether God could not have given man another chance to attain salvation or holiness by his own ability." This reminds me of a statement of H. J. Cadbury that Machen's *Origin of Paul's Religion* had proved that every naturalistic theory to date had failed to explain the origin of Paul's religion but had not proved that another naturalistic theory could not come along that would explain it!

A fourth objection to this dispensational view of the purpose of dispensations is that it is an insult to the honor and character of God in that it represents God as holding out false hopes to mankind. He would virtually be saying, "This do and thou shalt live," knowing full well that man cannot do it and, even if he could, he could not live thereby. This is like the second argument but not a mere repetition. It makes it all the more awesome because it involves God in duplicity. Since no dispensationalist would want to do that, I hope that this rationale will be withdrawn.

It has been frequently observed, as we will see later, that the kingdom offer to the Jews is open to the unavoidable charge that it has God presenting something which cannot be a *bona fide* offer. Dreadful as that is, it was only during one dispensation. What we are observing here is that, according to dispensational thinking, God is doing this in *all* generations. Therefore, God not only can lie, but He does so in all dispensations.

Finally, even the dispensation of grace and its way of salvation was not necessarily successful, according to Dispensationalism. Even the dispensationalists admit this, empirically speaking. That is, they themselves acknowledge that vast multitudes of people in this age of grace are refusing the offer of salvation and being damned. So, even this dispensation which *would* save people, if they believed, does not necessarily save them. It is essentially no different from these other dispensations which were, as Chafer and Walvoord put it, fallen men's chances "to attain salvation or holiness by his ability."[17] This, too, is a chance for man to gain salvation by his own moral ability to believe, which ability the totally depraved do not possess.

I think that I have shown that regeneration is not the source of faith in dispensational theology. It is the man acting independently of, though not separate from, simultaneous regeneration who does indeed accept Jesus Christ. Using his own ability, he avails himself of the way of the Cross. Using his own ability, in other dispensations he never availed himself of the ways therein offered. So, the only difference at this point between this dispensation and the others is that some do avail themselves of their "chance" in this dispensation, but none avails himself of his chance in other dispensations with respect to the particular conditions of these dispensations.

The difficulty here, it should be noted, is with the dispensational theological *system*. The sequence of dispensations is seen, as noted above, in Scofield's definition of a dispensation as "a period of time in which man is tested in respect of obedience." The only possible conclusion from this is that faith is a "work." Faith is the one work required of us in this dispensation. If we exercise it we are saved, if we do not we are lost. Faith is our work and it entitles us to Christ and His grace. The orthodox doctrine of justification by grace through faith is not to be confused with the dispensational travesty of that doctrine. In ortho-

---

17. Ibid.

dox Protestant Christianity, faith is the instrumental means of union with Christ who *alone* "justifies the ungodly." By contrast, the dispensational view of faith is, ironically, legalistic.

If the dispensation of grace is not *necessarily* successful, empirically considered, it is not even *possibly* successful, theologically considered. If man is truly dead in trespasses and sins, an enemy of God and a hater of the Light of the World, then he never is "by his own ability" going to accept Jesus Christ as his Savior. This dispensation is no better than any other dispensation as far as possible success is concerned if it depends on man's "own ability." Man by his own ability, as a totally depraved sinner, will reject every offer to come to God in whatever dispensation or whatever manner or by whatever scheme. Dispensational theology is in the business (in this dispensation and every dispensation) of throwing lifesavers to *drowned* persons who must reach out and take if they would be saved.

It is rather ironic that Ryrie feels that Dispensationalism is strong in this area where other theologies, including Covenant theology, are weak. As he sees it, Covenant theology concentrates only on the salvific purpose of God and His glory therein. Dispensationalism is supposed, by contrast, to be concerned with the total glory of God. It is thought that, by viewing the Bible dispensationally, God is seen to be at work in many different ways, manifesting many aspects of His glory and not merely His saving mercy.[18]

Historically, Calvinism has been viewed, in distinction from Lutheranism for example, as being theocentric rather than christocentric. Calvinism's theocentric character compares favorably with the theological absurdity of Dispensationalism. Not only does Dispensationalism not glorify any of the attributes of God, it does not even glorify the salvific, merciful aspects of God.[19] We see that the stated purpose of the seven dispensations reveals nothing and obscures everything about God and destroys Dispensationalism in the process.

---

18. Ryrie, *Dispensationalism Today*, p. 18.

19. Craig A. Blasing notes that "John Feinberg acknowledged in a recent debate with John Gerstner that a doxological unity is not a distinctive of dispensationalism and therefore cannot define its essence." "Development of Dispensationalism by Contemporary Dispensationalists," *Bibliotheca Sacra* 145 (1988):268. Nevertheless, most contemporary dispensationalists seem loyal to the faith of their fathers though Johnson, Geisler, and even Ryrie are tiring of this burden. See Blasing, pp. 264–266.

The "Chafer Problem"

With Chafer, as with his mentor Scofield, dispensationalists have a problem *showing* that he taught one way of salvation, not to mention proving it. Chafer writes, "With the call of Abraham and the giving of the Law . . . there are two widely different standardized, divine provisions whereby man, who is utterly fallen, might come into the favor of God."[20] Again, he remarks in the final volume of his *Systematic Theology* that, in the Old Testament men were justified by the law, while in the New Testament faith was without works.[21]

The effect of these types of statements has led dispensationalists to offer various excuses for the Dallas Seminary founder. When questioned by Daniel Fuller on this point, John Walvoord conceded that Chafer tended to "over-emphasize the legal character" of the law and kingdom periods. More importantly, according to Walvoord, Chafer became "quite indignant when his writings were interpreted as teaching anything other than that salvation was always by grace and by faith."[22] We ourselves have no doubt that Chafer was (and Walvoord is) sincere in the desire to teach one way of salvation.

Good intentions are not sufficient however. Here is what Chafer actually wrote:

> As before stated, whatever God does for sinful men on any terms whatsoever [being made possible through the death of Christ] is to that extent, an act of divine grace; for whatever God does on the ground of Christ's death is gracious in character, and all will agree that a divine covenant which is void of all human elements is more *gracious* in character than one which is otherwise. These distinctions apply only to the divine side of the covenant. On the human side . . . there is no exercise of grace in any case; but the human requirements which the divine covenant imposes may be either absolutely lacking, or some so drastically imposed as to determine the destiny of the individual.[23]

Let us analyze what Chafer is saying. First, he asserts that whatever God does on the ground of Christ's sacrifice is gracious. We know

---

20. Lewis Sperry Chafer, "Dispensationalism," *Bibliotheca Sacra* 93 (1936):93.
21. Chafer, *Systematic Theology*, 7:219.
22. Fuller, "Hermeneutics," p. 158.
23. Chafer, "Dispensationalism," p. 430.

from other utterances that Chafer believes that Christ's sacrifice is for all time and this is what leads Chafer to affirm that no one is ever, at any time, saved except by the blood of Christ. Therefore, Chafer concludes, even in the dispensation of the law men were saved by the grace of God in Christ. The death of Christ is apparently thought, by Chafer, to provide the possibility for grace throughout human history which, regardless of other requirements which might be added, allows us to view salvation as "gracious." We have already seen that Chafer's view of the Atonement as making salvation "possible" functions in this way. In reality, for Chafer, the Atonement makes it "possible" for God to offer two different ways of salvation—one by works (which has always failed) and one by faith (which succeeds if the sinner generates the necessary faith). That this is indeed the case is evident from Chafer's discussion of the requirements involved. A covenant may have human requirements—either "absolutely lacking" or so "drastically imposed as to determine the destiny of the individual."

What we have seen is that Chafer's Dispensationalism, strictly speaking, does not teach *salvation* by works in the dispensation of the law, but damnation by works. Second, because faith is really a "work" for dispensationalists, Chafer does not teach salvation by grace, even in the dispensation of grace.

The Continuity of Faith

Another problem facing Chafer is demonstrating the continuity of salvific faith that he claims is present in the dispensation of law as well as the dispensation of grace. This is a problem to which one successor of Chafer, Charles Ryrie, has paid particular attention. Replying to Daniel Fuller, Ryrie attempts to vindicate Dispensationalism's claim to teach one way of salvation in all dispensations by making a number of distinctions with regard to faith. "The *basis* of salvation in every age is the death of Christ; the *requirement* for salvation in every age is faith; the *object* of faith in every age is God; the *content* of faith changes in the various dispensations."[24]

Daniel Fuller wrongly criticizes Dispensationalism, Ryrie argues, because he does not distinguish between the "basis" of salvation and the "content" of faith.[25] "By comparison with the grace of Christ, all

---

24. Ryrie, *Dispensationalism Today*, p. 123.
25. Ibid., p. 124.

previous revelations of grace were as nothing," he continues.[26] Waxing triumphant, Ryrie declares that "only dispensationalism can harmonize these two aspects of truth."[27] Speaking of the law, he explains that "the means of eternal salvation was by grace and the means of temporal life was by law."[28] "The sacraments were part of the law; the keeping of them did not save; and yet a man could respond to what they taught so as to effect eternal salvation."[29] They had "ulterior efficacy."[30] Thus Ryrie maintains, apparently, that the Old Testament sacraments "taught" the salvation that God was to accomplish in Jesus Christ.

Then our theologian starts to hedge his bets. It "cannot be implied that the Israelite understood what that final dealing with sin was."[31] Ryrie's whole building begins to totter. "For if he had had sufficient insight to the extent of seeing and believing on the finished work of Christ, then he would not have had to offer the sacrifices annually, for he would have rested confidently in what he saw in the prefiguration."[32] Finally, the house of cards collapses as Ryrie concludes: "Acts 17:30; Rom. 3.25; John 1:21; 7:40; I Pet. 1:10–11 — These passages make it impossible to say that Old Testament saints under the law exercised personal faith in Jesus Christ."[33]

Instead of Ryrie's Dispensationalism harmonizing the two dispensations, we see that he destroys the graciousness of either. Ryrie's goal is to prove that *salvation* is the same in all dispensations. This he attempts by showing that *faith* is the same in all dispensations. What he actually shows is vastly different—namely, that the *requirement* of faith is the same in all dispensations. He also irrelevantly discusses the basis, object, and content of faith.

Since he discusses these irrelevant matters, we must discuss them too, if only to show that they are not germane before proceeding to the one crucial point. Ryrie distinguishes basis, object, and content of faith. *Basis* means foundation or ground-work, something on which something else rests. *Object* is that toward which faith is directed. That toward which faith is directed and that on which it comes to rest should be synonymous. We are using two different words for the same

---

26. Ibid., p. 125.
27. Ibid.
28. Ibid., p. 126.
29. Ibid.
30. Ibid., p. 129.
31. Ibid.
32. Ibid.
33. Ibid., p. 130.

allusion. Nevertheless, Ryrie thinks he has a difference here because he differently defines basis and object of faith. The basis is the death of Christ; the object is God. So, faith rests on two different foundations — or are the two one? Surely, Ryrie would not want to claim two different foundations for faith. He will have to plead guilty to redundancy.

In any case, the *faith* is what is necessary, and it is said to remain the same in all dispensations. No, that is not what Ryrie says. He says that the *requirement* of faith remains the same. Faith itself is actually always *changing*. Now faith is one thing that cannot change in different dispensations. If it did, one would not be talking about the same thing — about the same requirement. What is troubling about Ryrie here is that he speaks of the "content" of faith when he is thinking of the "object" of faith. But he has already identified the object of faith as God, who changes not.

What does all this irrelevancy add up to? That God-the-giver-of-Christ-crucified is the basis or object of faith in all dispensations. That is true and truly beside the point. What Ryrie is supposed to do is prove that Dispensationalism *teaches* that doctrine and does not implicitly deny it.

In the light of all this, Ryrie enters the arena of debate to answer the charge of Fuller. Fuller's error (says Ryrie) is that he does not distinguish between basis and content. I will not enter into the discussion between Fuller and Ryrie directly but address myself to Ryrie's comment here. We have already seen that Ryrie's distinction between "basis" and "object" is wrong-headed. As we have also seen, he goes on to distinguish between "object" and "content." Again, Ryrie attempts to divide the indivisible. By any reasonable standard, an object of faith (that towards which faith is consciously directed) is identical with Ryrie's "content" of that faith. (A more normal usage of the term "content of faith" might be the orthodox Protestant conception of faith as consisting of knowledge, assent, and trust.)

Where does this distinction between "object" and "content" get Ryrie? In essence, it allows Ryrie to maintain that Old Testament believers were saved by faith in God while believers in the dispensation of grace are saved by faith in Christ. Apparently, according to Ryrie, Old Testament believers needed some vague sort of faith in divine benevolence while New Testament believers need faith in Jesus Christ specifically. Ryrie is either speaking about faith in Jesus Christ or he is not. As we have seen, in the case of Old Testament "believers," he is not.

I originally said that Ryrie was being more profound and sophisticated here than his mentor, Chafer. As we probe we find that his very effort to go deeper has taken him deeper into the mire. The more he struggles the more he sinks. Chafer made a simple, easily refuted statement. Ryrie gives a more complex statement less easily refuted. It is less easily refuted merely because it is obfuscatory and not because it is profound.

Ryrie's argument may appear to gain plausibility by the introduction of what, on closer examination, is revealed to be a red herring. Ryrie claims that the question is, "How much of what God was going to do in the future did the Old Testament believer comprehend?"[34] Apparently nothing, according to Ryrie, because the Old Testament sacrifices did not give a "clear foreview of Christ."[35] Because Covenant theology maintains that Old Testament believers did exercise faith in Christ, it is guilty of an "historical anachronism" in reading New Testament faith back into the Old (according to Ryrie).[36] Dispensationalism is thus justified in maintaining that the "content" of Old Testament faith was different from saving faith today.

Ryrie's argument regarding the distinction between the basis of salvation and the content of faith will be examined below. What is crucial to note at this juncture is that the charge of Covenant theology "anachronism" is unjustified. Covenantal theologians have never maintained that the Old Testament sacrificial system gave a perfectly "clear foreview" of all the details of the life and work of Christ. It would not be possible, from an Old Testament perspective, to write one of the four gospels of the New Testament. Nevertheless, covenant theologians have adamantly maintained that the Old Testament in its entirety (see Luke 24:44–47) refers to Christ and that the Old Testament sacrificial system in its entirety (see Hebrews 10:1–18) points forward to Christ. Thus, the faith of Old Testament believers, however hazy that may have been with regard to details, can be meaningfully described as faith *in Jesus Christ*. As we have seen, Ryrie would substitute, in the case of Old Testament believers, some sort of vague faith *in God* for faith *in Christ*.

Why does Ryrie think that the believing Israelite could not have exercised faith in Christ? A number of reasons, none of them compelling, are advanced. First, Ryrie suggests that the believing Israelite would not have had to offer the sacrifices annually for "he would have rested confidently in what he saw in the prefiguration."[37] This resting

---

34. Ibid., p. 131.
35. Ibid., p. 129.
36. Ibid.
37. Ibid.

"confidently in what he saw in the prefiguration" was precisely the reason for offering the sacrifices. Why would he have slain millions of
bloody sacrifices if he had not realized that the blood of bulls and
goats did *not* take away sin. After all, John the Baptist, who knew very
well about the Lamb of God who takes away the sin of the world (see
John 1:29), continued to offer those sacrifices, as did that Lamb of
God Himself!

Trying to prove his point by New Testament texts, Ryrie cites five
and concludes that "these passages make it impossible to say that the
Old Testament saints under the law exercised personal faith in Jesus
Christ."[38] Since the dispensationalist makes such an astonishing and
unwarranted deduction from these portions of the Word of God which
teach the very opposite, we will have to look at them one by one.

Acts 17:30. "Therefore having overlooked the times of ignorance,
God is now declaring to men that all everywhere should repent"
(NASB). This statement was part of Paul's famous Mars Hill sermon before the Areopagus *Gentiles*. The apostle to the Gentiles was not referring to "Old Testament saints." Therefore, when he referred to the
"ignorance" which God "overlooked." Paul was not referring to the
Jewish believers at all.

Romans 3:25. "[Christ Jesus] whom God displayed publicly as a
propitiation in His blood through faith. This was to demonstrate His
righteousness because in the forbearance of God He passed over the
sins previously committed" (NASB). I will not here attempt to prove that
"passing over of sins" (*paresis*) was the equivalent of the forgiveness of
sins (*aphesis*). We are presently concerned with what the Israelite saw
in the prefigurations. Paul says here that God "displayed publicly"
and "demonstrated" His righteousness in Christ Jesus and His propitiation. Christ is now displayed as the antitype of all those ancient
types. He is "our passover" just as the Baptist said: "Behold, the
Lamb of God" (John 1:29, NASB). *All those millions of sacrificial
lambs were pointing to one—the Lamb of God.* John and all the
others could see, as no doubt Abraham did when that ram was
caught in the thicket, that all were prefigurations of Him who was to
come, for without the shedding of blood (of the Lamb of God) there
could be no remission of sins.

John 1:21. "And they asked him, 'What then? Are you Elijah?'
And he said, 'I am not.' 'Are you the Prophet?' And he answered, 'No'"

---

38. Ibid.

(NASB). One wonders why Ryrie chose this text for his purpose. Presumably because the Israelites did not know who the Christ was and wondered whether the Baptist was claiming to be He. If that is Ryrie's argument, the passage actually proves our point. The Jews knew the Christ was coming from the prefigurations. Of course, He had to be identified. In other words, they knew from the Old Testament who the Christ would be but not which person was He. They would not even have asked John if he were "the Prophet" if they had not known that "the Prophet" was coming. It was just a few verses later (John 1:29) that John identifies the Lamb of God, saying, "Behold"!

John 7:40. "Some of the multitude therefore, when they heard these words, were saying, 'This certainly is the Prophet'" (NASB). Everything just said above applies here and more so. In John 1:21 it was religious leaders who were asking. Here we see that even some of "the multitude" of Israelites knew, from the Old Testament prefigurations, that the Prophet was coming and were convinced, from the mounting evidence, that Jesus was He. In other words, even the laity could see Jesus Christ was the prefigured One.

1 Peter 1:10–11. "As to this salvation, the prophets who prophesied of the grace that would come to you made careful search and inquiry, seeking to know what person or time the Spirit of Christ within them was indicating as He predicted the sufferings of Christ and the glories to follow" (NASB). We doubt if Ryrie could have chosen five better texts more thoroughly to disprove his point but this one could do it all by itself. The passage shows clearly that the prophets "prophesied of the grace that would come." So also, Christ had pointed out on the way to Emmaus as he exclaimed:

> "O foolish men and slow of heart to believe in all that the prophets have spoken! Was it not necessary for the Christ to suffer these things and to enter into His glory?" And beginning with Moses and with all the prophets, He explained to them the things concerning Himself in all the Scriptures." (Luke 24:25–27, NASB)

So, from the Old Testament the Israelites should have learned clearly of the very grace that was to come—the grace of God in Christ. They knew it was to be in a "person" at some future "time." They knew from the prefigurations of the prophets that the Messiah in whom they believed was certainly coming in person at the appointed time. They needed only to recognize Him when He came.

The only explanation for Ryrie's peculiar exegesis here is that he has forgotten that people can very well see a particular person as described and defined before they meet him visibly in person. The Old Testament saints *knew* Jesus Christ although they did not know all about Him. Ernst W. Hengstenberg wrote four volumes sketching the Old Testament prefigurations of the Messiah.[39] For centuries, they had been looking for Him. To be sure, some misinterpretations had confused and obscured the prophecies (which were plain enough in themselves). Christ rebuked rather than excused the disciples for not believing. It remained only to locate the "person or time the Spirit of Christ within them was indicating" (1 Peter 1:10).

The only way dispensationalists will clear themselves of the charge of teaching multiple ways of salvation is by resting on the solid rock of teaching that saints in all dispensations do believe in Christ and in Him crucified and that there is *no essential difference* between one dispensation and another. As long as they are going to think of dispensations as they do, they are going to sink into legalism under the law and Antinomianism under grace. That means no salvation in any dispensation. Simply asserting one's intention without eschewing teaching to the contrary harms the church and places souls in jeopardy.

Eternal Life vs. Temporal Life

Thinking he has justified grace in the dispensation of the law, Ryrie goes on to explain what he thinks the law itself accomplishes: "the means of eternal salvation was by grace and the means of temporal life was by the law."[40] Here Ryrie is almost sound. If only he had a sound doctrine of grace, his understanding of law or "morality" as being temporally beneficial would be helpful. But, not having grace in his doctrine, he loses what he does have (the law). Temporal benefits are only beneficial if they are the fruits of grace; that is, only if they come to gracious persons. Otherwise, they are only instances of divine forbearance.

In point of fact, the dispensation of the law knows no such distinction as Ryrie defends. "This do and thou shalt live" surely does not refer only to temporal life. As a matter of fact, if a person is not made acceptable to God by grace, his temporal "benefits" become curses and not blessings.

---

39. Ernst Wilhelm Hengstenberg, *Christology of the Old Testament*, 4 vols., 2nd ed., trans. Theodore Meyer (Edinburgh: T. & T. Clark, 1861).

40. Ryrie, *Dispensationalism Today*, p. 130.

Dispensational Prospective Salvation
Excludes Actual Salvation

Dispensationalists teach that men and women in all dispensations are saved by the underlying blood of Jesus Christ. I have shown that the dispensational understanding of a "dispensation" and the dispensational system of doctrine in general contradict this claim. Having demonstrated that Dispensationalism does in fact teach a different way of possible salvation for the Old Testament dispensation in that Old Testament believers were *not* saved through faith in Christ, I now proceed to examine further the way in which this Old Testament salvation differs from the New. In this section, we focus on the way persons before the Incarnation are actually related to the sacrifice of Christ. It is, we shall see, by anticipation and not by participation. Dispensationalism teaches prospective rather than participative salvation.

C. I. Scofield himself makes our point here quite clear. In his note on Genesis 1:28, he writes that "before the cross man was saved in prospect of Christ's atoning sacrifice."[41] Now there is an infinite difference between being saved by Christ's sacrifice and living in "prospect" of it! If a dispensationalist replies that we are quibbling with language, he cannot have carefully reflected on this matter. That difference in the ways of salvation is the most crucial difference between the two theologies. If a dispensationalist gives up that distinction, he gives up his Dispensationalism!

This dispensational way of conceiving of the Old Testament believers is drastically different from the Biblical way. *According to dispensationalists, the Old Testament people are saved by believing in the coming of the Christ while, in the Biblical view, Old Testament people are saved by believing in the Christ who is coming incarnate.* In one system, a person is saved by the anticipation of a coming event. In the other system, a person is saved by the Person in the anticipated event. It is as simple as this — in Dispensationalism a person is saved by anticipation while, in the Biblical system, a person is saved by Christ.

We have seen that this is no artificial distinction. Because Old Testament people are not saved by Jesus Christ, according to Dispensationalism, they do not benefit from what Christ actually achieves when He comes. They are not regenerated, their hopes are not heavenly, and they are an earthly "herd of swine" (Calvin). In point of fact, they are

---

41. Ryrie, *Dispensationalism Today*, p. 126.

not even saved by hope in the coming of Christ since, according to dispensationalists, their faith was in divine benevolence rather than in a specific coming figure.

The truth will inevitably manifest itself. It has in dispensational soteriology. The truth is that another way of salvation which is somehow connected with Christ but not resting on Christ is a *different* way. The dispensationalist at this point is, unconsciously perhaps, consistent with himself. He does not regard the Old Testament people of God as second, third, or fourth class citizens of the kingdom of God. They simply are not citizens at all. While dispensationalists roundly assert that Old Testament people were saved by Christ, there is no way *in their theological system* they could be.

Conclusion

Thus we see that the charge that Dispensationalism teaches more than one way of possible salvation is well founded. Not only did the early dispensationalists teach this heresy, but more recent dispensationalists have failed to exonerate their predecessors and have, in more subtle ways, fallen into the same error. The problem here, as we have seen, is the understanding of a *dispensation* as a "period of time during which man is tested in respect of obedience" which is central to the dispensational system. As we have seen, dispensational adherence to this definition results in a denial of the gospel. More recent dispensational attempts to correct their theological system at this point are only another pathetic instance of putting on a band-aid to heal a fatal internal wound.

NINE

DUBIOUS EVANGELICALISM: THE "KINGDOM OFFER" TO THE JEWS UNDER- MINES THE GOSPEL

I n dispensational thinking of even the most moderate character, Jesus Christ came to offer an earthly kingdom to Israel. That kingdom, according to dispensational thinking, would have been a full establishment of the Old Testament legal system and its expansion through the whole world under the leadership of a revived Israel and her Messiah. Fortunately for the dispensationalist and all of us, the Jews did not do their duty but sinfully rejected Christ's offer. That spelled Christ's doom on the cross. Christ's death on the cross, which came about only because Israel did not do her duty and accept Him as the king of Israel, is the basis of our salvation in this dispensation of grace and every dispensation. In other words, the gospel was a happy accident. It depended entirely on the faithlessness of the Jews. *Had they responded as they ought to have responded, there would never have been a gospel of Jesus Christ*!

This is the standard dispensational position, and no one states it more clearly than the articulate Donald Grey Barnhouse. "When Jesus came, He made a *bona fide* offer of the Kingdom and power to the people of Israel." Barnhouse adds, trying to save an unsalvable situation, "He knew before He came that they would refuse it — knew it from all eternity; hence, there are prophets which speak of His coming to die for us."[1] A

---

1. Donald Grey Barnhouse, *He Came Unto His Own* (New York: Revell, 1933), p. 17.

little later, he adds: "The essence of Christ's teaching in the first part of His ministry that in which He was offering the Kingdom to the Jews, His own people, is to be found in the Sermon on the Mount."[2]

Two key dispensational ideas are closely related to this doctrine. The first is a supposed distinction between the "kingdom of heaven," or the earthly millennial kingdom offered to the Jews, and the "kingdom of God," or the eternal spiritual kingdom associated with the dispensation of grace. Appealing to the fact that the gospels portray Jesus as using both terms, dispensationalists contend that the distinction between the two is of the utmost importance while non-dispensational exegetes, of all theological stripes, maintain that the two terms are virtually synonymous.[3] The second idea is the view of the dispensation of grace as a *parenthesis*; that is, a period that was not predicted by the Old Testament prophets. Because these matters will be discussed later in connection with the dispensational view of Israel and the church, we need not pursue them fully here.

The Problem

This "kingdom offer" is surely an appalling notion. How a Christian person could entertain it, even momentarily, is very difficult to understand. Needless to say, weighty criticism of this dispensational teaching has been made, and dispensationalists have felt the need to respond. In addition to my critique, I will look at a number of dispensational attempts to vindicate this novel doctrine.

The primary objection is a moral one. A clear implication of the dispensational view is that God was offering Israel a very wicked option. According to Dispensationalism, the Lord Jesus Christ was offering something to the Jews in good faith which, had they accepted, would have destroyed the only way of man's salvation. God is an honest God. He is a sincere God. He, therefore, truly offered to the Jews the setting up of a kingdom which would have made the Cross impossible. *Obviously, if God did offer a kingdom which He could not have permitted to be established, He could be neither honest nor sincere.*

---

2. Ibid. p. 23.

3. See the *Scofield Reference Bible*, p. 996. For the more standard scholarly treatment of this question see the *Theological Dictionary of the New Testament*, 10 vols., ed. Gerhard Kittel, trans. Geoffrey Bromiley (Grand Rapids: Eerdmans, 1964–76), 1:582.

We know the way the dispensationalists themselves account for such a concept. They feel that they are absolved from guilt by their view of divine sovereignty. Because they believe in divine foreknowledge, they say that God knew from all eternity that, when the Jews were presented with the kingdom by Christ, they would refuse it. Consequently there was no possibility of Christ setting up His kingdom at that time and making the Cross unnecessary. But this knowledge of God does not make Him honest and sincere. He is doing it safely, as it were, because He knows that this dishonest and insincere offer will never be accepted.

The fact of the matter is He could not possibly have redeemed His promise. If the Jews had embraced Christ's offer, God would have had to say, "I am sorry, Christ cannot be elevated to the throne at this time. He must die on a cross." If the Jews expostulated and said, "But you offered us this," He would have had to say that it was not a sincere offer. I thought that you would never accept it. Of course, the dispensationalist in the background is saying, "No, that would never happen because God knew it would never happen."

We are granting that it never could have happened. Still, such a divine offer would have been insincere. God was making an offer that He could never have redeemed though He dishonestly said that He would if it were accepted. It is as if I safely offered a million dollars (which I do not have) to a debt-ridden relative who detested me because I knew, his hatred of me being what it was, he would never accept it.

Another objection to the kingdom offer is that it clearly implies, if we take dispensational assertions about the *bona fide* character of the offer with any seriousness, that it implicitly treats the sacrifice of Christ as virtually superfluous. Dispensationalists maintain that all are saved through the death of Christ but, if they are serious about the offer of the kingdom, that sacrifice was not, strictly speaking, necessary. Dispensationalists would not want to argue that the "kingdom of heaven" could have been fully established (that which the kingdom offer allegedly proffered) without there being some way of eternal salvation apart from the death of Christ. If the death of Christ was not necessary, our accepting it in the present time is the acceptance of a gratuitous event.

This, in turn involves a basic conflict with the Christian understanding of the nature of God. Manifestly, if the death of Christ were not necessary, then it is not necessary now because God is the same yesterday, today, and forever. He is not an arbitrary being who lays down arbitrary regulations in any given time that it pleases Him so to do. He is an immutable being who cannot clear the guilty by arbitrary fiat. Scripture tells us that "without shedding of blood there is no remission" (Hebrews 9:22, KJV). Dispensationalists will concede that, now that Christ has shed His blood, it becomes necessary to be saved by that method. It should be noted, however, that this necessity is not built upon the nature of God but simply reflects an arbitrary fiat of God. The most that the dispensational system can say about the death of Christ is that it was one possible way of making salvation possible. This picture of an arbitrary God and a gratuitous sacrifice can hardly be considered as glorifying God.

A final objection to the dispensational kingdom offer theory is that such a notion cannot be harmonized with the gospel accounts in the New Testament. Particularly problematic for the dispensational view is the following passage:

> Jesus therefore perceiving that they were intending to come and take Him by force, to make Him king, withdrew again to the mountain by Himself alone. (John 6:15, NASB)

The problem for dispensationalists is that here the Jews are recorded as asking Christ to accept the very temporal kingship which dispensationalists say the Jews were always refusing. As we see in this text, however, it was Christ who rejected the offer of a temporal kingdom.

While many dispensational works fail to deal with this passage, *The Ryrie Study Bible* has this note: "Jesus had to escape from the enthusiasm of the crowd, which would have forced Him to lead them in revolt against the Roman government. Jesus refused to become a political revolutionist."[4] This note, however, raises another question: How could Christ ever have offered to be King of the Jews without that bringing the wrath of Rome and war? It was this *false* charge (that Jesus claimed to be king) by which the Jewish leaders were literally able to nail Him to the cross (see John 19:19).

There has been some movement on this issue in recent years. For instance, a number of dispensationalists are presently rejecting the spurious distinction between the kingdom of heaven and the kingdom of God and thus obviating this terrible problem. Still, this notion of a kingdom offer remains dispensational "orthodoxy." Mainline dispensationalists, including popular figures such as Billy Graham and Hal

---

4. *Ryrie Study Bible*, p. 1610.

Lindsey,[5] are still teaching the kingdom offer and no dispensationalist, to my knowledge, whether accepting or rejecting the kingdom of God/ heaven distinction, has acknowledged the awful implications of the kingdom offer. Thus, we continue to indict the theological system and listen to its continued defense.

Dispensational Defenses of the Kingdom Offer

In my survey of dispensational defenses of the kingdom offer, I will first examine the arguments of Lewis Sperry Chafer and then briefly note defenses of the doctrine offered by Robert Saucy and Charles L. Feinberg.

Lewis Sperry Chafer

We can consider Chafer's argument as representative since he was one of the outstanding modern dispensationalists and also because he offers the two basic "reasons" that are usually offered by way of explanation. His first answer is "that Jehovah's lamb was in the redeeming purpose slain from the foundation of the world."[6] This is, of course, basically the appeal to divine foreknowledge and sovereignty which we noted above. Chafer simply *assumes* that a sincere offer is compatible with such foreknowledge rather than demonstrating how it is compatible.

Chafer's second argument is more substantial. Here he contends, essentially, that the sincere offer must be compatible with such foreknowledge because this situation is analogous to others which are readily accepted. In technical terms, this is referred to as a *tu quoque* argument. All Calvinists are supposed to have the same problem at other points that dispensationalists have at this point. Chafer asks, "Had Adam *not* sinned there could have been no need of a redeemer. Why did Jehovah tell Adam not to sin? And what would have become of the redemptive purpose had Adam obeyed God?"[7] Other dispensationalists raise a parallel question, "What would God have done had the reprobate accepted the gospel offer?" The question is essentially the same. Chafer is saying that God had decreed the Fall of Adam and yet He exhorted Adam not to fall. Is that consistent? What would have

---

5. See Jon Zens, *Dispensationalism*, p. 13, and Hal Lindsey, *The Late, Great Planet Earth*, pp. 20–21.
6. Chafer, "Dispensationalism."
7. Chafer, "Dispensationalism."

happened if Adam had done his duty and not fallen? Was God being honest in offering Adam a way of life and a way of death when the way of death was the foreordained way? The assumption is that Calvinists cannot answer that, and the dispensationalists are at no greater disadvantage if they cannot answer the objection to the kingdom offer.

Closer analysis of this alleged parallel shows that the analogy breaks down rather quickly. A number of important differences are evident. First of all, a major problem with the *bona fide* kingdom offer is that it amounts to an ethical indictment of God while the imagined problem that Chafer and other dispensationalists raise concerning Adam poses no ethical problem. In the kingdom offer, God is represented as being dishonest in offering something He could not have honored if accepted. In the case of Adam, if he had persevered, God could have given him the life He had promised. God told Adam no lie.

Second, if it be granted that the covenant with Adam did not involve implicit dishonesty in God, can it still be argued that it did involve inconsistency with His eternal sovereignty, omniscience, and foreknowledge? We think not. Will anyone say, least of all a Calvinist as Chafer claimed to be, that God could not have foreknown and even predestined that Adam would violate the command of God and at the same time offer Adam a reward if he did not do so? We are now asking the question only concerning God's eternal predestination and foreknowledge—nothing else. On the surface of it, there is nothing here that involves denial of those two doctrines. Unless, that is, someone can show that God's having decreed what free moral agents will choose makes it impossible for free moral agents to choose. The Reformed have refuted that charge time and time again, and I hardly need to go into any detail here, especially for the benefit of theologians claiming to be Reformed.

The thing that really bothers many people, not only dispensationalists, about this point is not that it implies non-veracity or non-sovereignty in the deity but that they have a hard time conceiving of responsible human choices which are known or decreed from all eternity. But mystery is no argument against the truth of anything, least of all things pertaining to the eternal decrees of God.

As we noted above, some dispensationalists, in a variation on the above argument, contend that the *bona fide* kingdom offer is analogous to the proclamation of the gospel. Dispensationalists counterattack at this point with some persuasiveness because this is a difficult point, dealing with the question of hypotheticals in the mind of God. They insist that what they are saying is no different from the usual Calvinistic interpretation of the "offer of the gospel." God knows who will and who will not accept it. The dispensationalist asks the authentic Calvinist whether, supposing a non-elect person had actually chosen to believe, God would have accepted that person's faith. God knows who and who will not accept it, yet He offers the gospel to everybody. If everybody actually did accept it, then God could not actually save everybody because He had already declared that everyone would not be saved. If He saved everybody, He would prove Himself to be ignorant of what was going to happen and frustrated in all of His counsels and purposes. So what difference, the dispensationalist asks, is there between the dispensational idea of a kingdom offer and the Calvinist saying that the gospel is *offered* to all while God designs the Atonement only for the elect and hence could save only the elect.

This might be a compelling argument except that the dispensational representation of Reformed theology is a caricature at this point. We do *not* teach that God invites reprobates to believe and be saved knowing full well that He will not give them a heart of faith. In fact, God does not call reprobates! He calls persons who recognize and admit themselves to be sinners. Those who confess themselves to be sinners, and they only, are called. Any one of them who comes will be saved. God *never* invited anyone who, if he responded, would be refused. God would never be embarrassed, even hypothetically, by someone coming and being rejected because he was not predestinated and foreknown. Every convicted sinner who has come, would come, will come, has been, would be, or will be accepted.

We have admitted (see chapter 7) that even Reformed theologians sometimes state this "universal call" incorrectly as if Christ were inviting the "righteous" to come. He never invited the self-righteous to Him. Christ specifically said that He did not "call the righteous" (Matthew 9:13). Only the "poor in spirit" inherit His kingdom because only they were ever made welcome or ever will be made welcome. When any of *them* comes, He welcomes them in perfect accord with His eternal election of them.

Robert Saucy

Another variation on this dispensational theme is offered by Robert Saucy. According to Saucy, those who say that Christ offered a spiritual kingdom and not an earthly kingdom do not escape the problem of the kingdom offer. Note that he is not defending his position here but simply arguing that its critics are just as guilty as its defenders. Saucy writes:

Assuming that Christ was offering a spiritual kingdom, as most objectors to dispensationalism do, is there a satisfactory answer to the place of the cross if this kingdom would have been accepted by Israel prior to the cross? If the nation had accepted His message no matter which kingdom was offered, what of the prophecies that He was to be rejected by His own?[8]

In other words, according to Saucy, if all the Jews had been converted and believed in Christ they would never have crucified Him either! The plan of salvation would have thus been thwarted. The main answer to Saucy is that Christ never offered His true spiritual kingdom to *all* Jews but only to Jews who acknowledged that they were sinners. All those Jews did accept the kingdom offer. In other words, all those Jews to whom Christ offered His kingdom did accept it and those who did not were never offered it. The latter could and did account for the Cross.

Saucy asks, if the offer was a spiritual kingdom and the Jews accepted that, how could it have been true that Christ "was to be rejected by His own?" What he means is that *if* Christ made a universal offer of the spiritual kingdom, that too could not have been fulfilled without destroying the possibility of the Cross. Saucy's logic is quite correct but his premise is quite wrong. Christ did not make a universal offer of the spiritual kingdom. He voiced the invitation universally (to all who heard Him), but the invitation when heard was perceived to be to sinners only and not to those who considered themselves righteous (see Luke 5:32; Matthew 9:13). Furthermore, even if everyone who heard that call did accept it, that would not have made the cross unnecessary in Reformed thinking. All who had accepted before the death of Christ did so on the basis of that Atonement before it had happened. Dispensationalists err at two points: First, that Christ ever offered the kind of Kingdom they imagine; second, that it would have obviated the cross if it had been!

Charles L. Feinberg

C. L. Feinberg offers a traditional dispensational defense of the traditional dispensational kingdom offer. In addition to a variety of *tu quoque* arguments, the substance of which I have examined above, he offers a number of other reasons which, in the interests of thoroughness, I will briefly examine.

First, Feinberg argues that Daniel 9:25 "places in juxtaposition the cross and the matter of the Kingdom, Messiah is to be cut off (the cross

---

8. Robert Lloyd Saucy, "The Relationship of Dispensationalism to the Eternal Purpose of God" (Th.D. dissertation, Dallas Theological Seminary, 1961).

clearly) and have nothing (the Kingdom)."[9] We reply that even if this is a correct interpretation of Daniel 9:25, the "juxtaposition" is no problem. The Jews could very well have rejected Christ as their rightful king and thereby brought about His crucifixion. That is not saying that Christ offered them a kingdom *in lieu* of the Cross.

Against Masselink, Feinberg argues that if there was not a kingdom offer, the "triumphal entry" is "inexplicable."[10] We would simply note that a king riding on a donkey with children as his heralds and palm branches for swords is not exactly the picture of the world-conquering ruler the dispensationalists have in mind.

Feinberg goes on to contend that, if Christ was not offering an earthly kingdom, He would have told his disciples from the beginning.[11] Against this somewhat odd argument I would simply note that Christ never taught error, though He taught truth gradually as the disciples were able to "bear" it (see John 16:12).

Finally, Acts 2:23 is cited to show it was determined of God that Christ was to be crucified, yet sinful of men to crucify Him.[12] But what is the problem? God determines evil *permissively* by leaving men to their wicked devices in His providential setting. Thus they carry out sinfully and culpably what He has decreed virtuously and admirably for the benefit of His people. "But where sin abounded, grace did much more abound" (Romans 5:20, KJV) by His gracious, sovereign, and holy decree. How this is supposed to justify a *bona fide* offer which God could under no circumstances have honored is, to us, a mystery. This supposed analogy is, in fact, a matter of "apples and oranges."

Conclusion

It would appear, therefore, that devastating criticisms of the dispensational *bona fide* kingdom offer to the Jews remain unanswered. Such an offer is a direct affront to the righteousness of God, involving as it does the implication that God can and did lie. Since God cannot lie, such a kingdom offer makes the cross of Christ *unnecessary*!

---

9. C. L. Feinberg, editor. *Jesus The King Is Coming* (Chicago: Moody, 1975), p. 88. See also C. L. Feinberg, *Premillennialism or Amillennialism* (Wheaton, Ill.: Van Kampen, 1954), p. 200.

10. Feinberg, *Premillennialism or Amillennialism*, p. 199.

11. Ibid., p. 200.

12. Ibid.

DUBIOUS EVANGELICALISM: DISPENSATIONALISM'S VIEW OF ISRAEL AND THE CHURCH DENIES THE GOSPEL

Having shown that Dispensationalism's view of "dispensations," its salvation by anticipation doctrine, and its kingdom offer are essentially incompatible with evangelicalism, I will now endeavor to show that Dispensationalism's view of Israel and the church denies the gospel in both dispensations. Dispensationalism's opposition to the gospel is no more blatant here than elsewhere. Nevertheless, it is more important because this doctrine is so central in all dispensational thinking and teaching. Before criticizing the doctrine, I will give considerable space to presenting it as the dispensationalists do, so that the reader may understand it and see its centrality in their system.

The Dispensational Doctrine of Israel And the Church

According to Dispensationalism, Israel and the church are different in almost every way. Israel is an ethnic group, the Jews, the descendants of Abraham and Sarah. The church is composed of all nationalities. The Abrahamic covenant which made his descendants God's chosen people was absolutely unconditional while the covenant of grace which brings the church into being is conditional in that it requires faith. Consequently, regeneration or the new birth is required, whereas one becomes an Israelite by being born, not by being reborn. Israelites never received a baptism by, or indwelling of, the Spirit which is essential for a member of the church. Israel is national and visible; the church is individual and invisible. Israel is an earthly people, with earthly promises and an earthly destiny eternally. The church is a spiritual people with eternal life in heaven for its destiny. Presently, Israel as God's people is in eclipse, but soon (probably) to be fully restored to the Promised Land and dominion over the earth. The church is now alive, growing, and soon to be raptured to heaven.

Great stress is placed on Israel as an ethnic group descended from Abraham and Sarah. Though it was Jacob who was given the name *Israel*, dispensationalists teach that Israel as God's chosen people began with Abraham. *The Ryrie Study Bible* follows the consensus commentary on Genesis 12:2. "When God made this promise, Abraham had no son. The reference is to the Jewish nation, i.e., the descendants of Abraham through Isaac and Jacob."[1]

The church, on the other hand, is composed of all nationalities. The church began at Pentecost following Christ's Great Commission to make disciples of all nations (see Matthew 28:19–20), and His saying to the apostles immediately before Pentecost that they were to be His witnesses "to the remotest part of the earth" (Acts 1:8, NASB). Thus far, the dispensational doctrine is rather obvious.

The covenant with Abraham which made his descendants God's chosen people was, according to dispensationalists, absolutely unconditional. "The ultimate fulfillment is made to rest upon the divine promise and the power of God rather than upon human faithfulness,"[2] Ironside put this matter very plainly. "His covenant with Abraham was pure grace. He was the only contracting party. Whatever Israel's failures, He could not break His promise."[3] In this context, Ironside expressed irritation with a man who had pointed out that Israel (see Acts 2:38) was called upon to repent.[4] That, according to Ironside, had nothing to do with the covenant God made with Abraham. When Israel later broke the law, they did not lose the Abrahamic Covenant

---

1. *Ryrie Study Bible*, p. 24.
2. *New Scofield Reference Bible*, p. 20.
3. Ironside, *Eternal Security*, p. 116.
4. Ibid., p. 117.

which was "unconditional."[5] Allan MacRae graphically presents this unconditionality:

> Even though Israel should fall into sin, and should seem no longer to be a recipient of God's blessing, it would still be true that God has promised that those who bring blessing to His earthly people will themselves be blessed, while those who curse His earthly people will themselves suffer the results of God's displeasure. All history is full of examples of this fact. Anti-Semitism is never justified, and never can receive God's approbation. The fate of the nations that have injured Israel is a terrible warning that God never goes back on His promises. From Haman to Hitler, history shows how dangerous it is to hate His chosen people.[6]

Dispensationalists seek to harmonize their view of the unconditional nature of the Abrahamic covenant with the Old Testament passages which enjoin covenantal sanctions for disobedience. According to L. S. Chafer and John Walvoord, the Abrahamic Covenant to provide redemption for Israel was unconditional but personal blessings were dependent on obedience.[7] Ryrie is also sensitive to the problem of an unconditional or one-sided covenant and, like Chafer and Walvoord, he attempts to solve it by pointing to the conditional features for personal blessings which are also a part of this covenant. Erich Sauer says, "the covenant is a pure gift of divine grace, that man neither works nor co-works therein, that God does all, and that man is simply the recipient."[8] Thus man's receiving, believing faith is the non-meritorious condition.

Nevertheless, dispensationalists seem to have a problem at this point. It would seem that title to the land of Palestine is a "personal blessing" which was, in the Old Testament, clearly conditioned upon faith and obedience. Dispensationalists appear to believe that the Jews have an eternal title to that piece of real estate regardless of faith and obedience, and so they contend that the Jews are to come back (as some of them have) to the land in unbelief.

---

5. Ibid., pp. 118–119.

6. Allan A. MacRae, "Hath God Cast Away His People?" in *Prophetic Truth Unfolding Today*, ed. Charles L. Feinberg (Westwood, N.J.: Revell, 1968), p. 95.

7. Chafer and Walvoord, *Major Bible Themes*, p. 143.

8. Erich Sauer, *The Dawn of World Redemption; A Survey of Historical Revelation in the Old Testament* (Grand Rapids: Eerdmans, 1952), p. 99.

The covenant of grace which brings the church into being is conditional in that it requires faith. Even Jews, as well as Gentiles, must believe if they are to be saved. A Jew may go to Palestine without faith but not to heaven. As Dwight Pentecost puts it, "A man is justified not by works, but by faith. That is why we continually invite men to receive Jesus Christ by faith as a personal Saviour, for apart from faith it is impossible to please God."[9]

Dispensationalists think it crucial to note that membership in Israel is by natural generation only.[10] The church, however, is by supernatural regeneration. "Israelites," says Chafer, "become such by a natural birth while Christians become such by a spiritual birth."[11] Later, he comments that Nicodemus, "apparently a most perfect specimen of Judaism was told by Christ that *he* must be born again, and the Apostle Paul prayed that the Israelites who had a 'zeal for God' might be saved."[12] Israel is national and visible. According to Chafer, Israel is an eternal nation, heir to an eternal land, with an eternal kingdom, on which David rules from an eternal throne.[13]

Dispensationalists generally contrast the earthly, national character of Israel with the spiritual character of the church. The church is individual and spiritual. Every Jew belongs to Israel, but not all Gentiles and Jews by any means belong to the church. The offer of the gospel is to all but only those individuals who believe are saved and become members of the church. Although American dispensationalists are usually members of an organized church, it is the invisible church which dispensationalists have in mind by the term *church*. Darby, as we have seen, though an ordained Anglican clergyman, gave up orders as he became convinced the organized, visible church was in ruins. He conceived of the church as local and consisting informally of true believers only.[14] He believed that purity was to be maintained by constant separation from evil. Chafer and Walvoord see no need to belong to any denomination.[15] This tendency to exalt the invisible church at the expense of the visible has been noted by Sandeen and others as an historical feature of Dispensationalism.[16]

---

9. Pentecost, *Things Which Become Sound Doctrine*, pp. 109–110. See also Charles Caldwell Ryrie, *The Best Is Yet to Come* (Chicago: Moody, 1981), p. 42f.

10. See Ryrie, *Dispensationalism Today*, pp. 137–140.

11. Lewis Sperry Chafer, *Systematic Theology*, 4:30.

12. Ibid., p. 34.

13. Ibid., pp. 315–323.

14. See Bass, *Backgrounds*, chapter 4.

15. Chafer and Walvoord, *Major Bible Themes*, p. 240.

16. Sandeen, *Roots of Fundamentalism*, p. 67.

In line with this, dispensationalists tend to see the organized denominations as apostate, and Walvoord is sure they will be when the Rapture takes the true believers away. "What today is a world church movement with some redeeming features will become totally apostate once the rapture of the church takes place."[17]

Consistent with their view of the Abrahamic covenant as an eternal pact pertaining only to ethnic Jews, dispensationalists view Israel and the church as having distinct eternal destinies. Israel is an earthly people with an earthly promise and an earthly destiny eternally. As we saw, Israel is an eternal nation, heir to an eternal land, with an eternal kingdom, on which David rules from an eternal throne. There will be an endless succession of human generations upon the earth but never the twain, Israel and church, shall meet. As Darby wrote, "The Jewish nation is never to enter the Church."[18] Said Scofield, "Comparing, then, what is said in Scripture concerning Israel and the Church, we find that in origin, calling, promises, worship, principles of conduct and *future destiny* all is contrast."[19]

The church is a heavenly people with an eternal life in heaven for its destiny. Saints, said Louis Talbot (the founder of Biola, now Talbot Theological Seminary in Los Angeles), when they die, go immediately to be with the Lord. "A true child of God goes immediately to heaven at the time of physical dissolution of body and soul."[20] J. A. Seiss maintained that, while Israel was the heir of the earth, the church inherits heaven.[21] Ryrie considers this the most important dispensational distinction, and he approves of Daniel Fuller's statement that the "basic promise of Dispensationalism is two purposes of God expressed in the formation of two peoples who maintain their distinction throughout eternity."[22]

It is interesting to note that dispensational discomfort with this notion of two separate eternal destinies for Israel and the church may be

---

17. John F. Walvoord, "Where is Modern Church Going?" in *Prophecy in the Seventies*, ed. C. L. Feinberg (Chicago: Moody, 1971), p. 119.

18. John Nelson Darby, *The Hopes of the Church of God* (London: G. Morrish, n.d.), p. 106, cited in Zens, *Dispensationalism*, p. 17.

19. Scofield, *Scofield Bible Correspondence Course*, pp. 23–25, cited in Zens, *Dispensationalism*, p. 17 (emphasis mine).

20. Louis T. Talbot, *Bible Questions Explained* (Grand Rapids: Eerdmans, 1938), p. 178.

21. Joseph Augustus Seiss, *The Apocalypse. A Series of Special Lectures on the Revelation of Jesus Christ*, 3 vols. (Philadelphia: Sherman, 1881), 3:442f.

22. Ryrie, *Dispensationalism Today*, pp. 44–45.

increasing. One possible example of this is found in Charles Ryrie's *The Best Is Yet to Come* which discusses a glorious millennium with Christ ruling perfectly the whole world but without Ryrie's especially mentioning the Jews at all.[23] This book ends with an evangelistic appeal to all to believe on Christ and live forever. Nothing about a new earth for Jews separate from heaven above. Is Dispensationalism beginning to disavow (at least at the eternal end) this perpetual separation of Israel and the church?

Particularly emblematic of this eternal distinction between Israel and the church is the doctrine of the premillennial, pretribulational rapture of the church. It is difficult to exaggerate the dispensational emphasis on the Rapture since it seems to outweigh all other eschatological matters. Dispensationalists take comfort in the teaching that the church will not have to endure the Tribulation, and rapture speculation has spawned a number of immensely popular books and movies. This popular preoccupation with eschatology is fueled in part by the doctrine of *imminency*—the idea that nothing else need transpire prior to the rapture of the church.[24]

As we noted in previous chapters, another characteristic of this dispensational separation is the contention that the church is, from the perspective of Old Testament prophecy, an unknown entity, a "parenthesis" during which the "prophetic clock" stops ticking. This is indeed a crucial issue for the viability of Dispensationalism in that, as we shall see, the criticism of Dispensationalism on this matter hinges on the fact that numerous Old Testament passages referring to Israel are applied to the church in the New Testament.

The Traditional Doctrine of the Unity
Of Israel and the Church

We have already noted that, historically speaking, this dispensational denial of the unity of Israel and the church represents a surprising novelty. From the earliest period of Christian theology onward, the essential continuity of Israel and the church has been maintained. This historic doctrine of the church is based on both the clear implication of Old Testament texts and the clear teaching of the New Testament.

---

23. For a focus on Israel's return to the land, see Walter Kaiser's "The Promised Land: A Biblical-Historical View," *Bibliotheca Sacra* 138 (1981):302ff.

24. Ryrie, *Dispensationalism Today*, pp. 159-160.

It will readily be seen that, from an Old Testament perspective, the church was not an unforseen entity or prophetic "parenthesis" as dispensationalists claim. A cursory comparison of a few prophetic passages with their New Testament fulfillment will illustrate this: Hosea 1:10 (Romans 9:22–26), Hosea 2:23 (1 Peter 2:9–10), Amos 9:11 (Acts 15:16).

Likewise, there are many Old Testament passages referring to Israel which, in the New Testament, are applied directly to the church. A few examples will suffice to demonstrate the point: Exodus 19:5–6 (1 Peter 2:9); Jeremiah 24:7 (2 Corinthians 6:16); Jeremiah 31:31–34 (Luke 22:20); Leviticus 19:2 (1 Peter 1:15).

Finally, there is the clear teaching of the New Testament that true membership in Israel is ultimately a matter of spiritual rather than physical relationship. Paul writes that "those who believe are children of Abraham" (Galatians 3:7, NIV). Later in the same epistle he writes, "If you belong to Christ, then you are Abraham's seed, and heirs according to the promise" (Galatians 3:29, NIV). Similarly, Paul teaches that Israel and the church constitute an organic unity. They are the same olive tree with the Gentiles of the church being grafted into the tree that was Israel (Romans 11:17–21).

Dispensational Exegesis in Support Of the Israel-Church Distinction

Nevertheless, this scriptural unity of Israel and the church is directly challenged by Dispensationalism, wrongly dividing asunder what God's Word has joined together. I will now examine this attack on the unity of Israel and the church as dispensationalists interpret particular New Testament passages.

The Sermon on the Mount (Matthew 5–7)

Without doubt the single most important question for dispensationalists about the Sermon on the Mount is the Lord's Prayer, and the single most important question about the Lord's Prayer is the petition, "forgive us our debts, as we forgive our debtors" (Matthew 6:12, KJV). Scofield did not hesitate to call that "legal ground" which is not applicable to the church.[25] L. S. Chafer and virtually all other dispensationalists see it the same way.[26] This dispensational stance has greatly disturbed many other evangelicals. Martin Lloyd-Jones, for example, referred to this interpretation with great distress:

> Now take this idea that there was ever a time when men were for-given on strictly legal grounds, or that there is to be some time in the future when men will be on strictly legal grounds before God, and will be forgiven even as they forgive. Do we realize what that means? It means, of course, that such people will never be forgiven."[27]

Dispensationalists are sensitive to this charge and usually try to an-ticipate and blunt this criticism. Frank Gaebelein, for example, while regarding the Sermon on the Mount primarily as kingdom legislation for the Millennium, maintains that it has application to the present be-liever. Charles Ryrie, following the same basic kingdom interpretation, speaks of "secondary application" and he goes on to add:

> Dispensationalists believe that anger, lust, divorce, and murder are sin, and they believe it on the basis of the Sermon on the Mount. Dis-pensationalists believe that the Golden Rule and the Lord's Prayer are excellent guides.[28]

Dispensationalists criticize those who accuse them of assigning no relevance to the Sermon on the Mount. They maintain that the Ser-mon has "dispensational" relevance—but not the kind of relevance it once had and will have again, according to Dispensationalism.[29] This approach reduces these commands of Christ to the status of "sugges-tions" which the Christian is perfectly free to ignore. Of course, dis-pensationalists admit that "anger, lust, divorce, and murder are sin," but the fact that they view those commands as the "legal ground" of acceptance in law and kingdom dispensations, but not in the present

---

25. *Scofield Reference Bible*, p. 1002.

26. Chafer, *Systematic Theology*, 4:221.

27. D. Martin Lloyd-Jones, *Studies In The Sermon On The Mount*, 2 vols. (Grand Rapids: Eerdmans, 1971), 2:75.

28. Ryrie, *Dispensationalism Today*, p. 108. See also his *Biblical Theology of the New Testament* (Chicago: Moody Press, 1959), pp. 81–82.

29. See Ryrie, *Dispensationalism Today*, pp. 105–106.

one is further evidence that the dispensational system of theology pre-supposes more than one way of salvation.

Before we leave this text, we note a rather unusual (for a dispensationalist) interpretation by Stanley D. Toussaint.[30] He does not see the Sermon on the Mount as for the kingdom age or for the correction of sin in this age. What it does is exhort righteous living in view of the coming kingdom. This idea is fairly common among non-dispensationalists, especially in Britain and Europe, but we have not noticed it before in dispensational circles. In any case, Toussaint's interpretation does not touch the fundamental question—whether it is *necessary* to obey Christ's commands to be a Christian.

So we must say that dispensationalists, past and present, do indeed take the Sermon on the Mount away from Christians as Lloyd-Jones complained. In so doing, they clearly and wrongly separate Old Testament Israel and the New Testament church at the very point of their forgiveness by God by basing it on two entirely different grounds—legal and antinomian—neither of which is compatible with the Old Testament or the New.

Matthew 16:18-20

The dispensational interpretation of this passage provides a good example of the lengths to which dispensational exegetes will go to force a passage to teach dispensational "truth." This passage is thought, by dispensationalists, to refer to a change in kingdom proclamation from a kingdom offer to the Jews to church-age proclamation of salvation by grace. It speaks of the *futurity* of the church. Notice the comment of the *New Scofield Reference Bible* on Matthew 16:20:

> The disciples had been proclaiming Jesus as the Christ, i.e. the covenanted King of a kingdom promised to the Jews and at hand. The Church, on the contrary, must be built upon testimony to Him as crucified, risen from the dead, ascended, and made "head over all things to the church" (Eph. 1:20-23). The former testimony was ended; the new testimony was not yet ready because the blood of the new covenant had not yet been shed, but our Lord began to

---

30. Stanley D. Toussaint, "A Biblical Defense of Dispensationalism," in *Walvoord, A Tribute*, ed. Donald K. Campbell (Chicago: Moody, 1982), pp. 81-91.

speak of His death and resurrection (v. 21). It is a turning point of immense significance.[31]

Here again, the so-called *messianic secret* becomes a source of confusion and it is a sheer flight of fancy for dispensationalists to read as much into this passage as they do. There is, first of all, no evidence that the disciples had heretofore been proclaiming Jesus "as the Christ"; that is, as the *political* Messiah who was about to set up an earthly kingdom. On the contrary, the ministry of the disciples was at this time apparently limited to the proclamation of the imminence of the kingdom and to the healing of the sick and demon-possessed (see Matthew 10:7–8). Indeed, there is good evidence that Jesus was very concerned that proclamation of Himself as Messiah was open to misunderstanding by the Jews. Thus, He takes pains to silence the witness of demons and even those whom He healed (see Mark 1:25, 44; 3:12). That such a concern was warranted is evident from the episode where the people sought to make Jesus an earthly king by force (see John 6:1–15).

Every dispensationalist I can ever remember reading has taken Christ's words "I will build my church" (Matthew 16:18) as implying that the church was strictly future and not existing at all when Christ spoke those words. This is notwithstanding the testimony of one of the greatest of Greek scholars, A. T. Robertson:

> The future [tense] likewise presents accomplished action which in any case may be either momentary, simultaneous, prolonged, descriptive, repeated, customary, interrupted, attempted, or begun, according to the nature of the case or the meaning of the verb.[32]

In other words, even the tense of the verb does not require *absolute futurity*. What is more important, the meaning of the verb does not require absolute newness. It can well mean that Christ is building up His church into its new and final form.

Matthew 21:43

"The kingdom of God shall be taken from you and given to a nation bringing forth the fruits thereof" (KJV). On the surface of it this is the

---

31. *New Scofield Reference Bible*, p. 1021.
32. A. T. Robertson, *Short Grammar of the Greek New Testament* (New York: Doran, 1908), p. 141.

end of the nation of Israel as the chosen people of God. They have been tried and found wanting. God's patience has been exhausted. If there were any doubts about that being the obvious meaning of the words, the parable on which they are based would utterly eliminate any lingering procrastination. O. T. Allis spoke for an almost universal tradition when he wrote concerning this text:

> Jesus declared to the Jews that the kingdom should "be taken from" them (Matt. xxi. 41f.). The children of the kingdom (the natural and lawful heirs) are to be "cast out" (viii. 11f.). None of those "bidden" are to taste of the marriage supper (Lk. xiv. 24). The vineyard is to be given to "other husbandmen"; to "a nation bringing forth the fruits thereof"; men are to come from the "highways," from "the east and west and north and south," to partake with Abraham, Isaac, and Jacob of the marriage supper.[33]

It is virtually impossible to imagine any other interpretation of this passage. The Greek word for *nation* in verse 43 (*ethnos*) is the word characteristically (although not exclusively) reserved for Gentile peoples. Furthermore, the parable of the tenants (verses 33–41), which verse 43 explains, clearly refers to the disobedience of the Jewish *nation* throughout its history.

One would suppose that dispensationalists, with their view of Israel, would be at least temporarily embarrassed and hasten to explain that Christ was referring to the *temporary* rejection of Israel instead of the "end of the world" or final rejection. Far from it. Dispensationalists transform this clear statement into a prediction of Israel's *receiving* —not losing—the kingdom! No less a theologian than Charles Ryrie writes that the word *nation* in the text refers to Israel. Thus Christ would be saying "The kingdom of God shall be taken from you (leaders of Israel), and given to a nation (Israel) bringing forth the fruits thereof."[34]

Even the *New Scofield Reference Bible*, which hopelessly distorts the passage, is not quite so bold. Relying on the common but artificial distinction between "kingdom of God" and "kingdom of heaven," it reads the parable as saying that the impious Jewish leaders are not fit to be in the spiritual domain of God's kingdom which is given to "any people who will bring forth the fruits of salvation."[35] Thus it avoids

---

33. Allis, *Prophecy and the Church*, p. 78.
34. Ryrie, *Basis of Premillennial Faith*, p. 72.
35. *New Scofield Reference Bible*, p. 1029.

having the Jews rejected without going so far as making this a prediction of their future glory.[36]

Other dispensationalists are not quite so bold. Chafer and Walvoord avoid even a single reference to Matthew 21:43 in a book (*Major Bible Themes*) which has a seven and a half page index of Biblical references (in very small print). Arno Gaebelein (considered by Scofield to be interpreter of prophecy *par excellence*), though he considered many other New Testament texts, was curiously silent on Matthew 21:43 in his *Harmony of the Prophetic Word.*

Acts 2:1; 16–40; Joel 2:28–32

The dispensational interpretation of this passage in the book of Acts (which certainly teaches that the New Testament church was foreseen by the prophet Joel) is another example of the penchant for reading dispensational theology into a portion of Scripture which teaches the very opposite.

Dispensationalists teach that the kingdom which Christ came to offer to the Jews was rejected by them, and so He turned to others and offered them the church. Various individuals responded and the church was beginning to take shape. However, it was not formally instituted until Pentecost. Darby, speaking of Acts 2–4, says, "These three chapters present the first forming of the assembly, and its blessed character through the Holy Spirit dwelling in it. They present to us its first beauty as formed of God, and His habitation."[37] Earlier he had written, "the mission of the Holy Ghost led them [the early church] at the same time, out of the Jewish field of purely temporal promises."[38]

At the same time that the dispensationalists believe that the church came into formal being at Pentecost, they do not believe that its nature was understood until its revelation to the Apostle Paul (the divinely chosen expositor of the "mystery" of the church which had never before been revealed). Darby was very emphatic on the point that the church had not been foreseen in prophecy before Paul.

---

36. We are pleased to note that veteran dispensationalist Clarence Mason quietly critiques Scofield on this point while resoundingly critiquing him on his false distinction between "kingdom of heaven" and "kingdom of God." See his "Two Kingdoms in Matthew?" in *Prophetic Problems With Alternate Solutions* (Chicago: Moody, 1973), pp. 87–109.

37. Darby, *Synopsis*, 4:14.

38. Ibid., p. 3.

The grace that sets us in heaven is not prophesied of at all; prophecy belongs to what is earthly, and so far as it relates to the Lord Jesus, contains the revelation of what He was to be upon the earth at His first coming, and then continues with what He will be upon the earth when He comes again, without alluding to that which should take place in the interval between those two events.[39]

The prophecies of the book of Daniel, and even of the book of Revelation, have nothing to do with the church, except for one feature which we will note later.[40] Only the epistles, especially those of Paul, deal with the church.

The Jews were set aside and the clear and positive doctrine of no difference between Jew and Gentile (by nature alike the children of wrath), and of their common and equal privileges as members of only one body, has been fully declared and made the basis of all relationship between God and every soul possessed of faith. This is the doctrine of the apostle in the Epistles to the Romans and Ephesians.[41]

Acts 2 presents the dispensationalist with an interesting challenge, however. The day of Pentecost is thought by all dispensationalists (except the Bullingerites) to mark the founding of the church and the dispensation of grace. In Peter's sermon on the day of Pentecost, however, he maintains that the giving of the Holy Spirit on this day was foretold by the Old Testament prophet Joel (Acts 2:16).

How do dispensationalists deal with this difficulty? The answer is — with difficulty. The *Scofield Reference Bible* attempts to sidestep the problem by calmly stating that a "distinction must be observed between the 'last days' when the prediction relates to Israel, and the 'last days' when the prediction relates to the church."[42] The text that follows in this note goes on to explicate this supposed distinction in great

---

39. Darby, *Inspiration of the Bible*, p. 5. Even Allis has some sympathy for this viewpoint, noting that there were "prophecies which seemed to declare with equal clearness that the pre-eminence of the Jews was to continue without end. Consequently, the statements of the prophets might be regarded as ambiguous, and the carnally minded Jews would naturally interpret them all in terms of their selfish, nationalistic desires and expectations . . . it was not there [in the Old Testament] made known, 'as it hath now been revealed' to the apostles and prophets of the Lord." Allis, *Prophecy and the Church*, p. 95.

40. See Darby, *Collected Writings*, 11:70; 4:70.

41. Darby, *Synopsis*, 4:100.

42. *Scofield Reference Bible*, p. 1151.

detail without, of course, demonstrating that such a distinction is operative here in this passage.

Allis, commenting on the Scofield note, critiques it neatly. The quotation from Joel, he says, is:

> clearly applicable to that mystery Church in which there is neither Jew nor Greek, the nature of which was most fully revealed to and declared by the apostle Paul. Darby and Scofield both admit that the Church was "formed" at Pentecost. So Scofield says of Joel's prophecy as cited by Peter: "A distinction must be drawn between 'the last days' when the prediction relates to Israel, and the 'last days' when the prediction relates to the church." This is an admission that Joel's words do concern the Church, and amounts to a confession that the Church is the subject of prophecy. How then are we to understand the statement that "The church, corporately, is not in O. T. prophecy"? What does "corporately" mean?[43]

We add to this that Joel's prophecy being made to Israel and fulfilled in the church shows the identity of the two bodies. His prophecy is not directly related to the Gentiles. The Pentecost sermon itself is addressed by a Jew to Jews. But even dispensationalists consider this the establishment of the church. Consequently, when Joel prophesied and Peter applied, Israel was being identified with the church. Speaking to Israel and to the church was one and the same thing. The promise to Israel was fulfilled in the "formation of the church," to use Scofield's expression. The "latter days" of Joel were the "last days" of Peter and the Christian church. Geerhardus Vos has well shown how this expression "in the last days" refers to the whole era between the first and second advents.[44]

The revised note on this passage in the *New Scofield Reference Bible* is significant. While continuing, with Scofield, to distinguish between the "last days" of the church and the "last days" of Israel, it makes the fatal (to the dispensational system) concession that Joel 2 is applicable to the church. According to this note, the prophecy in Joel apparently refers to both Israel and the Church.

> While Acts 2:17 is part of this context and therefore relates to the Church, it should be remembered that it has reference to Israel as well and, therefore, points to a future day (see Joel 2:28, note).[45]

---

43. Allis, *Prophecy and the Church*, pp. 135–136.

44. Geerhardus Vos, "Eschatology of the New Testament," *International Standard Bible Encyclopedia*.

45. *New Scofield Reference Bible*, p. 1164.

Thus, it would seem that more recent dispensational exegesis of this passage is moving in a covenantal direction. It is interesting that in a recent dispensational work, *Joel and the Day of the Lord*, Walter K. Price does not differ from Allis.[46] He too sees Joel's prophecy as initially fulfilled at Pentecost, continuously fulfilled in the church age, and ultimately, at the Second Coming.

Acts 15:13-21; Amos 9:11-12

Here again we see a New Testament application to the church of an Old Testament prophecy to Israel. Because of this, the interpretation of this passage has been a bone of contention between dispensationalists and their critics. The irony is that this passage is cited in support of the dispensational system when it in fact teaches the opposite. If any reader perusing my words is not already aware of the controversy about the meaning of these words of Amos quoted by James, I suggest that, before he reads another line of this book, he look again at Acts 15:13-21 with the obvious question—what is James trying to prove by that quotation from Amos? Try to forget that the verses are controversial and just simply read with that question in mind before proceeding. You may have to read further back into Acts more fully to understand the issue in chapter 15.

I will summarize and let the reader determine what is obvious. The issue before the Jerusalem council was whether to receive professing Gentiles into the church without Jewish rites, especially circumcision. Peter's argument for accepting believing Gentiles without circumcision was that God revealed this duty to him by a vision and confirmed it by the actual pouring out of the Spirit on uncircumcised believing Gentiles. This latter argument was confirmed by the testimony of Paul and Silas about their experiences among Gentiles. James cites Joel's prophecy as having been fulfilled in what these men had described. Therefore, Gentiles were to be admitted as they were, with only a few minor stipulations not at issue. Thus, the church and Israel are essentially identified as the building again of the "booth of David." The building of the "booth of David" and the erecting of the Christian church are one and the same.

What is abundantly clear is that James cites the Amos prophecy as referring to what was then actually taking place. Incredibly, the *New Scofield Reference Bible* sees in James' citation of Amos a reference to the Millennium.

---

46. Walter K. Price, *Joel and the Day of the Lord* (Chicago: Moody, 1976).

With the exception of the first five words, vv. 16–18 are quoted from
Amos 9:11–12. James quoted from the LXX, which here preserved
the original text (see Amos 9:12, note). Amos 9:11 begins with the
words "in that day." James introduced his quotation is such a way as
to show what day Amos was talking about, namely, the time after the
present world-wide witness (Acts 1:8), when Christ will return. James
showed that there will be Gentile believers at that time as well as
Jewish believers; hence he concluded that Gentiles are not required to
become Jewish proselytes by circumcision.[47]

The Scofield revisers have James saying that at some future time
there will be Gentile believers as well as Jewish believers and therefore
Gentile believers at James' time need not be circumcised. Against this
bizarre suggestion we simply note the following considerations. First,
as we say, this is far-fetched in this context (already nearly two thousand years far-fetched). Second, there had always been some Gentile
believers as well as Jewish and that did not prevent their circumcision
previously. Third, there is nothing more in the nature of a Gentile
being a believer that would preclude the possible necessity of his being
circumcised than would prevent the necessity of his being baptized.

Finally, we should note that the traditional interpretation affords a
reasonable explanation of James' conclusion. He recognized that Israel
(the church) was now becoming really international and that such
changes were appropriate "in order that the rest of mankind may seek
the Lord" (verse 17, NASB). Even the less patriarchal character of the
new dispensation had a bearing.

Romans 11:26

This interpretive crux is worth quoting in full:

> and thus all Israel will be saved; just as it is written, "The Deliverer
> will come from Zion. He will remove ungodliness from Jacob. And
> this is my covenant with them, when I take away their sins." (NASB)

This passage is crucial for dispensationalists, and most of them feel
that this verse proves that Israel and the church remain forever distinct. All dispensationalists see this as a prediction of some general
conversion of Jews, and they seem to feel that this interpretation is
something of a dispensational distinctive.

---

47. *New Scofield Reference Bible*, p. 1186.

Interestingly, most Reformed theologians agree that this passage does indeed foretell a general conversion of the Jews. Jonathan Edwards, for example, expresses this view confidently:

> Nothing is more certainly foretold than this national conversion of the Jews, in Rom. xi. There are also many passages of the Old Testament which cannot be interpreted in any other sense, which I cannot now stand to mention. Besides the prophecies of the calling of the Jews, we have a remarkable providential seal of the fulfilment of this great event, by a kind of continual miracle, viz. their being preserved a distinct nation in such a dispersed condition for above sixteen hundred years. The world affords nothing else like it. There is undoubtedly a remarkable hand of providence in it. When they shall be called, that ancient people, who alone were God's people for so long a time, shall be his people again, never to be rejected more. They shall then be gathered into one fold together with the Gentiles; and so also shall the remains of the ten tribes, wherever they be, and though they have been rejected much longer than the Jews, be brought in with their brethren. The prophecies of Hosea especially seem to hold this forth, that in the future glorious times of the church, both Judah and Ephraim, or Judah and the ten tribes, shall be brought in together, and shall be united as one people, as they formerly were under David and Solomon; (Hos. 1. 11, &c.) — Though we do not know the time in which this conversion of Israel will come to pass; yet thus much we may determine by Scripture, that it will be before the glory of the Gentile part of the church shall be fully accomplished; because it is said, that their coming in shall be life from the dead to the Gentiles (Rom. xi. 12, 15).[48]

While many Reformed exegetes view this passage as does Edwards, not all do. Among the Calvinists who do not is John Calvin. In his commentary, he saw "all Israel" as all the elect — the total number of the elect of the ages.[49] Others, especially Dutch Reformed theologians, are more restrictive and interpret "all Israel" as the total number of elect Jews.[50] Still others, more restrictive, limit the expression to the elect remnant of Jews.

Hendriksen, admiring of Calvin and sympathetic with his fellow Dutch Calvinists, wrestles with the exegesis before coming gradually to

---

48. Jonathan Edwards, *Works*, 2:607. See also Charles Hodge, *Systematic Theology*, 3:792, 805.

49. John Calvin, *The Epistles of Paul to the Romans and to the Thessalonians*, trans. Ross Mackenzie (Grand Rapids: Eerdmans, 1960), p. 255.

50. See William Hendriksen, *Israel in Prophecy* (Grand Rapids: Baker, 1972).

the national Israel interpretation. Observing that all uses of *Israel* from Romans 9 to 11:26a indisputably refer to Jews distinguished from Gentiles, and the verses which follow likewise, he concludes that Israel in this verse "in all probability does not indicate the church universal. It has reference to Jews, not to Gentiles."[51] He then asks whether the reference is to the Jews as a whole or to the "entire Jewish remnant." Based on Romans 11:5, 14, and 31, Hendriksen argues that it is evident that "the salvation of 'all Israel' was being progressively realized until 'all Israel' shall have been saved. When the full number of the elect Gentiles will have been gathered in, then the full number of elect Jews will also have been gathered in."[52] Thus, "all Israel" refers to the elect remnant.

It is not my purpose here to adjudicate these various Reformed interpretations. Rather, I simply note that the recognition of a continuing divine purpose for ethnic Jews does not at all imply the eternal distinction between Israel and the church that dispensationalists imagine. The metaphor of the olive tree which immediately precedes the verse in question illustrates the truth well. While most ethnic Jews had been cut off from the olive tree (Israel) because of unbelief (verses 22–23), they could be grafted back in (verse 24) and so form (with believing Gentiles) the Israel of God.

Ephesians 3:4–6

This passage, which speaks of the fact that Gentiles "are fellow-heirs and fellow-members [with Jews] of the body" as a "mystery of Christ" (NASB) which had not been made known to previous generations, is considered by dispensationalists to be a bulwark of their view of the church as a "mystery" which was unknown to the Old Testament writers. This doctrine of the mystery has continued to be a major characteristic, if not actual hallmark, of the dispensational school. Thus, the *New Scofield Reference Bible* comments: "The church, corporately, is not in the vision of the Old Testament prophecies (Ephesians 3:1–6)."[53]

John Walvoord continues to defend the doctrine of the mystery church.[54] Commenting on Colossians 1:26–27, he offers five arguments in favor of his doctrine. First, the mystery is said to have been hidden in the past. Second, the content of the mystery, "Christ in you," was never predicted in the Old Testament. Third, in the Old Testament, the

---

51. Ibid., p. 43.
52. Ibid., pp. 48–49.
53. *New Scofield Reference Bible*, p. 711.
54. Chafer and Walvoord, *Major Bible Themes*, p. 240.

glory of the Lord is outward rather than inward. Fourth, appealing to Colossians 2:9-19, Walvoord says that it represents Christ as the head of the church, while in the old theocracy, God merely dwelt among His people. Fifth, Christ in the heart of the believer is the hope of glory, while Israel was looking for His glorious advent.

Against this "mystery" doctrine of the dispensationalists I submit a number of considerations. First, just as we saw in our examination of dispensational "literalism," here too the dispensationalist confuses fulness of prophecy with the substance of prophecy. It is one thing to say that all the details of the church were not revealed to Old Testament believers but quite another to say that the church was not in view at all.

Second, we have already noted that many Old Testament prophecies to Israel are applied to the church by the New Testament (Joel 2:28-32) and that the fact that Gentiles were to be included in the worship of God was revealed in the Old Testament (Amos 9:12). While the details of this "mystery" were undoubtedly the cause of great perplexity, this "mystery" was not a complete unknown.

Finally, the meaning of the word *mystery*, both within the Bible and in popular usage, is against the dispensational interpretation. In common usage mystery means something *partly* unknown. For example, the church speaks of the "mysteries of the faith" as articles of belief which she now sees through a glass darkly. More importantly, the Bible also uses the word in this sense. O. T. Allis wrote:

> The word "mystery" occurs 29 times in the New Testament, most of which are in Paul's epistles, six being in Ephesians. It is important, therefore, to observe how the word is used, especially by Paul. Paul speaks of several mysteries; "the mystery of God and of the Father and of Christ" (Col.ii 2), "of Christ" (Col.iv 3), "of the gospel" (Eph.vi 19), "of his will" (Eph. i 9), "of the faith" (I Tim.iii 9), "of godliness" (I Tim.iii 16), "of iniquity" (2 Thess.ii 7). These passages show that to describe a person as a mystery, does not necessarily imply that he or it was entirely unknown. It might be known yet still be a mystery because not fully known: God was known in Israel—that was Israel's preeminence . . . yet Paul speaks of "the mystery of God." Christ was God "manifested in the flesh." He had been on earth and the facts of His earthly life were known. Yet Paul speaks of the "mystery of Christ." Especially noteworthy is I Tim.iii 16 where Paul speaks of the "mystery of godliness"; and then refers to events in the earthly life of Christ which were known too and had been witnessed by Christians who were in Christ before him.[55]

---

55. Allis, *Prophecy and the Church*, p. 90. See pages 90-102 for a full discussion.

Thus, it cannot be said that the dispensational doctrine of the church as a parenthesis or "mystery" which was wholly unknown to the Old Testament can stand close scrutiny. None of the passages traditionally cited by dispensationalists support the notion. Rather, the dispensational exegesis of these passages is controlled by an *a priori* commitment to a radical theological distinction between Israel and the church—a theological distinction without exegetical support from Scripture.

Ultradispensationalism on Israel and the Church

If Dispensationalism has failed to recognize the unity of the Bible, Ultradispensationalism (or Bullingerism) has utterly destroyed it. If anything should show a dispensationalist the error of his way, it is the possibilities implicit in his system which are revealed in Bullingerism. Virtually all of the beliefs of this more radical movement are drawn consistently from dispensational principles.

In Ultradispensationalism, the dispensational commitment to a radical distinction between Israel and the church is given full rein. While Scofield regarded Matthew as "Jewish" or "kingdom" teaching up to the rejection of Christ as king, E. W. Bullinger much more consistently regarded all of the four gospels as strictly and purely Jewish. In my earlier criticism of the dispensational teaching, I showed the injustice of drawing the line where Scofield and other dispensationalists do. The kingdom continued to be offered after Matthew 16:21 as well as before, and personal invitations were undoubtedly given before as well as after this passage in Matthew. The dispensationalist is obliged to see the kingdom being offered throughout the gospels and, therefore, must do one of two things—either he must continue to interpret the kingdom as purely legalistic Judaism (in which case he must go with Bullingerism), or interpret it as roughly synonymous with the Christian church (in which case he must return to traditional theology).

If the dispensationalist will go with Bullinger, he should count the cost. For one thing, it means that the great prophecy of the church in Matthew 16:18-20, which he now regards as a prediction of Pentecost, must be abandoned as such and given over to the "Jewish remnant church." "There was no beginning of a church on that day of Pentecost."[56] He must say with Bullinger that this is in no way connected with

---

56. E. W. Bullinger, *Foundations of Dispensational Truth* (London: Eyre and Spottiswood, 1931), p. 34.

the "mystery" or Christian church. For this future *ecclesia* of the Jews spoken of in Matthew 16 is yet to be built on Christ, the returned Messiah, as the foundation stone. This church is to be built *on* Christ, while the mystery church is now a spiritual building *in* Christ. This church of Matthew 16:18 is to consist of remnant Jews only, while the present church is composed of Jews and Gentiles, predominantly the latter.[57]

Commenting on Acts 26:22–23, Bullinger writes:

> This positive statement that Paul was not only *confirming* the word which "began to be spoken by the Lord"; but that, like the Lord's own ministry, Paul's was based entirely on the Old Testament prophetic Scriptures, "Moses and the Prophets." From this it is conclusive that there can be no Dispensation of the Church in Acts of the Apostles, and certainly no revelation of the mystery (or Secret) as subsequently made known in the later epistles written from his prison in Rome.[58]

It is the later epistles which refer to the "riches of grace" and the church. In the same vein, ultradispensationalist John O'Hair writes:

> In Acts 10:28 we learned that it was unlawful for the messengers of the risen Christ to have fellowship with Gentiles some seven years after the day of Pentecost. In Acts 11:19 we learned that Jewish disciples preached to none but Jews only. In Acts 11:1–6 we learned that the Christian Jews condemned Peter for preaching to a Gentile some seven years after the day of Pentecost. Therefore, all Christians should know that there was no Joint-Body (Ephesians 3:6) during those years covered by the first ten chapters of Acts.[59]

A second price the dispensationalist will have to pay if he goes with Bullinger is the loss of Christ as a sacrifice. Darby had come dangerously close to that position in his own lesser heresy, when he said that Christ offered Himself as a sacrifice only because Israel had refused Him as a king. Some of the Brethren had actually denied that Christ was a priest while on earth, but this was not unanimous even with them, and non-Brethren have been most reluctant to say this. But, if they will go with Bullinger, they must say that Christ "never was a priest on earth."[60]

---

57. Bullinger, *How to Enjoy the Bible*, 3rd ed. (London: Eyre and Spottiswood, 1913), p. 148.

58. Bullinger, *Foundations*, p. 219.

59. John O'Hair, *W. W.*, p. 19.

60. Bullinger, *How to Enjoy the Bible*, p. 128.

Why is this a necessary step given the radical distinction between Israel and the church? Here Bullinger saw the implications of Dispensationalism more clearly than many. Citing Christ's words at the Last Supper, "This cup which is poured out for you is the new covenant in My blood" (Luke 22:20, NASB) (which the Christian church has always taken to refer to His sacrifice on Calvary), Bullinger noted that this referred back to the prophecy given in Jeremiah 31:31–33 — a prophecy to Israel and not to the church. Bullinger would agree that the cup of the Lord's Supper is the new covenant, but precisely for that reason it has no reference to the mystery church, but to Israel. The Lord's Supper, therefore, should not now be administered to the "mystery" church. It should not be observed except by the Jewish church and it is to be reestablished only in the kingdom age.[61] Indeed, Christ is the mediator of the new covenant, but that has nothing to do with the mystery or "body" church. The body church is Christ, and it does not need any mediator — end of Christ's sacrifice!

Third, if the dispensationalist will go with Bullingerism, or consistent Dispensationalism, he will pay a heavy price in that there is precious little left of Scripture which applies to the Christian today. The reason for this is quite simple. As we have seen, virtually all of the New Testament events are implicated in Old Testament prophecies to Israel and, if the Israel/church distinction is to be preserved, none of this can apply to the church. The ultradispensational rejection of the idea that the church began at Pentecost is a case in point. The church could not have begun at Pentecost because the Pentecost outpouring of the Spirit was predicted, according to Peter in Acts 2:16, by the prophet Joel!

If there is any point at which the Bullingerites can teach the dispensationalists some lessons in drawing conclusions from principles, it is in their interpretation of the book of Acts.[62] First of all, they show that if the dispensationalists can refuse to let Stephen's use of the word *church* (*ecclesia*) with reference to Israel in Acts 7:38 mean "church," the Bullingerites can, with equal justification, refuse to allow the word *church* in Acts 2:47 mean "church." They take it as a reference to the Jewish church which is assumed to be radically different from the "mystery" church. In exactly the same manner, the dispensationalists take Stephen's "church" as the Jewish church and, therefore, radically different from the mystery church.

---

61. John O'Hair, *Pentecostalism, Bullingerism, and the World Wide Grace Testimony*, p. 23.
62. E. W. Bullinger, *Mysteries*, p. 40.

Consistent with their interpretations, ultradispensationalists extend the offer of the kingdom to the Jews throughout virtually the entire period covered by the book of Acts. "The public preaching of the Kingdom ends with Acts 19:20."[63] Paul continues privately to preach the kingdom to the very end of the book of Acts and even two years afterwards. In fact, everything prior to the prison epistles of the Apostle Paul has no relevance for the church.

If this is a true view of Acts, what becomes of the other books of the New Testament? James died twenty years before the mystery church was announced. Therefore, he was not in the mystery church.[64] John O'Hair does not hesitate to continue by saying that all the others of his time before the mystery church, as well as James, were not in the mystery church. The epistles of John were written before the prison epistles. Therefore, they were directed to the Jewish church of the book of Acts and not to the mystery church of Christ.[65] The appearing of Christ anticipated by the Apostle John (1 John 3:1–4) is, according to the Bullingerites, the appearing of Christ as king for Israel. The book of Revelation was written before Colossians, and therefore, it too is entirely Jewish.[66] Consistently, Bullinger relegates the seven churches of the book of Revelation to the Jewish church. The dispensationalists tend to regard these opening chapters of the book of Revelation as having reference to the time before the end-time and thus as a reference to the mystery church. But, why draw the line at this point? If this was written before the mystery church was revealed, it does not have to do with the mystery church but with the Jewish church as all the rest of the book does.[67]

The fact that many will not accept the dating of New Testament books proposed by the ultradispensationalists should not obscure the central challenge they pose to all dispensationalists. This challenge, quite simply, is that it is impossible completely to disassociate Israel and the church in the New Testament. If one feels that it is a matter of prime theological importance that the two be separated, we cannot be confident that we have thoroughly done so unless we have relegated most if not all of the New Testament to the Jews. This raises the question what relevance the Bible, as a whole, has for the Bullingerite. O'Hair speaks to this point and claims complete relevance:

63. A. P. Pollock, *The Kingdom and the Church*, p. 14.
64. O'Hair, *Pentecostalism*, p. 22.
65. Ibid., p. 22.
66. Ibid., p. 22.
67. See Ethelbert William Bullinger, *Apocalypse or the Day of the Lord* (London: Eyre & Spottiswood, 1909).

The World Wide Grace Testimony teaches that every line and word in
the Bible is for every member of the Body of Christ, but that every
line and word is not about the Body; and therefore, all of the Bible
which is not about the Church must be studied, applied and appropriated in the light of the Bible that is about the Body of Christ.[68]

In spite of the pious-sounding flow of these words, one who
reveres the Bible senses intuitively an almost complete rejection of the
Word of God. It is true that the Christian church has always recognized
that some parts of the Bible have been abrogated — such as the ceremonial laws of Moses and Saturday observance as Sabbath. But, with
such qualifications, the entire Bible is both *about* and *for* the church of
God. To restrict the preceptive relevance of the Bible to the prison
epistles of Paul is surely to make almost all of the Word of God of no
effect by the traditions of the Bullingerites.

Thus we see that the ultradispensationalists go to the end of the
dispensational line while the more moderate dispensationalists, at the
cost of consistency, try to get off at midpoint. Both varieties of dispensationalists believe that there is a qualitative difference between Israel
and the church. Ultradispensationalists have no question whatever
about it, and Charles Ryrie, as we have seen, considers it the most fundamental difference between dispensational and Covenant theology.

How does the Scofieldian get off the dispensational train? By simply insisting that Christ starts to preach the gospel of individual salvation after the Jews had rejected His kingdom offer. Christ then declares
His intention to establish the church which actually took place at
Pentecost. Ultradispensationalist John O'Hair states candidly that at
this point Scofield errs; that is, at the point that Christ was about to establish His church. As a matter of fact, according to O'Hair, even John
3:16 is not a part of the Christian church message. Not even Pentecost
was the beginning of the Christian church for the Bullingerites. People
could not be saved merely by being told that Jesus was the Messiah
whom they had killed. Even the early teaching of the Apostle Paul was
not an articulation of church doctrine. That did not come until Ephesians 2 where Paul refers to the breaking down of the wall of partition
between Israel and the Gentiles which marks the beginning of the
"body church."

Why do we say that this is the necessary implication of traditional
Dispensationalism? Well, if Scofieldians will not acknowledge that the

---

68. O'Hair, *Pentecostalism*, p. 15.

dispensation of the law is simply the covenant of grace in a legal dispensation, then how can they insist that Pentecost is the beginning of the dispensation of grace without actually extending that terminal point? The Scofieldians have arbitrarily tended to focus on Matthew 11:28 where Christ invites persons individually to come to Him and find their rest, as the beginning of the church age. But Christ does not use the word *church* there and, as even the traditional dispensationalist insists, when He does use the word in Matthew 16:18, He uses the future tense. So if there is no basis for saying that the church exists at Matthew 11:28 or 16:18, the question is on what basis would the Scofieldians say that it originates in Acts 2? How can they refute O'Hair's contention that there was no preaching of the gospel explicitly on that occasion but a mere indication that Israel had sinned in crucifying its Messiah? There is still no reference to the word *church*. Traditional dispensationalists will not grant that Stephen in Acts 7:38 is using the word *ecclesia* (translated "church" in KJV) with reference to ancient Israel as part of the church. So once again we join with the ultradispensationalists and ask how the Scofieldians can say the church is in existence in Acts 7? How are they going to stop the Bullingerites who insist that the "body church" of Ephesians 2 is the very initiation of it and only the prison and post-prison New Testament literature is immediately relevant to this church age?

The moral of all this for the Scofieldian dispensationalist is that if he will not build on the covenantal continuity of the earlier dispensations, there is simply no way by which he can make room for the church at a later stage. The ultradispensationalist has been pointing this out for a century. Covenant theologians have been showing it for millennia. Modern Dispensationalism is halting between two opinions. It must either come to a fundamentally covenantal theological basis which it sometimes senses and vaguely articulates or it must take the consequences of its refusal to do so and embrace the very unwelcome invitation of the Bullingerites.

One option is not open to it. Dispensationalism cannot continue to vacillate between the two. We say with Elijah to those Israelites who were halting between two opinions – "How long will you hesitate between two opinions? If the LORD is God, follow Him; but if Baal, follow him" (1 Kings 18:21, NASB). This analogy is not too extreme. Bullingerism is surely another gospel, as even dispensationalists sense, and sometimes say.

Conclusion

The dispensational distinction between Israel and the church implicitly repudiates the Christian way of salvation. I have already discussed this problem with more than a hint of its implication. As we have seen, dispensationalists make a qualitative distinction between Israel and the church. They are two different peoples. They are not the same people of God. They have a different relationship in this life and, as we shall see later, a different future.

If these are two different types of people, how can they have the same salvation? If, as dispensationalists maintain, Israel as well as the church is saved by the blood of Jesus Christ, how can there be this qualitative difference between them as peoples? Jesus Christ is the same yesterday, today, and forever. His salvation is the same yesterday, today, and forever. It may be administered in somewhat different ways and in different contexts, to be sure. But that which is administered is the same — redemption by the blood of Jesus Christ. If that is the case, as the whole church has taught down through the centuries and as even the dispensationalists profess to believe, how can there be two different categories of people? How can those who are saved in the same way by the same Savior, through the same redemption, be a different people? How can Israel be reduced to an earthly, temporal people and at the same time be the spiritual beneficiaries of the same blood of Christ from which Christians benefit?

It will not do to say that Israelites were the beneficiaries of the same redemption when they obviously benefit in an entirely different manner. According to dispensationalists, the Old Testament people are not the heirs of the Holy Spirit, are not regenerated by Him, and are not grafted by Him into Christ in the same way that the New Testament people are. If Christ purchased the same thing for the Old Testament saints before He came that He did for the New Testament saints after He came, there cannot be a qualitative difference between them. There being clearly that difference, as the dispensationalists *vigorously maintain*, then there must be what the dispensationalists *vigorously deny* — a different basis of their acceptability with God.

The Bible teaches that the people of God are the same in all dispensations. They are, as Ephesians 2:20 says, built on the same foundation, "the apostles and prophets." The prophets of the Old Testament and the apostles of the New Testament are together a foundation for the church of God. There is no difference between prophets and apostles in the role which they perform. The church which is built on them is built on prophets as well as on apostles, apostles as well as on prophets. Just as the Apostle Paul recognizes the identity of the Old and New Testament peoples of God, so the Apostle Peter uses the same language for the New Testament church of God which was used for the people of God in the Old Testament. "But ye are a chosen generation, a royal priesthood, an holy nation, a peculiar people, that ye should show forth the praises of him who hath called you" (1 Peter 2:9, KJV; see Exodus 19:6; Deuteronomy 7:6; 10:15; Isaiah 61:6).

In Paul's famous metaphor, the Jews were the original olive tree into which the Gentile believers were grafted (see Romans 11:17). They are the same plant; they have the same source of life; there is no difference between them except a temporal one. The early form of organization was displaced by the present form of organization, but the living source of their lives, Jesus Christ, is the same in all periods. The Bible says this because it maintains what the dispensationalist only claims; namely, that Christ is the one and only Savior of all time. It does not split the church, as dispensationalists do, but unifies the church in all ages, because it sees that all members are saved by the same undivided Lord Jesus Christ.

The dispensationalists may object, saying that the covenantalists recognize some differences between Israel and the church. We grant that there are temporal differences of administration between the Old and New Testament dispensations, but there is no essential or qualitative difference. The Old Testament church was restricted largely to one land, one ethnic group, an agricultural society, a theocratic organization, a childhood state of development, and a preparatory stage. But if it had the one and only basis of salvation, the Lord Jesus Christ, the only name ever given whereby men must be saved, it is one with the New Testament church. We are all one in Christ Jesus. If we are not one, we are not in Christ Jesus.

In addition to the serious theological error involved in the dispensational distinction between Israel and the church, there are very unfortunate practical consequences as well. One result is a powerful tendency to obliterate the distinction between Jews today as unbelievers in desperate need of Christ for salvation and their possible future status as redeemed. Events at a 1982 conference of evangelicals and Jews show how Dispensationalism is breaking down the theological barriers between Christian belief and Jewish unbelief. Joint worship services (with Jewish rabbis, John Walvoord, Jerry Falwell, Pat Robertson, and other dispensationalists present) were held. One paper at this 1982 conference "identified both groups as 'descendants of Abraham' and 'chosen under the terms of [God's] covenants.' It concludes by saying 'we are prepared to walk together as God's covenanted people because we are agreed on important fundamentals of our faiths.' " It is some slight relief to read that Homer Heater apprehensively remarked, "You can't get around the fact that salvation is through Jesus alone. Sure the Jews are God's people, but they are in unbelief."[69]

The dispensational distinction between a completely temporal, earthly people (Israel) and a completely spiritual, heavenly people (the church) has also yielded bitter fruit in Dispensationalism's attitude toward the organized Christian church. Dispensationalists often evidence intense suspicion toward the organized, visible church. Darby, for example, wrote that "the Year-books of Christianity are the yearbooks of hell."[70] Another Plymouth brother wrote of organized Christianity, "It is worse, by far, than Judaism; worse by far than all the darkest forms of Paganism."[71]

Such examples could be multiplied almost endlessly. The root of the problem is the Israel/church distinction which assumes that Israel is an entirely temporal matter and the church an entirely spiritual affair. As a result, dispensationalists retreat into a hyper-spiritual Gnosticism which spurns the structures of the visible church which God has graciously given to His people.

We are glad to see one noted dispensationalist admit, however qualifiedly and inadequately, the error of the dispensational distinction of Israel and the church. Robert Saucy writes that the "earlier" dispensational view

> that divided the people of God into an earthly and heavenly people (i.e. the Church and Israel), with fundamentally no continuity in the plan of God on the historical plane, must be rejected. . . .[72]

Yet how can this error be restricted to "earlier dispensational teaching" when it is found in *The New Scofield Reference Bible* and Charles Ryrie's *Dispensationalism Today*. The tone of its rhetoric aside, the new Dispensationalism still sounds very much like the old.

---

69. Beth Spring, "Some Jews and Evangelicals Edge Close on Israel Issue," *Christianity Today*, December 17, 1982, pp. 33–34.

70. See Steele, *Antinomianism Revived*, p. 15.

71. Ibid.

72. Robert Saucy, in *Prophecy and the Church*, ed. C. L. Feinberg (Chicago: Moody, 1971), pp. 239–240.

ELEVEN

DISPENSATIONAL ANTINOMIANISM— THE ANTITHESIS OF TRUE GRACE— PART ONE: EVIDENCE OF ANTINOMIANISM

I n this crucial chapter I will show that all traditional dispensational-ists teach that converted Christian persons *can* (not may) live in sin throughout their post-conversion lives with no threat to their eternal destiny. The following chapter will examine the underlying dispensa-tional teaching regarding the "two natures" of the Christian (carnal and spiritual) which gives rise to this fatal Antinomianism. After a brief glance at historic Antinomianism, I shall examine the teachings of a number of prominent dispensationalists, past and present, show-ing that there is essential continuity and agreement within the dispen-sational movement on this fatal error.

Historic Antinomianism

This phenomenon of Antinomianism, which seems to be an integral, though disavowed, part of Dispensationalism, has been with the church down through the centuries, especially since the Reformation. William K. B. Stoever gives an apt definition of this heresy:

The label "antinomianism" derives from the syndrome's distinctive mark, namely the denial of the relevance of the moral law to true Christians because of the ability claimed for the Holy Spirit to separate persons directly and radically from the obligations of ordinary worldly existence.[1]

One factor contributing to Antinomianism is a misunderstanding of the Reformation doctrine of justification by grace through faith. Luther and Calvin staunchly opposed any hint of the Roman Catholic doctrine of merit in justification with its complex of doctrines such as the treasury of merit and works of supererogation. At the same time, they insisted on the inseparability of faith and works, of justification and sanctification, for the simple but profound reason that all of salvation is to be found only through a genuine union with Jesus Christ. Thus, good works may be said to be a condition for obtaining salvation in that they inevitably accompany genuine faith. Good works, while a necessary complement of true faith, are never the meritorious grounds of justification, of acceptance before God. *From the essential truth that no sinner in himself can merit salvation, the antinomian draws the erroneous conclusion that good works need not even accompany faith in the saint.* The question is not whether good works are necessary to salvation, but in what way are they necessary. As the inevitable outworking of saving faith, they are necessary for salvation. As the meritorious ground of justification, they are not necessary *or acceptable.*

Another historic factor contributing to this heresy is an ontological dualism which denigrates the created order and places total reliance upon the direct and unmediated work of God. It is crucial to understand the point at issue here. The question is not divine monergism in salvation—whether salvation is entirely a work of God. Rather, the issue at stake is whether God works through the created order and whether God truly effects positive changes in the created order. Stoever notes that Antinomianism typically:

> exalted the unconditioned, unmediated operation of the Spirit in the application of redemption, to the point of seriously minimizing, if not altogether overruling, the Christian's continuing rootedness in the ontological and moral orders of creation. From the antinomian perspective the agency and instrumentality of creatures are incidental

---

1. William K. B. Stoever, *A Faire and Easie Way to Heaven: Covenant Theology and Antinomianism in Early Massachusetts* (Middletown, Conn.: Wesleyan University Press, 1978), p. 161.

to the Spirit's gracious work, which renders the Christian, morally and ontologically, a veritable "new being."[2]

This is to be contrasted sharply with the historic position of Reformed theology which maintains that God, in His saving work, instills the principles or "habits" of sanctified life which then become truly part of that person's being.[3] For the Reformed theologian, good works, while the *result* of divine grace, are genuinely human actions. For the antinomian, good works *are* divine actions, the direct action of God within the human person.

This dualism leads in turn to an odd, but understandable juxtaposition of licentiousness and Perfectionism — sometimes in combination. Because the direct agency of God is all that really matters and because God does not really change created human nature for the better, the actual conduct of the Christian may be seen as a matter of little importance. On the other hand, the presence and direct action of the uncreated deity within a person renders that person at least implicitly perfect — no matter how he actually behaves. We shall see, especially in the treatment of the dispensational doctrine of sanctification, that Dispensationalism fits this model of classical Antinomianism virtually to the letter.

The magisterial Reformers were very sharply opposed to Antinomianism. While they recognized that justification by faith alone was the article by which the church stands or falls (Luther), and the very hinge of the Reformation (Calvin), they never for a moment granted that the faith which justifies could be sterile. As a matter of fact, the formula was "*Sola fides justificat, sed fides non est sola*" (faith alone justifies, but faith is not alone). Luther strongly opposed antinomians such as Johann Agricola and Nikolaus Amsdorf, who went so far as to say that good works are harmful. Luther wrote two treatises against the antinomians.

Calvin stoutly defended the Protestant doctrine of justification by grace through faith against Roman Catholic charges that it would destroy good works.[4] He even went so far as to treat the doctrine of sanctification prior to the doctrine of justification in his *Institutes*, contending that the inseparability of the two is best understood in this way.

---

2. Stoever, p. 162.
3. See the helpful discussion of Stoever, pp. 170–174.
4. See John Calvin, *Reply to Sadolet* in *Calvin: Theological Treatises*, ed. J. K. S. Reid (Philadelphia: Westminster, 1954), pp. 234–237.

For when this topic is rightly understood it will better appear how man is justified by faith alone, and simple pardon; nevertheless actual holiness of life, so to speak, is not separated from free imputation of righteousness.[5]

Indeed, Calvin never tired of stressing the indissoluble connection between justification and sanctification—this bond being none other than the person of Jesus Christ.

Why, then, are we justified by faith? Because by faith we grasp Christ's righteousness, by which alone we are reconciled to God. Yet you could not grasp this without at the same time grasping sanctification also. For he "is given unto us for righteousness, wisdom, sanctification, and redemption" (I Cor. 1:30). Therefore Christ justifies no one whom he does not at the same time sanctify. These benefits are joined together by an everlasting and indissoluble bond, so that those whom he illumines by his wisdom, he redeems; those whom he redeems, he justifies; those whom he justifies, he sanctifies.[6]

In spite of the opposition of Reformation leaders, Antinomianism was a recurring phenomenon in the Reformation and post-Reformation period. The Anabaptist debacle at Munster in 1532 discredited Antinomianism in the eyes of many but the tendency remained. A tradition of English Antinomianism is associated with John Eaton, Tobias Crisp, and John Saltmarsh and this thinking was brought to seventeenth-century Massachusetts by Anne Hutchinson, her advocacy of the heresy resulting in the so-called "Antinomian Controversy" of 1636–38.

In Scotland, the Sandemanians were antinomians with a vengeance. All so-called "good works" were considered bad works. They almost sensed the fact that all works of the Christian are works of the created nature, and they consistently called for inactivity. They seemed to feel that the good works would have to come from God alone, as the dispensationalist is constantly inferring though seldom recognizing. These Sandemanians were the original champions of "Let go and let God," and the "deadliness of doing." Sanctification, consequently, was seen as no evidence whatever of justification, but, if anything, the opposite.

---

5. Calvin, *Institutes*, III.3.1.
6. Ibid., III.16.1.

Dispensational Antinomianism

In both historic and contemporary Dispensationalism, we see both of the factors mentioned above at work. Dispensational theologians fail to understand the Reformation doctrines of justification and sanctification, and this misunderstanding is rooted in a dualistic conception of the relationship between God and the Christian.

The classic dispensational distinction between "standing" and "state" is evidence of a persistent misunderstanding of the doctrines of justification and sanctification. According to the dispensationalist, man in innocence sinned, and he and his progeny have become totally depraved. That is man's present nature. At his so-called "new birth," nothing in *nature* changes. His *standing*, which is his legal relationship to God, is supposed to change. His *state*, which is his own condition, does not necessarily change at that time or even thereafter. The error of the dispensationalist lies, not in the *distinction* between "standing" and "state" (for justification and sanctification cannot be reduced to the same thing), but in the denial that there is any necessary connection between the two.

The dualism noted above is evident in the dispensational doctrine of regeneration. Here the old fallen nature remains untouched by the Holy Spirit. The Spirit regenerates and indwells the person — his temple or body, but He does not indwell his old nature — the old man. The regenerate man is made a partaker of divine nature, but this divine nature is not *his* nature. Quite literally, it is the *divine* nature.

In a certain sense, never the twain do meet. That is, the old sinful nature and the new sinless nature are poles apart in the same person. There is a real psychical schizophrenia here — an absolute and antithetical split between the finite, created, sinful, old human nature and the divine, uncreated, infinite, sinless, new divine nature. In a profound sense, the person is not changed at all. He is not regenerated; he is counter-balanced. Consistent with the underlying dualism, these two natures never meet. Neither influences the other. They go their separate ways — the old nature ultimately being destroyed and the new living forever.

These ideas give rise to the dispensational doctrine of the two kinds of Christians — the "spiritual" and the "carnal." The spiritual Christian is one who, for some reason, is controlled by the indwelling divine nature. The "carnal" Christian is one controlled by the old nature. There is no necessary reason why a Christian should not continue to be "carnal" all his life. Kraus, in his *Dispensationalism in America*, recognizes this as characteristic of American Dispensationalism. According to Dispensationalism there are

> two classes of Christians: Those who "abide in Christ" and those who "abide not"; for those who are "walking in the light," and those who "walk in darkness"; those who "walk by the Spirit," and those who "walk as men"; those who "walk in newness of life," and those who "walk after the flesh"; . . . those who are "spiritual" and those who are "carnal"; those who are "filled with the Spirit," and those who are not. All this has to do with the qualities of daily life of saved people, and is in no way a contrast between the saved and the unsaved.[7]

This is classic, historic Antinomianism.

In the rest of this chapter, I examine the teachings of numerous dispensationalists, past and present, with special focus on their persistent teaching that the Christian need not, and may never, forsake sin.

J. N. Darby

Darby taught this Antinomianism in its crudest form. Turner, in his biography of the Brethren leader, tells of an episode in his life that illustrates our point graphically. He was once asked about 1 John 1:7 ("But if we walk in the light, as he is in the light, we have fellowship one with another, and the blood of Jesus Christ His Son cleanseth us from all sin" [KJV].) He explained that the text deals with where you walk, not how you walk. Dr. Steele, who had asked the question, was somewhat perplexed by such an antinomian reply and asked further, "Suppose a real Christian turned his back on the light (meaning deliberately and permanently)?" Without hesitation, Darby replied, "then the light would shine upon his back."[8]

The question may arise whether there are more "carnal" than "spiritual" Christians. We suppose that dispensationalists think that there are vastly more carnal than spiritual Christians and that, therefore, this type of living is more common "Christian" behavior than the other. Nevertheless, the old man, Darby taught, is not crucified daily. He is now growing worse all the time. Steele tells of having asked him if he felt that he had been growing in grace since becoming a Christian. "In response to a question we once put to Mr. Darby, he said, his

---

7. Kraus, pp. 62, 121.
8. Turner, p. 23.

nature, or old man, had been growing worse and worse ever since he believed in Christ."[9]

C. I. Scofield

In Scofield, we see the basic pattern of dispensational thought on the relationship of works to salvation clearly articulated. We have already noticed the Scofield note on the forgiveness petition of the Lord's Prayer, "Forgive us our debts, as we forgive our debtors" (Matthew 6:12, KJV). According to Scofield, "Under the law forgiveness is conditioned upon a like spirit in us; under grace we are forgiven for Christ's sake and exhorted to forgive because we have been forgiven."[10] Scofield then refers his reader to a note where this theme is enlarged upon, "The sin of the justified believer *interrupts his fellowship*; it is forgiven upon confession, but always on the ground of Christ's propitiating sacrifice."[11]

One can see from this note that forgiveness is not necessary for a person's salvation; it is necessary only for fellowship. I may refuse all my life to forgive. God will, however, forgive this and all my other sins in which I may choose to persist. I will lose fellowship with Him and fellow Christians, but my salvation is an accomplished fact because I once professed faith in Christ. It is obvious that one could go on lying, blaspheming, fornicating, and murdering for a lifetime with no threat to one's salvation. The Christian's "disobedience does not affect his salvation, but fellowship, peace, and growth," he wrote in his *Question Box*.[12]

The Christian, in other words, is a carnal person. He was born so and he may remain so after regeneration, according to C. I. Scofield. I know that many dispensationalists will rally to Scofield's defense here, saying that he is simply defending the Calvinistic doctrine of perseverance of the saints. In an earlier chapter, we have shown that he is not defending the Calvinistic doctrine of perseverance of the saints (whatever he may have intended). In any case, that is not the point here. Whatever Scofield's motivation, he emphatically and dogmatically teaches that a Christian may be carnal all his life and yet be a Christian. These statements alone—and his writings are full of statements

---

9. Ibid., p. 15.
10. *Scofield Reference Bible*, p. 1002.
11. Ibid., p. 1039 (emphasis mine).
12. C. I. Scofield, *Question Box*, ed. Ella E. Pohle (Chicago: The Bible Institute Colportage Assn., 1917), pp. 13, 14.

like them—would prove that America's most famous and influential dispensationalist was an arch-antinomian.

Harry Ironside

Harry Ironside is especially interesting, for surely no classical dispensationalist has tried more strenuously to avoid Antinomianism (unless it be John Mac Arthur, who succeeded). He wrote:

> It is not easy in attempting to steer clear of the Scylla of legalism to keep from running into the Charybdis of license. In the effort to avoid Jewish legality, it is most natural to fall into antinomianism.[13]

Unfortunately, even Ironside does not avoid the "Charybdis" of Antinomianism. He acknowledges here, as elsewhere, that the Christian in this age of grace has the power to overcome or be delivered from the power of indwelling sin as well as from its penalty. There is no excuse, in his opinion, for a Christian not overcoming indwelling sin. He even goes as far as to insist that, "when you receive a new life, you love to follow Christ, and, if you do not, you are not a Christian. Take that home. Examine your own foundations a bit."[14] He says that the answer to the claim that it does not make any difference what you do if you are a true believer is: "It makes a tremendous difference what you do. If you do not behave yourself, it shows that you are not a real Christian."[15]

Nevertheless, if Ironside were truly anti-antinomian, why would he write the following:

> Backsliding there may be—and, alas, often is. But the backslider is one under the hand of God in government. And He loves him too well to permit him to continue the practice of sin. He uses the rod of discipline; and if that be not enough, cuts short his career and leaves the case for final settlement at the judgment-seat of Christ (I Cor. 3:14; 11:30–32; and II Cor. 5:10).[16]

If the Christian had the principle of holiness in him, he could not "continue the practice of sin" until God actually "cuts short his career" because he has nothing but bad works.

---

13. Harry Ironside, *Sutherland's Last Will, a Revelation of our Inheritance in Christ Jesus Being Also a Scriptural Answer to the Error of Seventh Day Worship*, p. 3.
14. Ironside, *Eternal Security*, p. 18.
15. Ibid.
16. Ibid., p. 124.

On the next page, Ironside shows that the virtue the Christian inalienably has is his "standing" in Christ: "It is the believer looked at as characterized by the new nature who does not sin."[17] Still again, he contradicts himself without being aware of it:

> True, he still has the old, carnal, Adamic nature; and if controlled by it, he would still be sinning continually. But the new nature imparted when he was born again, "not of corruptible seed, but of incorruptible," is now the controlling factor of his life. With this incorruptible seed abiding in him, he cannot practice sin.[18]

How could this man be an incorrigible sinner and unable to "practice sin"? Thus we see that Ironside does allow for the possibility that a genuine Christian will continue callously to live in sin with no threat to his eternal destiny.

Alva J. McClain

Former Grace Theological Seminary president Alva McClain has produced one of the ablest defenses of the antinomian doctrine that the Christian is in no sense under obligation to the law of God.[19] McClain (one of the editors of *The New Scofield Reference Bible*) argues that the New Testament expression "under the law," could only have one of two meanings. Either it referred to being under the law as the basis of salvation or as a way of life. Since no one was ever, in any age, saved by keeping the law, the former possibility is excluded and the expression can only refer to being under the law as a way of life. So, when the New Testament says, as in Romans 6:14, that the Christian is not "under the law," it means that he is free from it as a way of life or standard of duty.

What is McClain's mistake? The problem lies in McClain's failure to recognize that, *although the Bible never taught that the law was the basis of salvation, the Jews did so misconstrue the Bible.* The Pharisees and Jews generally *trusted in their own righteousness* as keepers of the law (see Luke 18:9; Romans 10:3). That "righteousness" is what, as a Christian, Paul found to be "dung," though he had cherished it before (Philippians 3:8).

---

17. Ibid.
18. Ibid.
19. Alva J. McClain, *Law and Grace* (Winona Lake, Ind.: Brethren Missionary Herald, 1954), see chapter 7.

In Romans 6:14, Paul is saying that we are not "under the law" precisely in that sense. He said that, when the Galatians had sought to be "justified by the law," they had, by putting themselves under the law, "fallen from grace" (Galatians 5:4). Consequently, Paul meant that his doctrine "established" the law *as the way of life, not as the meritorious ground of salvation.* What Paul's doctrine of grace established, McClain's doctrine of grace destroys. "Do we then make void the law through faith?" asks Paul. McClain's answer is, "Precisely!" What is Paul's answer? "God forbid!" (Romans 3:31).

Lewis Sperry Chafer and John Walvoord

Chafer and Walvoord, in *Major Bible Themes*, reveal themselves to be hesitating antinomians. After a long discussion of sanctification, they conclude lamely: "It is therefore *fitting* for us to 'abstain from every appearance of evil.' "[20] Once again, we note that the word *fitting* is no substitute for "mandatory" or "necessary" or "indispensable." *There is never a question that dispensationalists recommend virtuous living.* It has its rewards in this world and in the world to come. On the other hand, not to live godly in Christ Jesus spells misery here and loss of reward in the world to come. So, it is indeed "fitting" for Christians to live godly. But, is it necessary? That is the question. If it is not *necessary*, we have Antinomianism.

Chafer and Walvoord not only recommend virtue, at times, they seem emphatically to demand it as essential. Consider this from Chafer: "There can be no such thing as a Christian who is not indwelt by the Holy Spirit."[21] Walvoord writes, "Never in the dispensation of grace are Christians warned that the loss of the Spirit will occur as a result of sin."[22] Chafer is saying that every Christian is indwelt by the Holy Spirit, and Walvoord that he never loses the Holy Spirit. Most non-dispensationalists would think that such affirmations would guarantee Christian, spiritual conduct as inseparable from being a Christian. But that is never asserted, to our knowledge, by Chafer and Walvoord or any other dispensationalist. The Holy Spirit may indwell throughout a Christian's life without that Christian ever acting accordingly. He may, perhaps even *probably* will, behave as a Christian should. But the *dispensationalist* refuses to say that he is not a Christian if he does not.

---

20. Chafer and Walvoord, *Major Bible Themes*, p. 210 (emphasis mine).
21. Chafer, *Systematic Theology*, 6:122.
22. John L. Walvoord, *The Holy Spirit* (Findlay, Ohio: Dunham, 1958), p. 151.

If there were any doubt about the Antinomianism of these definitive dispensational authors, it is dispelled a few pages later:

A carnal Christian is as perfectly saved as a spiritual Christian; for no experience or merit or service can form any part of the grounds of salvation. Though but a baby, he is, nevertheless, in Christ (I Cor. 3:1).[23]

These dispensational writers seek to avoid the embarrassment posed by the "carnal Christian" by appealing to "normal Christian experience." "It is of fundamental importance to understand that a *normal* Christian experience is realized only by those who are Spirit-filled."[24] There never is any question among dispensationalists that *some* converted persons do live the Christian life. Nevertheless, as long as it is not the universal Christian experience, it is possible, though not "fitting," advisable, desirable, or rewardable for a true Christian not to live godly in Christ Jesus. *If total Christian carnality is a possibility, Antinomianism is a certainty.*

A close reading of dispensational writers reveals a recognition on their part that this "normal" Christian life is, in fact, the *exception* among dispensationalists. Chafer and Walvoord begin to hedge their case by appealing to "ordinary conditions." "Salvation which is of God will, under ordinary conditions, prove itself to be such by its fruits."[25] Add to this Chafer's own acknowledgement of "the great mass of carnal Christians" and one begins to sense the dimensions of this frightening tragedy.[26]

Charles Ryrie

Before I analyze Dr. Ryrie's thought, let me note his appreciation of the crucial nature of the issue before us. In his *Balancing the Christian Life* he sharply focuses the point at stake:

The importance of this question cannot be overestimated in relation to both salvation and sanctification. The message of faith only and the message of faith plus commitment of life cannot both be the gospel; therefore, one of them is false and comes under the curse of perverting the gospel or preaching another gospel (Gal. 1:6–9).[27]

---

23. Chafer and Walvoord, *Major Bible Themes*, p. 214.
24. Ibid. (emphasis mine).
25. Ibid., p. 223.
26. Lewis Sperry Chafer, *Grace* (Grand Rapids: Zondervan, 1922), p. 345.
27. Charles Ryrie, *Balancing the Christian Life*, (Chicago: Moody, 1969), p. 170.

In that appalling statement, Ryrie is saying that the orthodox, Biblical doctrine of Christian sanctification is "another gospel" under a divine curse.

In *The Ryrie Study Bible*, we have alongside each other two conflicting statements. First, "James 2:14–26. Nonworking faith is not faith that saves in the first place."[28] Second, however: "Christ's personal Lordship over the individual's life is not a condition for salvation." Thus: "nonworking faith" is not faith; but then Ryrie goes on to say that a person may deny Christ's Lordship and yet have salvation, which we know Ryrie thinks, comes only by faith. So, nonworking faith is not faith but, nevertheless, it may bring salvation, which is supposed to be by faith. Ryrie cannot have it both ways. Ryrie ends up where virtually all dispensationalists always do end up: "*It should be a consequence of salvation and is a condition for dedication in full discipleship.*"[29]

Charles Ryrie is hesitant about being labeled an antinomian but he is somewhat more outspoken on this subject than most others. "Carnal believers whose lives will not merit reward will, nevertheless be saved (1 Cor. 3:14)."[30] Indeed, Ryrie seems to go out of his way to see how *little* a person must do in order to be saved. Continuing, Ryrie asks, "Are there not examples of uncommitted, unsurrendered, though genuine believers in the Bible? Yes, there are. Lot, who the New Testament calls 'righteous' (2 Peter 2:7), is an example of life-long rejection of God's Lordship over his life."[31] Even "life-long rejection" of God's will is no bar to salvation according to Ryrie.

The allusion to Lot, who is a common example cited by dispensationalists, makes Ryrie's Antinomianism clear enough. He and other dispensationalists who cite Lot, take courage because they know that the New Testament calls Lot, "righteous." So, the dispensationalist feels comfortable that he has a prime illustration of a godless person who is nevertheless godly, an unrighteous person who is nevertheless righteous. They think they have a perfect illustration of their distinction between a good standing and a bad state. However, they never prove what Ryrie says here about Lot—that his life was a constant "rejection of God's Lordship." That is not demonstrated, and it cannot be. Admittedly, he made a foolish choice and lived in a bad location,

---

28. *Ryrie Study Bible*, p. 1950.
29. Ibid. (emphasis mine).
30. Ryrie, *Survey of Bible Doctrine*, p. 135.
31. Ibid., p. 136.

where his righteous soul was constantly vexed. Yet, he was rescued before destruction set in upon his city. None of these facts add up to a "totally godless life" in which the Lordship of God is always rejected. He committed incest to be sure, but his daughters had to trick him into drunkenness to make him unconsciously do it.

The "Lordship Salvation" controversy has apparently hardened Ryrie in his Antinomianism. In a recent volume, he maintains that *a Christian may even cease to believe in Christ and still be saved.*

> Normally one who has believed can be described as a believer; that is, one who continues to believe. But . . . a believer may come to the place of not believing, and yet God will not disown him, since He cannot disown Himself.[32]

Apparently for Ryrie, it is asking too much of a person even to require belief in Christ as a condition of salvation. Few dispensationalists have carried their Antinomianism to this obvious indubitable dead end.

Hal Lindsey

Hal Lindsey, too, believes that Christians should behave as Christians, but may not do so. He reveals his Antinomianism by his denial of the necessity of confession. Commenting on Hebrews 10:35–39 (a passage with a message rather different than Lindsey imagines), he writes, "The Lord warns us that to shrink back in unbelief, even under persecution, is displeasing to Him. He encourages them to put their thoughts on the imminent possibility of the Messiah's return."[33] We can see that Lindsey is following the usual dispensational pattern of recommending faithfulness under persecution but preparing to excuse the Christians who do not practice it. He continues:

> These believers had started out well, but had taken their focus off their hope and centered on their persecution. They were about to throw their eternal rewards away. . . . We can "shrink back" far enough to lose our rewards, but not so far that we lose salvation.[34]

Lindsey, unlike his Lord, is telling us that we may refuse to confess Him before men, but He will never refuse to confess us before God (see Luke 12:8).

---

32. Charles C. Ryrie, *So Great Salvation* (Wheaton, Ill.: Victor, 1989), p. 141.
33. Hal Lindsey, *The Terminal Generation* (Westwood, N.J.: Revell, 1976), p. 182.
34. Ibid.

M. R. DeHaan

DeHaan is clearly dispensational but just as clearly and emphatically *seems* to repudiate Antinomianism. On the one hand, in his *Galatians*, he strongly censures those who teach that,

> because we are saved by grace it makes no difference how we live and behave. One book of the New Testament is devoted to answering this Satanic error. It is the Book of James, summed up in James 2:17, "even so faith, if it hath not works, is dead, being alone."[35]

This statement of DeHaan sounds like a genuine rejection of Antinomianism and *is if one correctly interprets James 2:17* which De Haan does not. This erroneous understanding of James 2:17 becomes evident near the end of his volume:

> You ask me, "Do not Christians who are under grace have to keep the law?" No, there is no compulsion, but the truly born-again believer desires to keep the law, not because he MUST, but because he WANTS to, and goes far beyond the law itself. . . . If we love as we ought to love, we need no one to tell us what to do — for the grace of God will teach us through His Word and His Spirit."[36]

The one part of this expression that, if taken as verity, does condemn Antinomianism is that the true Christian's work "goes far beyond the law itself . . ." That statement is an extreme denial of Antinomianism because it actually asserts the opposite, Romish error of "works of *supererogation*." These are not merely perfect works but works beyond perfection. When this dispensationalist really did deny Antinomianism, it was only by affirming its absolutely opposite error. It is quite clear from his writings that DeHaan did not mean to assert the Romish error but as a true dispensationalist simply could not deny Antinomianism without falling into the opposite error of Perfectionism.

DeHaan's problem here is with the use of the word *must* and the idea of compulsion. He categorically rejects compulsion in sanctification, and reduces "must" to "want." Like McClain, DeHaan fails to understand that the law of God is a "must" law. The law of God consists of commands, not suggestions that we may take up if and when we *want* to. The Reformed and Biblical faith says that one *must obey from his*

---

35. M. R. DeHaan, *Galatians* (Grand Rapids: Zondervan, 1960), introduction.
36. Ibid., p. 160.

heart voluntarily. One is *commanded* to love God and his neighbor and himself with all his heart, soul, mind, and strength. That is *not optional.* It is *absolutely necessary.* DeHaan does not acknowledge that, or even understand it. Simple as it is the little ditty:

> Free from the law;
> Oh blessed condition;
> We can sin as we please;
> And still have remission,

is the motto of Dispensationalism. The dispensationalist will immediately protest that the Christian *will not be pleased* to sin. But all he *can* and ultimately *does* say *as a dispensationalist* is that the saint *ought not* to be pleased to sin.

Harold Barker

Barker provides an illustration of the lengths to which antinomian exegesis will go to avoid the clear teaching of Scripture. Commenting on John 15:2 ("Every branch in Me that does not bear fruit, He takes away" [NASB]), he writes:

> The phrase in John 15:2 would be better translated, "every branch in Me that beareth not fruit he lifteth up." There is no implication here that the branch is cut off and taken away. Rather, it is lifted up, evidently from trailing on the ground, that it may receive more sunlight, and thus become more fruitful.[37]

Of course, this is desperation exegesis. It is perfectly clear that this is a dead branch, that it is taken away, and that it is cast into the fire.

Barker comments on 1 John 1:9 ("If we confess our sins, he is faithful and just to forgive us our sins, and to cleanse us from all unrighteousness" [KJV]). He hurries to prevent us from thinking that, if we do not confess our sins, we will not have our sins cleansed, which is quite clearly the implication of this didactic passage. John's epistle is saying that we *must* go on confessing our sins and that makes Barker very uncomfortable. Why? Because Barker believes that, *once* a person confesses his sin, all his sins—past, present, and future—are forgiven forever whether he ever confesses again or not. So, how does he handle the problem? He hastens to add that "confession is a condition of

---

37. Harold Barker, *Secure Forever* (Neptune, N.J.: Loizeaux, 1974), p. 131.

fellowship and communion, not of salvation from the eternal penalty of sin."[38] Here is our constantly recurring dispensational Antinomianism once again. Barker is insisting that, if we once profess to believe, then, though we never for the rest of our lives again profess to believe, our salvation will be in no jeopardy, though our fellowship will be in ruins. That is, faith without works is not dead after all but very much alive, bringing everlasting life.

We need not continue with Barker here. He handles other verses in the same free way that he disposes of the two we have noticed. It is sad to see him saying, after commenting on 1 John 5:18, "that God will not let a Christian continually practice sin, and He may even call him home (to heaven)."[39] Once again, we have the notion that a converted person may be so incorrigibly wicked that there is nothing that God can do with him except take him to heaven! According to dispensational theology, the quickest way to heaven is by continually engaging in horrible wickedness after having believed in Jesus Christ! If heaven is your destination, crooked living is the straightest route.

W. W. Howard

Most dispensationalists will contend that confessing Christ before men and the ongoing confession of sin are not necessary for salvation, but W. W. Howard goes even further. Speaking of confessing Christ and its consequences according to Matthew 10:32, he remarks, "This teaching is not in any way related to the salvation of men in this age. . . . Can this be the same Saviour who in 1 John 2:1 is described as our Paraclete when we sin?"[40]

Howard does not hesitate to go on to the point of denying the propriety for praying for forgiveness:

To be propitiated to me is the cry of the publican. It is a pre-Calvary petition that no longer is befitting the sinner, for Christ has made propitiation with the Father by means of His blood (Heb. 2:17). . . . To pray for salvation is an admission of ignorance that salvation stands finished. God's solitary command is to take it by simple faith.[41]

---

38. Ibid., p. 132.
39. Ibid., p. 138.
40. W. W. Howard, "Is Faith Enough?" (Th.M. Thesis, Dallas Theological Seminary, 1941), p. 35.
41. Ibid., p. 37.

This is a step beyond most dispensationalists. We have already seen that classic dispensationalists do not believe that the prayer "forgive us our debts, as we forgive our debtors" belongs in this dispensation. Scofield has called it "legal ground." But there are very few dispensationalists hardy enough to go beyond that statement and say that we should no longer ask for forgiveness at all. Such a prayer is no longer fitting, because it has already been permanently answered in the Cross. To pray for forgiveness now is an act of unfaith rather than faith, according to Howard.

R. B. Thieme

This gentleman may have the distinction of being the frankest antinomian on the American scene today. Many examples of his totally unambiguous views could be produced, but one utterly typical statement should suffice. Addressing professed evangelicals he asks, "Do you know that if you were a genius, you couldn't figure out a way to go to hell?"[42]

Zane Hodges

In 1981, Zane Hodges wrote his *The Gospel Under Siege*. This volume states and argues the dispensational case for Antinomianism. In fact, as I shall show, the book should be entitled, "Antinomianism Under Siege." Because Hodges' book may be one of the most important dispensational volumes of this century, I will give it a more extended criticism. I stress this book's crucial importance though other, more recent volumes such as Charles Ryrie's *So Great Salvation* have replaced it on center stage.

At the very beginning of chapter 1, Hodges quotes those whom he thinks have the gospel under siege as saying, "Unless you persevere in good works, you cannot be saved," and "Unless you yield your life to the Lordship of Christ, you cannot be saved."[43] We will grant that is an accurate statement of our contention.

Yet, on the very next page the author shows that he does not understand what we are saying. There, he states that they insist that "to faith are added other conditions, or provisos, by which the essential nature of the Gospel is radically transformed."[44] Hodges funda-

---

42. R. B. Thieme, *A New Species*, p. 9.
43. Zane Hodges, *The Gospel Under Siege* (Dallas: Redencion Viva, 1981), p. 3.
44. Ibid., p. 4.

mentally misunderstands the nature of the issue when he thinks that works are some sort of addendum, something beyond the faith itself. We maintain that it is implicit in the faith from the beginning. It is merely an expression of the nature of that faith. The expression lacking, the faith is lacking. What we are saying is that justification is by faith alone, but not by the faith that is alone. It is a *working faith*. Nothing is added to the faith, but this is a part of the definition of the faith; namely, that it is genuine, authentic, true, saving, and therefore, a working faith.

So we see at the very beginning of the book (and this will persist throughout) that Hodges simply does not critique the traditional orthodox position accurately or respond to its critique of the antinomian position relevantly. Hodges, and virtually all dispensationalists, do not see the elementary difference between *non-meritorious* "requirements," "conditions," "necessary obligations," "indispensable duties," and "musts," as the natural outworking of true faith, in distinction from faith in the Savior *plus meritorious works* as the very basis of salvation. If it is a true faith, it is a working faith, and it will endeavor to meet these requirements, conditions, obligations, and necessities. Having done all, it will still say, "I am an *unprofitable* servant." At the end of a lifetime of discipleship (inevitably a very imperfect discipleship), it will still sing, "Nothing in my hands I bring, simply to Thy cross I cling."

In his fear of any "conditions" for salvation, Hodges is very hesitant to require very much of faith itself. This is quite evident in the following sentence: "To assert that a man may profess faith in Christ without knowing whether or not he has truly trusted Christ, is to articulate an inconceivable proposition."[45]

This proposition is not as inconceivable as Hodges thinks. There are two problems here. The first has to do with the object of faith and the second with the nature of the faith itself. First of all, it is by no means self-evident that the person who claims faith in Jesus Christ has necessarily believed in the Christ of Scripture. There are many popular definitions of Jesus Christ in circulation, but most of them are woefully inadequate. For example, if a person thinks of Christ as a sublime, but purely human teacher along the lines of Buddha, that person can hardly be said to have believed in the Christ of the Bible. If a person is aware of these divergent understandings of Christ and has not made a thorough examination of the matter, he may not know whether he is trusting the true Christ or one of the false ones who go by that name.

---

45. Ibid., p. 13.

Second, even if a person has an intellectual understanding of the person of Christ which is formally correct, the nature of that person's faith still must be examined. The Bible knows of at least five different meanings of the word *faith* — historical, temporary, miraculous, symbolic, and salvific.

For example, the individual may have what is commonly called "historical faith." That is, he may believe that Jesus is the Second Person of the Godhead, who was born of the Virgin Mary and became incarnate for the redemption of mankind, was delivered up for our offenses, and raised again for our justification. He may also be aware of the fact that the devils know that even better than he does. Ask this nominal Christian pointedly, "What is your trust in Christ? Is it a mere confidence that this Jesus, thus described, did indeed, and does exist? Or, are you really trusting in Him for your salvation?" How will he answer? We are not denying that some people *do* know that they do have saving faith in Jesus Christ. What we are denying is Hodges' contention that *no person* professing faith in Christ could be uncertain about the kind of faith which he actually has. I have known hundreds myself.

It is necessary to say something about Hodges' exegesis of a number of Biblical texts. Here we see both the tendentious character of his interpretation and the startling implications of his antinomian theology. In support of his position, Hodges cites the words of Christ in John 5:24:

> "Most assuredly I say to you, he who hears My word and believes in Him who sent Me has everlasting life, and shall not come into judgment, but has passed from death into life." Anyone who takes this statement at face value should be able to say, "I *know* I have everlasting life. I *know* I will not come into judgment." But if assurance arises from a simple promise like this, it can have nothing to do with works.[46]

This shows that Hodges conceives of faith as possibly existing without works. Here he is citing Christ's promise that whoever hears His word will be saved and can know it. We, of course, could not agree with him and our Lord more. We only note that, when Christ uses the words *believe*, or *faith*, or *trust*, He means "believe" or "faith" or "trust." That is, He means the real thing, a working faith and not a merely nominal faith. In fact, the faith that Christ speaks of has everything to do with works. The faith that Christ is talking about is a genuine, that is, a working faith.

---

46. Ibid., p. 10.

Commenting on the episode of the Samaritan woman at the well (John 4:4–42), Hodges insists that Christ simply promises her everlasting life. "There is no effort to extract from the woman a promise to correct her moral life. If she wants this water, she can have it. It is free!"[47] *Then Hodges forthrightly declares that had this woman continued to be the immoral person she had been up to that point, she would nonetheless have been a truly saved person*:

> If the mind of man recoils from so daring an expression of divine generosity, it recoils from the Gospel itself. If it should be thought necessary to add some intrinsic guarantee that the woman would not continue her illicit liaisons — and according to Jesus she was currently-engaged in one (4:18!) — that guarantee would add to the words of our Lord himself. The result could only be a false Gospel.[48]

That we are not misunderstanding Hodges' appalling doctrine is evident from the following statement:

> Did the woman therefore simply return to her former sinful lifestyle? The Scripture does not tell us. It is not at all the point of the story! . . . The bestowal of a superlatively valuable gift as an act of unconditional generosity was *precisely the kind of action most likely to woo her from her former ways*. It is more likely by far to have accomplished this result than any legalistic undertaking into which she might have entered. . . . her assurance did not rest on what she might later have done. It rested instead upon the uncomplicated promise of the Son of God Himself.[49]

We turn, finally, to Hodges' treatment of the Bible's *locus classicus* against Antinomianism — James 2. His reading of this passage is, to put it mildly, rather peculiar. We should also note that here the extremes of Hodges' Antinomianism become fully evident. Referring to James 2:26 ("For as the body without the spirit is dead, so also faith without works is dead" [KJV]), Hodges comments:

> No one who encountered a dead body whose vitalizing spirit had departed, would ever conclude that the body had never been alive. Quite the contrary. The presence of a corpse is the clearest proof of a *loss* of life. If we allow this illustration to speak for itself, then the presence of a dead faith shows that this faith was once alive.[50]

---

47. Ibid., p. 14.
48. Ibid.
49. Ibid.
50. Ibid., p. 20.

A number of comments are in order here. It is apparent that Hodges has missed the obvious meaning of this passage because he is fascinated by the expression of faith which, with his minimalistic understanding of faith, he always assumes is a live faith. The text says simply that faith without works is dead. It certainly says nothing about a faith which was once alive and then later died. Hodges has, in fact, made an allegory out of the word *dead* (an odd move for a professed literalist like Hodges) and thus compared it to a human corpse. James 2:26 makes the point of the passage perfectly clear. All that James says is that, just as you cannot have a man without a body and spirit together, so you cannot have a Christian without works and faith together.

On a more general level, we notice that here Hodges seems to concede what he elsewhere denies. Elsewhere he teaches that faith has "nothing to do with works," that saving faith need not issue in any fruit at all. Here he at least concedes that the lack of works is the evidence of a totally dead faith.

The second thing we notice is that Hodges states that this non-working but saving faith, which is now dead, was once actually alive. Now many readers might conclude from this that this loss of faith would result in spiritual death, that Hodges has abandoned the dispensational doctrine of "eternal security." Nothing could be further from the truth. That Hodges has not abandoned the dispensational doctrine of "eternal security" is evident in his treatment of James 2:14. In fact, the doctrine is radicalized. Hodges writes concerning James 2:14 that "James' point is quite simple: faith alone cannot save."[51] He then attempts to show that the word *saved* there means "saved from physical death."[52] Thus, Hodges contends that James is concerned with the relation of dead faith to physical life rather than eternal life. It is definitely fatal to physical life, but not at all to eternal life!

Hodges is actually defending the proposition that a dead faith may be fatal to temporal existence, but not to eternal life. What Charles Ryrie only suggests, Zane Hodges boldly proclaims. We can hardly believe what we are reading. Roman Catholicism ultimately teaches salvation by works; evangelicalism teaches salvation by working faith; Hodges teaches salvation by dead faith—by what is really no faith at all. Rather than the "perseverance of the saint," this is the "preservation of the sinner" in its most odious form.

There, in plain and candid speech, is the gospel according to Zane Hodges. We must also say that it is the gospel according to Dispensa-

---

51. Ibid., p. 23.
52. Ibid., pp. 23–27.

tionalism. Hodges is, as we have said, nothing but a consistent, if rather outspoken, dispensationalist. Our survey in this chapter has revealed that the "reasonable" dispensationalist (Ryrie) agrees with the "outspoken" dispensationalist (Hodges) that good works need not accompany faith for a person to be saved. Even more shocking, both agree that a person's faith can totally die and he will still possess eternal life. Horrible as this theology is, we cannot help but be grateful to Hodges for his candor. If this is the gospel according to Dispensationalism, it proclaims "another gospel" which is, in fact, no gospel at all.

Conclusion

Bad theology inevitably issues in bad consequences. We will conclude this general discussion with A. W. Tozer's lament—perhaps we should say dirge—regarding the tragic character of Antinomianism in so much of contemporary evangelicalism.

> Large assemblies today are being told fervently that the one essential qualification for heaven is to be an evil person, and the one sure bar to God's favor is to be a good one. The very word *Righteousness* is spoken only in cold scorn and the moral man is looked upon with pity. "A Christian," say these teachers, "is not morally better than a sinner. The only difference is that he has taken Jesus, and so he has a Saviour." I trust it may not sound flippant to inquire, *"a saviour" from what*? If not from sin and evil conduct and the old fallen life, then from what, and if the answer is, from the consequences of past sins and from judgment that comes, still we are not satisfied. Is justification from past offenses all that distinguishes a Christian from a sinner? Can a man become a believer in Christ and be no better than he was before? Does the gospel offer no more than a skillful Advocate to get guilty sinners off free at the day of judgment?[53]

In this chapter, we have seen that Dispensationalism clearly teaches Antinomianism. That is to say, it begins by teaching that men may be saved without the good works which bear witness to a living faith. It concludes, when pressed to its logical conclusion, by teaching that men may be saved with non-faith, with dead faith, with no faith, without faith. Justification without faith, and salvation without grace is its false gospel. It is ironic that Dispensationalism prides itself on its claim to exalt the free "grace" of God. The "grace" which allows the sinner to wallow endlessly in his sin on his way to heaven is certainly not grace at all.

---

53. A. W. Tozer, *Divine Conquest* (Harrisburg, Pa.: Christian Publications, 1940), pp. 35–36.

DISPENSATIONAL ANTINOMIANISM – THE ANTITHESIS OF TRUE GRACE – PART TWO: THE DOCTRINE OF SANCTIFICATION

I have shown at length that Dispensationalism is antinomian. Antinomianism has been seen to be constantly maintained both yesterday and today by representative writers. To depart from it is to depart from Dispensationalism. In this chapter, we will examine the dispensational roots of this heresy – its doctrine of sanctification.

Those who study theology for even a brief amount of time quickly learn that all of theology is interrelated. This issue is no exception. Because this chapter builds on material previously discussed, the reader may wish to review chapter 7 (which deals with the dispensational doctrine of salvation) as well as the description of historic Antinomianism at the beginning of chapter 11.

Sanctification and Justification

We begin our study of dispensational sanctification, which underlies Antinomianism, with justification which underlies sanctification. This doctrine is the crux of the Christian religion. Antinomianism is its counterfeit or caricature. It would seem, therefore, that if Dispensationalism teaches Antinomianism, it cannot consistently teach justification by faith alone.

We have seen that dispensational justification is made to apply only to the "new nature." The best way to understand the dispensational view of justification (and sanctification as well) is to understand its view of regeneration. According to the latter doctrine, a distinct ontological entity or new self, which indeed appears to be a part of the divine nature, is implanted in the soul. This results in two distinct natures in the Christian. Nothing actually happens to the old nature at all, except that it has an entirely different new nature placed alongside it.

This is to be contrasted with the traditional orthodox Reformed view in which a new foundation for action, a new disposition is implanted in the old ego, and, accordingly, the Christian is one person with two struggling principles, the new one destined to conquer the old. This is quite a different conception from the dispensational conception of two utterly distinct natures or selves.

We can see immediately that this view of regeneration has profound implications for the doctrine of sanctification. The old nature continues as before throughout earthly life only to be annihilated at death. C. H. Mackintosh illustrates this conviction well:

> Flesh is flesh, nor can it ever be made aught else but flesh. The Holy
> Ghost did not come down on the day of Pentecost to improve nature
> or to do away the fact of its incurable evil, but to baptize believers
> into one body, and connect them with their living head in Heaven.[1]

The new nature, on the other hand, is understood to be the actual indwelling divine nature of God. We have already seen that this new nature really *cannot be justified* because, being the very nature of God Himself, it could not possibly need justification.

A corollary of this is the total separation of justification from sanctification. This total separation is presupposed by dispensational Antinomianism with its conviction that one who has exercised faith in Christ may never show fruit. A person may be justified and not sanctified. Chafer speaks for the entire dispensational tradition when he says that the experience of sanctification is "absolutely unrelated to position in Christ." [2] It is one thing to say that sanctification is not the meritorious ground of justification and quite another to say that the two are "absolutely unrelated."

---

1. Steele, *Antinomianism Revived*, pp. 16–17.
2. Chafer, *Systematic Theology*, 7:279–284. See also Chafer and Walvoord, *Major Bible Themes*, p. 99.

Sanctification and Assurance

We have seen that the issue of assurance is involved in dispensational Antinomianism. Many dispensationalists will contend that sanctification and Christian experience play no role in the assurance of the believer. It was especially this doctrine of Darby that first influenced C. H. Mackintosh so greatly and decisively. Mackintosh found peace when he did not have to look for it as in any way connected with his own life; that is, in Christ's living in him, but only in the belief that Christ died for him.[3] Similarly, Scofield stated, "His own works can never be to the believer his own ground of assurance."[4] While some dispensationalists will admit that the changed life can provide some assurance that one is saved, none will concede that the lack of a changed life is positive evidence that one is *not* a Christian.

This provides further evidence of our theme in the previous chapter—that Dispensationalism has radically abstracted justification and sanctification from each other. If faith is union with Christ and union with Christ communicates both justification and sanctification, this dispensational insistence that only one's justification can alone provide assurance would seem to miss an important dimension of Biblical teaching.

The Scriptures teach that Christian experience and assurance are related. There is, first of all, the direct witness of the Holy Spirit to the Christian (see Romans 8:16). The believer's behavior also provides an important indication of the presence or absence of God's grace (see 1 John 2:3). For this reason, Reformed theology has placed a good deal of emphasis upon sanctification as evidence of the reality of one's faith. The Reformed view is summed up in the following statement often attributed to Luther and Cromwell: "The only way I can know I am saved is by knowing that I am being saved" (that is, sanctified).

It also reveals something further about the dispensational view of faith. We suppose that, when dispensationalists insist that experience is not necessarily involved in justification and salvation, they refer to a *sensing* of the presence of Christ. But, if faith is union with Christ how is faith possible without sensing Him? I will not press this point at the moment, though it is important. The dispensationalist tends to conceive of faith as merely intellectual fact. One trusts in Christ for his sal-

---

3. See Noel, *History,* 1:64–65.
4. *Scofield Reference Bible,* p. 1083.

vation. That is, he recognizes himself to be a sinner and Christ to be the proffered Savior and believing that fact he is thereby justified. If that is what Dispensationalism believes about faith, it is seriously defective. Such a non-experiential faith would be no faith at all but the kind of conviction that even devils can and do have (see James 2).

Sanctification and the Holy Spirit

Dispensationalists believe in the third person of the Trinity, but differ fundamentally from the orthodox churches with regard to the nature of His activities in different periods. They all seem to hold that the Holy Spirit was not active among the Old Testament saints in the same way that He was active among saints of the New Testament dispensation.

No one has stated the dispensational doctrine of the Holy Spirit more fully and completely than Lewis Sperry Chafer. His well-known book, *He That Is Spiritual* (which I will discuss below), is devoted to it but we will follow here the later treatment in his *Systematic Theology*. First of all, we note the denial of any work of the Holy Spirit in the Old Testament similar to that in the saints of the New Testament. "Especially to be observed is the fact that there was no provision for, and no promise of, an abiding presence of the Holy Spirit in the life of any Old Testament saint."[5]

We have seen that the Holy Spirit regenerates. What does He then do, according to dispensationalists? It seems that the Holy Spirit thereafter forever indwells the Christian believer. Unger writes, "God's dynamic to live the Christian life is the indwelling Holy Spirit, *whom every* regenerated soul possesses."[6] The Holy Spirit may be grieved and He may be quenched, but He will never, ever leave the Christian.

One would suppose that every Christian indwelt by the Spirit of God would be to some degree, at least, holy or spiritual. However, as we have seen, this is not necessarily the case. The Holy Spirit may indwell yet have no influence whatever on the Christian's life. The indwelling of the Holy Spirit does not insure that the Christian will be a spiritual person in any degree.

Kenneth Peterson spelled this out quite thoroughly in his thesis, "The Doctrine of Carnality." "Christians should not grieve or quench

---

5. Chafer, *Systematic Theology*, 7:71.
6. Merrill F. Unger, *Commentary on the Old Testament* (Chicago: Moody, 1981), p. 17.

but walk in the Spirit." But, he continues, "since the man who is carnal does not comply with these conditions, he is not filled with the Spirit."[7] Six definite effects of this follow. First, there is no spirituality and the person remains a babe in Christ. Second, there is no growth. Third, there is no godly walk. Fourth, there is no fellowship. Fellowship with God is literally "impossible." Fifth, there can be no fruit. Sixth, there is no victory but, instead, the distress of Romans 7.[8] These effects are seen in the church in the form of envy, strife, discord, ineffectiveness, and a miserable effect on the world.[9] Because of this there is no separation, no power, no witness, no intercession, no service.[10]

How can this deplorable situation be rectified? Peterson's answer is that the Spirit must be recognized. He must be "permitted" to fill the person. "That the Spirit cannot undertake in this ministry until the conditions of filling are met is obvious."[11] The "believer must open his life." "The believer is to depend upon the Spirit, and then to engage in certain positive activity himself."[12] Peterson goes on to assert that "it lies within his personal power to turn the battle over to the Spirit for solution."[13] The believer must drop things pleasing to the flesh from his life. He must feed the "Spirit nature" with the Bible. Finally, Peterson remarks, "when, such practices become the all-absorbing interest of the Christian, carnality will be again the cast off and discarded thing, right where it belongs!"[14]

So to live the life of sanctification one must yield to the Holy Spirit. We have seen that regenerate Christians — all Christians — are indwelt by the Holy Spirit. The Spirit's indwelling, however, does not imply the Spirit's outworking. According to Paul, the Spirit is working in us "to will and to do" (Philippians 2:13, KJV), but the Holy Spirit of Dispensationalism may remain — does remain in some cases — indwelling without ever leading the saint to "will and to do." In other words, the Christian may have Christ as Savior without His being Lord. The Christian may be justified without being sanctified. This is not "natural" but it may

---

7. K. N. Peterson, "The Doctrine of Carnality" (Th.M. Thesis, Dallas Theological Seminary, 1943), pp. 44–45.

8. Ibid., p. 48.

9. Ibid., p. 55.

10. Ibid., p. 59f.

11. Ibid., p. 63.

12. Ibid., p. 64.

13. Ibid. I may remark here that according to this view, the sinner controls the Holy Spirit. He must turn the battle over to the divine Spirit. "He" being the "flesh" will never do that (Galatians 5:17). So sanctification depends on the fleshly, fallen, human nature (not the Holy Spirit), and he will never choose it. This is not merely possible Antinomianism but certain Antinomianism.

14. Ibid.

happen. It *should* not be but it *may*. Indeed, as I have shown in foot-note 13, it *must* happen according to dispensational hagiology.

So, strictly speaking, what is usually called sanctification may not occur in the Christian, according to Dispensationalism. Sanctification has been called "the Christianizing of the Christian." If this doctrine be true, a dispensational Christian may—really must—exist without being Christianized.

The Mysterious "Third Nature"

Being fruitful depends, apparently, on being Spirit-filled. But being Spirit-filled depends on what? It does not depend on being Spirit-indwelt. Though one cannot be Spirit-filled without first being Spirit-indwelt, he may be Spirit-indwelt without being Spirit-filled. Again we ask, on what does being Spirit-filled depend? If it is not on the Spirit Himself, it must be on the person himself. Who is the crucial person himself? Let us examine this more closely.

On the dispensational view, a distinct ontological entity, or new self, which indeed appears to be a part of the divine nature is implanted into the soul. This results in two distinct natures in the Christian. Nothing actually happens to the old nature at all, except that it has an entirely different new nature placed alongside it. The old nature, as we noted earlier, is not sanctified; it is counterbalanced by the new. In chapter 7, we noted the irony involved in this dispensational doctrine of regenera-tion. This allegedly totally depraved old nature is, nevertheless, able of its own accord to exercise faith in Christ. A similar problem arises in connection with the doctrine of sanctification. Although the regenerate person is really the old, completely unrenovated nature, he is, never-theless, supposed to yield to the Holy Spirit and become spiritual.

The problem with this is quite simple. There is simply no way for the dispensationalist to account for the phenomenon of spirituality us-ing this model of psychology. There is, first of all, the old nature, which is really the person and which is supposed to yield to the new nature but cannot because it remains untouched. The new nature need not yield to itself for it is, in actuality, divine Spirit. The result is a stand-off with no motion toward spiritual improvement.

One way of accounting for spirituality is to say, with Reformed theology, that the Spirit begins to effect real and positive changes in the human nature of the regenerate person and that, because of this mirac-ulous grace, the Christian is enabled to grow spiritually. Dispensation-alists, as we have seen, do not say this. The only other way to account for spirituality would seem to be the positing of a third entity within the person, a mysterious "third nature" which mediates between the old and the new natures and somehow makes the crucial choice to yield or not to yield to the new nature. We should note that dispensationalists do not explicitly adopt this theory, incoherent as it is, although their system seems to demand such.

So we have seen that dispensationalists make it impossible for the person to become spiritual even though he has an obligation to be spiritual. We now come to an even more paradoxical statement. That is, in spite of the fact that the saint cannot become spiritual, he actually does become spiritual. This does not seem to bother the average dispensationalist because, when he is talking about the subject of actual spirituality, he does not think about its theoretical foundation which he has undermined.

There are some dispensationalists, however, who are aware of the problem we have noted here. Sidlow Baxter, a very moderate dispensationalist, is most interesting here. He shows sensitivity to the weaknesses of Dispensationalism and to the strength of Reformed theology, but never quite breaks with the one or embraces the other. He aptly critiques Scofield and dispensational sanctification in this astute observation:

> A regeneration which does not regenerate me, but only transplants into my being a so-called "new nature" which is not really "me," and which is always distinct from what I am in myself, is not regeneration at all.[15]

Unfortunately, most dispensationalists simply go on asserting the necessity of yielding to the Spirit without any real recognition of the problem that their theology poses at this point. Reginald Wallis is a case in point. I cite it partly because it is a sort of straight line articulation of the viewpoint, but also because it is especially lucid:

> The flesh can only be reckoned dead by the power of the new life. Such life is imparted by the Holy Spirit when the whole being—that is, spirit, soul and body—is surrendered to Him (Rom. 8:13). If your will is unyielded all your reckoning will be futile.[16]

As we say, this simply restates the dispensational position that the person is supposed to yield to the Holy Spirit if sanctification is to be produced.

---

15. J. Sidlow Baxter, *Christian Holiness Restudied and Restated* (Grand Rapids: Zondervan, 1977), p. 241. See also p. 103f.

16. Reginald Wallis, *The New Life* (New York: Loizeaux, 1932), p. 63.

Wallis views the person as spirit, soul, and body, to be sure. Nevertheless, it is the will which is crucial and which does, if anything does, the yielding which is required. How a will which is totally carnal and unregenerate can actually choose to yield goes totally unexplained. The problem is apparently unrealized.

Charles Ryrie fails, in a similar manner, to address the real problem. Using the curious metaphor of "two tapes," Ryrie maintains that the Christian has two capacities—the power for doing evil and the power for doing good. These powers, as it were, are taped out on two recorders. "It is I in pushing the button on each action who determines from which tape it comes."[17] Elsewhere, he writes that "the believer through the action of his will pushes the button which determines which nature is permitted to act."[18] We see in this that the believer is the invisible man who pushes the tape which releases one nature or the other.

What this third nature is, which determines the first and second nature's activity, is nowhere explained. Nor is it, in fact, capable of explanation. This dispensational theory of sanctification is seen to be utterly incapable of making any sense of the phenomena of spirituality.

Dispensational Perfectionism

We have already seen that, according to dispensational hagiology, the regenerate person cannot be spiritual but he must be spiritual. Though he cannot be spiritual, he nevertheless does yield and becomes spiritual. Now to cap the climax, this turns out to be an instantaneous event. That the dispensationalist would think so should not really surprise us. It is a logical deduction from his view of regeneration and its relationship to faith and sanctification. We have noticed that dispensationalists believe that regeneration is an implantation of the new, divine nature. This implantation is within the person and not in his old corrupt fallen nature. This new divine nature never does choose to do anything except what is divine or perfectly excellent. Just as truly as the old nature sins and does nothing but sin, this new nature does nothing but virtue.

Going along with this gratuitous assumption of theirs, let us suppose that the new nature does spring into action. If that action were to happen it would be instantaneous. There would be no struggle, no progress, no eradication. This is the new nature acting of itself and of

---

17. Ryrie, *Balancing the Christian Life*, pp. 35–36.
18. Ryrie, *Survey of Bible Doctrine*, p. 107.

itself alone. Being utterly divine, it always and invariably acts divinely. So its behavior is, in the nature of the case, instantaneous and perfect.

The dispensationalist may respond that there is, in fact, struggle in the Christian life. To this we simply note that the struggle of the Christian life, for the dispensationalist, is the struggle to yield to the divine nature. Once this struggle (which we have seen cannot be accounted for) is completed, the divine nature is then free to act. To the extent that the new nature acts at all, it acts divinely and perfectly.

In the previous chapter, we noted that historic Antinomianism often tends, because of its pantheistic tendency, toward implicit perfection in tandem with actual Antinomianism and its attendant licentiousness. Here we see that Dispensationalism fits this model of historic Antinomianism exactly. The actual Antinomianism proceeds from the fact that the old nature is utterly unchanged and therefore acts invariably in a sinful manner. This is considered, however, not to be inconsistent with a person being a Christian in whom the new nature actually dwells, in this instance passively. On the other hand, if the new nature is said ever to spring into action, then, to the extent that it acts, it acts instantly and perfectly. So the born-again Christian, according to the dispensationalist, is at any given moment either perfectly sinful or perfectly virtuous and instantaneously so in each instance. It all depends on which button the invisible man pushes.

It can be shown that the very words of the dispensational teachers, once they are examined, weighed, and carefully interpreted, do teach Perfectionism explicitly, just as they teach Antinomianism explicitly.

J. N. Darby

That this perfectionist tendency has been present in Dispensationalism from the very beginning is evident from the work of the founder of the movement — John Nelson Darby. Speaking of the ideal Christian life, Darby says:

> No one in the Christian state but has this life; and all this belongs to whomsoever is quickened now; but till he is sealed with the Holy Ghost, his state and condition, as alive in Christ, is not known to him, he has not got into that state in relationship with God. It is his, no doubt, but he has not got it.[19]

This is Darby's basis for a slogan that was to be oft repeated in Brethren teaching — the difference between "standing" and "state." A man's

---

19. Darby, *Letters*, 2:408.

standing is perfect before God, though his state may not be. This might seem to be only the traditional distinction between justification and sanctification but it is not. In Reformed teaching this difference is one of fact; in Dispensational teaching it is one of knowledge only. That is, according to the Reformed view, the justified person is not perfectly sanctified; according to the other view, the justified person is implicitly perfectly sanctified but he does not know or feel it. That is the point of Darby's remark, "till he is sealed with the Holy Ghost, his state and condition, as alive in Christ, is not known to him." When he is sealed then he becomes aware of the fact. Sealing does not create the fact. Just as an unconscious man is alive but does not know it, when he regains consciousness, he knows he is alive. His regaining of consciousness does not make him alive, it only enables him to recognize himself as alive all the while he was unconscious.

All of this is implicit, as we have seen above, in the dispensational doctrine of regeneration. Thus, Darby could say that "conduct is the display of the divine nature in Christ."[20] Naturally, if conduct is the display of the divine nature in us, it must needs be perfect. What better statement of sinless perfection could be found than this by Darby?

> He that is born of God does not practice sin. The reason is evident; he is made partaker of the nature of God; he derives his life from him. . . . This new nature has not in it the principle of sin, so as to commit it. How could it be that the divine nature could sin?[21]

L. S. Chafer

Lewis Sperry Chafer is as clear as anyone on this implicit Perfectionism. We are fortunate in having a review of his book, *He That Is Spiritual*, by the Princeton theologian, B. B. Warfield, which demonstrates the perfectionist commitment of Chafer.[22] Warfield argued that, in Chafer, two traditions were struggling for expression—the evangelical Presbyterianism in which he was reared and the "Higher Life," or Keswick movement thinking of the coterie of Bible teachers with whom he had come in contact. The former was Reformed, the latter Arminian. In line with the latter, Chafer maintained that becoming a

---

20. Ibid., p. 478.

21. Darby, *Collected Writing*, 5:403–404.

22. B. B. Warfield, "Review of L. S. Chafer, *He That Is Spiritual*, *Princeton Theological Review* 17 (1919):322–327; Lewis Sperry Chafer, *He That Is Spiritual* (New York: 1918).

spiritual man was at the option of the individual, a mere claiming of the blessing is all that there is to it.[23] He speaks of "letting God" and "engaging" the Holy Spirit, and "making it possible for God" to do things. The spiritual life was accomplished "not by trying but by a right adjustment."[24] By this an "unbroken victory" was altogether possible.[25] "The Christian may realize *at once* the heavenly virtues of Christ."[26]

In spite of all these statements, Chafer ostensibly repudiated Pentecostalism, second blessing theology, and sinless perfection.[27] Chafer's indictment of sinless perfection is tantamount to a rejection of the claim that sin can be completely eradicated in favor of the notion of suppression (called "control"). But Dr. Warfield rightly concluded that his teaching was indistinguishable from what is ordinarily understood as the "second-blessing," and other hall-marks of Perfectionism. Warfield contends that this belief in possible complete suppression is of the essence of Perfectionism, which has always maintained that a fall from a state of sinless perfection is possible.

That Chafer did not benefit from the salutary criticisms of Warfield is apparent from his later writing, indeed his last writings. We now consider Chafer's response. In a later edition of Chafer's book, he gives a detailed response to Warfield's criticisms, and so today we enjoy the benefit of a major work, articulating the dispensational view, a major critique from a Reformed theologian, with an extensive reply by Chafer himself.

The first thing Chafer notices in Warfield's criticism is that the latter says that Chafer, "subjects the gracious working of God to human determination."[28] What Warfield was saying at that point was in reference to the control of the new nature by the mysterious "he" in dispensational sanctification. We have already presented that thinking in considerable detail—as a matter of fact, in much more detail than Warfield ever enters into in his review. Warfield, not having probed the matter as deeply as we have necessarily had to do, simply notices that the Chaferian thought has the Christian himself determining the Spirit's activity in sanctification. When Warfield wrote that, Ryrie had

---

23. Chafer, *He That Is Spiritual*, pp. 129, 146.

24. Ibid., p. 39.

25. Ibid., p. 96.

26. Ibid., p. 39.

27. Ibid., pp. 47, 31, 107, 139.

28. Ibid., pp. 68–69, note. Note the discussion of the Chafer-Warfield matter in Curtis I. Crenshaw and Grover E. Gunn, III, *Dispensationalism Today, Yesterday, and Tomorrow* (Memphis: Footstool Publications, 1985).

not yet coined his metaphor about the two tape recorders, with its assumption of a third entity. But the thought was already present, without that metaphor, in Chafer also. Warfield is simply taking Chafer at face value on this matter, though not without considerable doubt about the identity of this controlling human agent.

What is Chafer's reply? First, he insists that he believes with Warfield that God determines everything and that He realizes everything that He determines. Chafer insists that he is as Calvinistic as Warfield on this matter. But, he adds:

> there is equal emphasis in the Scriptures upon the fact that lying between these two undiminished aspects of His sovereignty—His eternal purpose and its perfect realization—He has permitted sufficient latitude for some exercise of the human will. In so doing, His determined ends are in no way jeopardized. There is difficulty here, but what, in Scripture, is difficult for the finite mind to harmonize is doubtless harmonized in the mind of God.[29]

Chafer misses Warfield's point. Warfield never denies the reality of human choices. He is simply teaching the Reformed doctrine that God works grace into the soul before the soul works grace out. We work out because He is working within. He accuses Chafer of reversing the process, thus subjecting the gracious working of God to human determination. We have noted this repeatedly in the writing of Chafer and other dispensationalists.

The situation is even worse than Warfield realized. This human determination is either by the corrupt human, fallen, depraved nature, which would never make such a choice as that, or by this invisible, nonexistent human person. In other words, it is a human sinner or else a nonentity who actually determines the gracious working of God. Chafer's reply, that he believes in the reality of Christian choices, does not touch Warfield's point, which is that genuinely human Christian choices follow, rather than precede, God's gracious working.

As Chafer goes further in his reply to Warfield, he sinks deeper and deeper into error:

> Though it is revealed that God must impart the moving, enabling grace whereby one may believe unto salvation (John 6:44, cf. 12:32), or whereby one may yield unto a spiritual life (Philippians 2:13), it is as clearly revealed that, within His sovereign purpose and power,

---

29. Ibid., p. 68.

God has everywhere conditioned both salvation and spiritual life upon these human conditions.[30]

This is a flat contradiction. Chafer is saying in the first part of the sentence that he acknowledges Warfield's point, that God does initiate faith unto justification and grace unto sanctification. Having genuflected at the Calvinistic shrine, Chafer then goes on to contradict what he has said by his concluding remark, that God has "everywhere conditioned both salvation and spiritual life upon these human conditions." How can the divine activity be conditioned upon human activity and human activity be conditioned upon divine activity at the same moment in time? (It is agreed by Warfield and Chafer that God's working *in* leads to the saint's working *out* which in turn leads to God's working *in* etc., but that is not what is being debated here.) It has to be one or the other. It cannot be both. In the first part of the sentence, Chafer is talking as a Calvinist. In the end of the sentence he is a pure Pelagian. He has the option of being a Calvinist or a Pelagian, but not of being both.

Next, Chafer addresses himself to the charge, discussed above, that the dispensational theory of sanctification involves instantaneous change from carnality to spirituality:

The same reviewer objects to the teaching that there is any sudden change possible from the carnal state to the spiritual state. To quote: "He who believes in Jesus Christ is under grace, and his whole course, in its process and in its issue alike, is determined by grace, and therefore, having been predestined to be conformed to the image of God's Son, he is surely being conformed to that image, God Himself seeing to it that he is not only called and justified but also glorified. You may find Christians at every stage of this process, for it is a process through which all must pass; but you will find none who will not in God's own time and way pass through every stage of it. There are not two kinds of Christians, although there are Christians at every conceivable stage of advancement towards the one goal to which all are bound and at which all shall arrive."[31]

Here the reader can see that Warfield is objecting to this notion of the two natures which alternately are in operation in perfect sinfulness or perfect spirituality. As a Reformed theologian, he sees instead a

---

30. Ibid.
31. Ibid.

gradual struggle toward conquest of the remaining corruption, with a mixture of good and evil in all of the actions of the regenerate person.

What is Chafer's reply to this fundamental criticism? In the light of Chafer's teaching, the first part of his reply is incredible: "Doubtless there are varying degrees of carnality as there are varying degrees of spirituality."[32] We are fully aware of the fact that Chafer and others are constantly saying this but, as I have pointed out more than once, they have no basis in their view of sanctification for saying it. As we have seen, the carnal nature is counterbalanced rather than changed by the spiritual. Thus, Chafer's claim that the carnal nature is subject to "varying degrees" is, in terms of his system, an incoherent statement.

Chafer is not yet finished. He believes that the matter may be clarified by resorting to a distinction between "spirituality" and "growth." He remarks with reference to Warfield, "In this reviewer's mind, the change from carnality to spirituality is evidently confused with Christian growth."[33] Chafer goes on to write:

> Christian growth is undoubtedly a process of development under the determined purpose of God which will end, with the certainty of the Infinite, in a complete likeness to Christ; but spirituality is the present state of blessing and power of the believer who, at the same time, may be very immature. A Christian can and should be spiritual from the moment he is saved. Spirituality, which is the unhindered manifestation of the Spirit in life, is provided to the full *for* all believers who "confess" their sins, "yield" to God, and "walk not after the flesh, but after the Spirit." When these conditions are complied with, the results are immediate; for no process is indicated. Jacob, an Old Testament type, was completely changed in one night.[34]

These sentences simply make no sense. Their incoherence is easily seen by asking a simple question—what is it that "grows"? Certainly it is not the old carnal nature, for this nature remains as it was although it may possibly be counterbalanced. Certainly it is not the new nature for this new nature is the indwelling Spirit of God and the divine nature is certainly not subject to "growth." The only thing which might be said to grow is the mythical "third nature" which again seems to be implied by the dispensational system but is, alas, nowhere to be found.

The speciousness of Chafer's distinction between "growth" and "spirituality" is also evident when one examines the true nature of

32. Ibid.
33. Ibid.
34. Ibid.

Christian growth. Chafer's distinction implies that spiritual immaturity is generally a state of childishness, innocent and undeveloped. But the acts of the old nature are not innocent and undeveloped; they are acts of wickedness. If Chafer was really trying to talk about a process of "spiritual growth" he would talk about a person growing out of his sensuality or sinfulness into greater and greater spirituality. That is exactly what Warfield is saying, and that is what spiritual growth does mean. There is no confusion in such a statement. But for Chafer, that is not the way sanctification operates. Men do not daily die more and more to sin and live more and more to righteousness. Corrupt human nature is not changed for the better by the miracle of God's grace. Rather, a man bounces back and forth between dominion by the carnal nature and control by the spiritual nature. He momentarily lives totally to sin or totally to righteousness.

We have seen that the later dispensationalists examined above, such as Ryrie and Peterson, operate with precisely the same conceptual schema as Chafer. Whether one speaks of a carnal and a spiritual nature or of Ryrie's "two tapes," the basic idea is the same—a carnal nature which is never really changed for the better and a spiritual nature which is, in reality, the infinite being of God.

The Historical Context of Dispensational Perfectionism

The perfectionist strain in Dispensationalism that we have considered is, in fact, super-perfectionism. It imputes the perfection of God to the Christian. The new nature, as we have seen, is the divine nature and that never needed perfecting, but has always, everlastingly, in and of itself, and immutably, been perfect. When that nature acts, it cannot act any other way than perfectly. So when the action of the new nature is attributed to the Christian person, that Christian is perfect with the perfection of deity.

This perfectionist element in Dispensationalism is what led Warfield to identify it with that type of movement. As we have seen, however, dispensational theologians do not take kindly to such a label. Chafer, as we saw, took pains to distinguish his own views from Wesleyan and Keswick Perfectionism. This repeated charge has created a problem for the dispensational self-understanding. They know that Protestantism, generally, is anti-perfectionist. Claiming to be four-point Calvinists, they think of themselves as Reformed, and Reformed theology is always anti-perfectionist. Consequently, when Dispensationalism

lapses into the perfectionist heresy, it is bound to be somewhat unconscious of it. That being the case, it is going to be very reluctant to
use the word *perfection* favorably. So one must listen carefully for
synonyms for the same idea and for tendencies that indubitably imply
that conclusion.

Nevertheless, recent historical research has confirmed the existence
of a genetic link between Dispensationalism and Perfectionism.
George Marsden has noted the wave of interest in holiness and in the
work of the Holy Spirit which characterized American evangelicalism
in the late nineteenth century. This had been preceded by over a century of complex interaction between the Wesleyan perfectionist
groups, which stressed the possibility of actual freedom from known
sin and viewed sanctification as a single event or "second blessing," and
Reformed thinkers who dismissed the possibility of actually attaining
to a state of sinless perfection and who viewed sanctification as a process. Marsden writes:

> These two opposed views clashed at first and were then synthesized
> during the evangelical revivals of the first half of the nineteenth cen-
> tury in America. Charles Finney brought the two views together and
> by 1840 was introducing something very similar to the Methodist
> holiness teaching into Reformed circles.[35]

The addition of British elements to this American matrix of holiness
concerns eventually gave birth to the so-called "Keswick Movement."
As Marsden notes, the Keswick theory of sanctification involved the
notion of the "counteraction" of the sinful nature by the "filling of the
Spirit." Marsden writes:

> The rest of Keswick teaching follows from these concepts of sin and
> counteracting grace. There are two stages of Christian experience:
> that of the "carnal Christian," and that of the "spiritual." To move
> from the lower to the higher state takes a definite act of faith or "con-
> secration," the prerequisite to being filled with the Spirit. This conse-
> cration means an "absolute surrender," almost always described by
> the Biblical term "yielding." Self is dethroned, God is enthroned.[36]

The similarities of Keswick sanctification theory to the Dispensationalism described above are patently obvious. This is entirely under-

---

35. Marsden, *Fundamentalism and American Culture*, p. 74.
36. Ibid., p. 78.

standable in that Charles Trumbull, Scofield's protégé, was a central figure in the Keswick movement and Scofield "eventually more or less canonized Keswick teachings in his *Reference Bible*."[37] Marsden is undoubtedly correct in saying that "Dispensationalist and Keswick teachings were two sides of the same movement."[38] (Though, of course, its opposite, dispensational Antinomianism, must never be forgotten.)

Although there are some slight differences of emphasis, dispensational and Keswick sanctification theories reduce to the same basic set of concerns—the counterbalancing of the sin nature by the indwelling divine Spirit, the necessity of yielding to the divine presence within, the possibility of living without sin when controlled by the Spirit, and the division of Christians into the categories of carnal and spiritual. Thus, it is clear that Dispensationalism teaches a form of Perfectionism and that it has clear historical connections to explicitly perfectionist movements. There is, therefore, little reason to deny Dispensationalism the label of Perfectionism—however loathe dispensationalists themselves may be to accept it, and however inconsistent their undeniable Antinomianism.

The Cost of Error

The cost of theological error is often high and the dispensational doctrine of sanctification has exacted a particularly heavy toll on the church. This doctrine of sanctification has contributed to the desiccation of the personal spirituality of many Christians. Furthermore, the Antinomianism which inevitably attends this doctrine has severely compromised the witness of the church before a watching world. Perhaps most tragic is the false assurance given by Dispensationalism to many who have no valid reason to consider themselves Christians.

Personal Spirituality

We have seen that the dispensational theory of sanctification is utterly incapable of accounting for the phenomenon of true Christian spirituality. Instead of a steady pattern of genuine spiritual progress and growth through dependence upon divine grace, Dispensationalism offers the Christian an endless pattern of vacillation between the poles of carnality and spirituality. Instead of growing personal wholeness

---

37. Ibid., p. 79.
38. Ibid., p. 80.

and inner healing, Dispensationalism offers the believer a schizophrenia of two mutually exclusive natures.

Dispensationalism implicitly counsels the Christian to "let go and let God," but it cannot empower him to do so. The Pauline formula for sanctification is very different. Rather than counseling passivity and nonresistance to an indwelling new divine nature, the Apostle urges the positive action of obedience. Paul understood that it is only as we actively obey that we recognize our dependence on God's grace. His words to the church at Philippi illustrate this truth well:

> So then, my beloved, just as you have always obeyed, not as in my presence only, but now much more in my absence, work out your salvation with fear and trembling; for it is God who is at work in you, both to will and to work for His good pleasure. (Philippians 2:12–13, NASB)

This point cannot be overemphasized. After all, Dispensationalism is a popular movement and people live their lives by these formulae. I am myself one of those who, at one time assuming this view of sanctification to be correct, can remember the psychological anguish I went through trying to cultivate spirituality by such a fallacious theory of sanctification. There are many people in the dispensational school of thought, including, I am afraid, most of the teachers, who simply do not see the error of this teaching. They endeavor, undoubtedly in great agony, to live out its impossible principles.

Antinomianism

Probably the most pernicious error to spring from this dispensational theory of sanctification is its Antinomianism. It is the most pernicious because it immediately affects a person's very behavior, and it makes it possible for a person to be considered a true Christian while acting in a way that would make Satan proud of him. It also allows a person to have false assurance of salvation in spite of adultery, murder, or other crimes as part of his standard behavior.

Even if a person does not fall into the grosser forms of sin, Dispensationalism offers little incentive for total commitment. When I stressed Christian discipleship on a certain Christian campus, a student asked me in utter earnestness, "Are you trying to say that to be a Christian one must follow Jesus Christ?" Undoubtedly, this person and thousands and thousands of others have learned from Dispensationalism that there is no need to fear the judgment seat of Christ.

Antinomianism springs from the dispensationalists' view of sanctification because it supposes sanctification to be merely the manifestation of the perfect, divine, new nature by the agency of the Holy Spirit. It is apparent that, if sanctification is but the manifestation of the divine nature within, there is no need of holding by the law which is fundamentally negative. This new nature has no inclination to do the things forbidden in the law, therefore it is irrelevant for the new nature. We have seen that dispensationalists view the Christian as not under the law in any sense at all—even as a rule of life.

All of this is bad enough; what is worse is that dispensationalists consistently proceed to regard violations of the commands of the law as not related to one's salvation by grace. This horrible error may appear inoffensive because it is sometimes stated as if it were a proper corollary of the doctrine of justification by faith. If one is justified by faith, it is true that no infraction of the law can destroy that justification. "The just shall live by faith" (Romans 1:17, KJV). Having begun in faith, Christians know that they cannot be perfected by the flesh (see Galatians 3:3). Their righteousness came "apart from the law" (Romans 3:21) in the sense of not being based upon their perfect keeping of the law. Believers in perfect justification also believe in imperfect sanctification in this life.

All this may resemble the dispensational doctrine superficially, but only superficially. In substance, Dispensationalism is radically different. It believes that regeneration brings a new divine nature that is separate from the old nature and unaffected by it, and that justification applies only to this new nature. The old nature continues to sin, and indeed, does nothing but sin, because it is utterly unaffected by sanctification. But since the dispensationalists do not really believe in the salvation of the sinner (who desperately needs it), but only of the saint (who as a part of God does not need it), he does not care what this old nature does. How the old nature behaves does not affect the "salvation" of the new nature at all. The old nature may violate the law of God all the day long, but that does not affect the new nature. A person may actually have the old nature operating all the time in the business of sin and nothing but sin, but, since it is the old nature, it does not affect his salvation. Therefore, a person may be a murderer, adulterer, thief, blasphemer, hater of God and man all the moments of all the days of his life, without ever "losing his salvation" or being in the slightest danger of doing so. That all this is a frightful travesty on the Biblical doctrine of being saved by grace apart from the works of the law is manifest.

The Reformed doctrine, which recognizes that the man himself is regenerated (that is, that the old nature is given a new principle of life and this new principle, though it does not eradicate the other, becomes dominant over it), states that this regenerated person will strive after holiness without which no man shall see the Lord (see Hebrews 12:14). If he does not do so, it is manifest that he has not had the new birth at all. He does not rest his new birth or his justification on the excellence of the life he lives, but he rests the ascertaining of the presence of a new nature on the life he lives. He does not establish his election *on* his works, but *by* them he makes it sure to himself. He does not work out his justification, but he does work out his sanctification if God is working in him to will and to do. If he is not working out, he knows that God is not working in. There is no possibility, on the one hand, of legalism; nor, on the other hand, of carnal security. As Luther, Calvin, the Reformation, and all sound teachers, we are justified by faith alone, but not by a faith that is alone.

We notice, with relief, that many dispensationalists are better Christians than their theology allows. Mercifully, many have not worked out their principles in life with the consistency that logically should have been. Nevertheless, there is a definite degree of approximation in life to what is held so tenaciously in thought. There is no question that Dispensationalism has been relatively indifferent to strict morality and usually indifferent to reform activities. Its preaching has always been very lopsidedly balanced in favor of their notion of grace with a conspicuous absence of moral stress. As a matter of fact, in some of their circles it would be assumed that a man is a liberal if he preached on humility or self-discipline.

Let it be noted that we are not simply hanging up in public view some of Dispensationalism's dirty laundry. Every movement in every branch of the Christian church has its dirty clothes, and to speak of it publicly would not tend to advance the interest of the kingdom of God in most cases. Nor is it denied, on the other hand, that Dispensationalism has some good features that are worthy of commendation. For one thing, these men are notably zealous—but alas for an unsound system of doctrine and practice. For another, they make an attempt to ground their positions on the Scriptures. But, we mention the above faults because they grow directly out of their faulty doctrine of sanctification. They illustrate their Antinomian teachings, and dispensationalists cannot properly point to these things as deviations from their teachings.

THIRTEEN

THE LORDSHIP CONTROVERSY AND THE DEMISE OF DISPENSATIONALISM

T he last chapter of this book deals with current history. The church is presently faced with a struggle equal in importance to the fourth-century Nicene battle for the deity of Christ and the Reformation struggle for the doctrine of justification by faith. In both of these previous controversies, the very gospel of Jesus Christ was at stake. The situation is no different today. We have shown throughout this volume that Dispensationalism teaches a different gospel. The gospel of dispensational Antinomianism declares that a person may have Christ as Savior but refuse to accept Him as Lord of one's life. This battle has been called the "Lordship Salvation" controversy.

The Historical Context of the Controversy

This controversy is especially important because of the historical context in which it occurs. In the last decade of the twentieth century, mainline "Christianity" is in decline—both theologically and sociologically. Liberal theology is "another gospel," and the mainline churches which espouse it are increasingly becoming the "sideline" churches as their memberships vote with their feet. Liberalism, secularism, and "post-Christianity" dominate the scene, especially in Europe and

America. Only those denominations out of the mainstream and fighting against its heavy flow are spreading a gospel that bears any resemblance to the Biblical original.

Among these would-be-faithful, dispensationalists have, in the twentieth century, been the most numerous, though they bear a twisted gospel. In the historical section of this volume, we saw that this prominence is due to an accident of history, to the fact that dispensationalists were able to market their theology as a viable alternative to the theological modernism or liberalism which swept into the major denominations during the early part of this century. It is perhaps not surprising that the Lordship controversy erupted during a period in which the decline of the mainline churches became evident and during which evangelicalism has turned its attention somewhat from a discredited external enemy to the task of getting its own theological house in order. The evangelical world is gradually realizing that, in spite of its great zeal, Dispensationalism really lacks the Biblical wisdom it claims so uniquely to possess.

All this dispensational defection from the gospel has come to a head in the Lordship controversy. Indeed, the debate itself has hardened many in their Antinomianism. Of course, dispensational Antinomianism has been pointed out since the earliest days of the movement, but there has been a veritable explosion of it in recent years. The fact that the antinomian tendencies of Dispensationalism were previously held somewhat in check is due to the fact that, early in its history, Dispensationalism was grafted on to theologies and church traditions, such as Calvinism, where the law of God and obedience to it were held in high esteem.

The parallel between the present situation and the Reformation period may be extended. Luther and Calvin undertook the Reformation struggle because of the doctrine of justification by faith alone, even though the Roman church held to many other indispensable verities of the Christian religion. Why so? They recognized that the doctrine of justification was central to God's grace and that justification is *only* through the faith which unites the believer with Christ. All the truths of the Roman faith were of no value if redemption could not reach perishing sinners. Luther was willing even to keep the papacy if only the pope would let God's people have a completely gracious salvation. When he would not, the pope had to go.

The situation is the same today. Scofield and his followers exercise a kind of papal infallibilism over thousands and thousands of evangelicals. In spite of numerous contemporary fringe changes, Dispensationalism in America is still essentially Scofieldian, and teachers with the imprimatur of dispensational "orthodoxy" wield tremendous power and influence over many Christians. That they have not exercised that authority wisely is abundantly evident.

The Terms of the Debate

As early as 1969, Charles Ryrie had called attention to differences within evangelicalism over this issue in his *Balancing the Christian Life*. When I was lecturing on church history at Campus Crusade's conference grounds in Fort Collins, Colorado in the late seventies, I called attention to the various appearances of Antinomianism in the church through the centuries. After a class a student asked me to read Dr. Ryrie's book and tell the class whether it was antinomian. I did read it and regretfully reported to the class of some four hundred crusaders that, in fact, it was. Later I spoke and corresponded with Dr. Ryrie and published my little *Primer on Dispensationalism* in 1982, where I noted this fundamental and fatal error of Antinomianism.

Without question, the most serious and effective attack on dispensational Antinomianism has come from within dispensational ranks. Though many others had said the same things before him, when John MacArthur, almost universally recognized as a respected dispensationalist himself, wrote *The Gospel According to Jesus*, the fat was in the fire.[1]

A brief summary of MacArthur's epochal book as it applies to the Lordship controversy is in order. The essential declaration of *The Gospel According to Jesus* is that Jesus Himself insists that if a person does not take up Christ's cross and follow Him that person does not have saving faith in Him and will be disowned and damned by Him at the day of judgment. That is shown through parable after parable, teaching after teaching, and illustration after illustration. The appendix adds insult to injury against Dispensationalism's antinomian teaching by showing that the church's historic understanding of the gospel has always recognized the necessity of obedience. The question in the mind of the non-dispensational reader is why would such an obviously sound book cause the flicker of an eye, not to mention an ecclesiastical earthquake.

---

1. John MacArthur, Jr., *The Gospel According to Jesus* (Grand Rapids: Zondervan, 1988).

But a controversy of enormous proportions has resulted none the less. Since then there has been an explosion of materials written on both sides of the question. The evangelical journal *Christianity Today* aptly referred to the Lordship controversy as a "volcanic issue" and the controversy shows little signs of dying down.[2] It is possible to mention only a few of these works although a very lengthy list could be compiled. Notable dispensational statements have been written by Charles Ryrie, Zane Hodges, G. M. Cocoris, and Livingston Blauvelt, Jr.[3] Whatever the other effects of the controversy may be, it has forced such dispensationalists to be much more baldly explicit in their Antinomianism.

Recent materials critical of Dispensationalism on this issue have not been lacking either. Curtis I. Crenshaw and Grover E. Gunn, III, made a notable contribution in 1985 with their *Dispensationalism Today, Yesterday, and Tomorrow*.[4] Coming from two scholars who knew Dispensationalism from the inside as students at Dallas Theological Seminary, this volume is a thorough study of crucial Biblical passages with an especially fine examination of eschatology and a masterful defense of the Reformed faith.

Vern Poythress, professor of New Testament at Westminster Theological Seminary, has continued the tradition of O. T. Allis and B. B. Warfield with his incisive Reformed criticism of Dispensationalism. His irenic yet penetrating *Understanding Dispensationalists* is well worth reading—especially the treatment of dispensational hermeneutics.[5]

Christianity Today, sensing the significance of the Lordship controversy, gave us the responses of three well-known dispensationalists—S. Lewis Johnson, Jr., Charles C. Ryrie, and Zane Hodges. Uninformed readers would hardly realize the momentous significance of the controversy from Dr. Johnson's low-key survey article, which tended to emphasize commonalities rather than differences. Johnson explained the battle as largely a failure to communicate: "The problem of definitions accounts for the fact that persons holding the same theological views

---

2. *Christianity Today*, September 22, 1989, p. 21.

3. Charles Ryrie, *So Great Salvation*; Zane Hodges, *The Gospel Under Siege*; *Absolutely Free* (Grand Rapids: Zondervan, 1989); G. M. Cocoris, *Lordship Salvation—Is It Biblical?* (Dallas: Redencion Viva, 1983); *Evangelism: A Biblical Approach* (Chicago: Moody, 1984); Livingston Blauvelt, Jr., "Does the Bible Teach Lordship Salvation," *Bibliotheca Sacra* 143 (1986):37–45.

4. Curtis I. Crenshaw and Grover E. Gunn, III, *Dispensationalism Today, Yesterday, and Tomorrow* (Memphis: Footstool, 1985).

5. Vern S. Poythress, *Understanding Dispensationalists* (Grand Rapids: Zondervan, 1987).

debate and disagree with one another."[6] The reality of the matter is that Johnson is about half right — this is not a two-sided but a one-sided fault. Lordship teachers generally have defined the issue correctly while the dispensational antinomians have routinely failed to grasp the basic issues at stake. Johnson should have so ruled rather than give the impression that the whole affair is a logomachy.

Let me illustrate this striking failure to comprehend the issues by briefly examining the responses of a number of noted dispensationalists to the controversy.

Charles Ryrie

In his book, *So Great Salvation*, Ryrie is feeling the pressure of his Antinomianism more keenly than ever before in his long-term opposition to Lordship teaching. Indeed, the book itself is curiously double-minded. On the one hand, he is virtually driven to the wall of the deathbed convert. The only believer who didn't follow the Lord he says, didn't because he didn't live to do so! He "never had time to show he was a disciple."[7] Ryrie is virtually admitting that believers immediately follow Jesus Christ in this world unless death prevents them.

> Every Christian will bear spiritual fruit. Somewhere, sometime, somehow. Otherwise that person is not a believer. Every born again individual will be fruitful. Not to be fruitful is to be faithless, without faith, and therefore without salvation.[8]

"Somewhere, sometime, somehow." That is not enough, Dr. Ryrie. The Holy Spirit never leaves or forsakes the saint, and the Holy Spirit *always* bears the fruit of the Spirit.

Ryrie goes on to show that he has missed the point, contending that "learning and obeying are not *prerequisites* for believing, they are *products* of believing."[9] What Lordship teacher ever said otherwise? Does this champion of Antinomianism not understand that the issue is the *immediacy* of that product? Obedience is not prior to faith; neither is it subsequent in time. If faith came at the very minute of death, obedience would come with it. Of course, the dying individual would not

---

6. S. Lewis Johnson, "How Faith Works," *Christianity Today*, September 22, 1989, pp. 21–25.
7. Ryrie, *So Great Salvation*, p. 103.
8. Ibid., p. 46.
9. Ibid., p. 105.

be able to show it or even say it before he dies, but the Lord knows it and so do we because the Lord tells us so.

That Ryrie cannot grasp the distinction between a necessary condition and a meritorious condition is apparent in the following passage:

> The question is not whether believers will sin, or whether they will bear fruit. They will sin, and they *will* bear fruit. . . . The question is whether commitment . . . is a necessary part of faith and thus of the gospel.[10]

On the other hand, in spite of all of his concessions, Ryrie simply will not give up his Antinomianism or understand the Biblical doctrine of sanctification. To the statements cited above must also be added his suggestion that it is possible for one who has truly believed, not only not to show fruit, but to cease believing in Christ altogether and still to receive eternal life.[11] This is Antinomianism of the most radical sort. Instead of the perseverance of the saint, this is the preservation of the sinner.

Zane Hodges

We dealt with this chief figure in the Lordship controversy more extensively in the previous chapter. Nevertheless, a few comments are in order here. The title of Hodges recent volume, *Absolutely Free*, points graphically to the extent of his misunderstanding of the matter. He extends his finger into the light for a moment by granting that a true believer does become an obedient disciple. But he quickly draws back that timid finger by saying that true Christians *can drop out of Christ's school but not out of Christ*. Obedience is still an elective course in Christ's academy—not required. Antinomianism is still the gospel.[12]

Salvation is "absolutely free" but not in the way Hodges imagines. It is absolutely free because Christ has fulfilled all the meritorious requirements for it. It is, however, not *absolutely free from good works*. If the gospel is free from good works, it is not the gospel. Salvation is God's great gift whose very purpose is to produce good works. The words of Christ cannot be more clear on this matter: "Not everyone who says to me, 'Lord, Lord,' will enter the kingdom of heaven, but only he who does the will of my Father who is in heaven" (Matthew 7:21, NIV).

---

10. Ibid., p. 107.

11. Ibid., p. 141, critiqued above.

12. Hodges, *Absolutely Free*, see chapter on "Dropping Out."

Livingston Blauvelt, Jr.

Blauvelt remarks that MacArthur's teaching regarding Lordship salvation "is false because it subtly adds works to the clear and simple condition for salvation."[13] Again, this fundamental failure to comprehend is evident. Lordship teaching does not "add works," as if faith were not sufficient. The "works" are part of the definition of faith. It is a working faith which unites the believer with Christ, not a mere nominal or dead faith.

J. Dwight Pentecost

Pentecost writes, "Good works in the believer's life are the *result* of salvation; they are not the cause."[14] Here, in a principal disputant, is the loose use of the word *salvation*. We have seen that Christ repeatedly makes good works a condition for salvation (see Matthew 7:21). "Salvation," in the broadest sense, includes good works. "Salvation" is more than salvation from the penalty of sin; it is also salvation from the misery of sinful practices. The "work" of Philippians 2:13 and elsewhere is *identified* with "salvation" and is not merely a "result" of it.

We could hope that what Pentecost means is that "good works" are an immediate corollary and not a cause of *justification*. This is exactly what Lordship advocates teach, but Pentecost thinks he is defending anti-Lordship teaching by making his observation.

Ray A. Stanford

Antinomians typically misunderstand the relationship between faith and repentance, and this is especially evident in this statement by Stanford: "Notice that the Bible states here that we are to proclaim repentance toward God. Nothing here about turning from sin."[15]

How does one "proclaim repentance" without thereby proclaiming a hatred of sin and a turning from it? If there is "nothing here about turning from sin," there is nothing here about repentance. Repentance (*metanoia*) is mentally and spiritually turning from sin (implying outward action). This is precisely what repentance does proclaim.

---

13. Blauvelt, "Does the Bible Teach," p. 38.
14. J. Dwight Pentecost, "A Christian Perspective," *Bibliotheca Sacra*, Winter, 1988, p. 11.
15. Ray A. Stanford, *Handbook of Personal Evangelism*, p. 87.

I occasionally see a practicing homosexual who understands this issue far more accurately than the antinomians. He believes that Jesus Christ is the Son of God and only Savior of mankind. This man knows that if he ever came to saving faith in Christ, Christ would have saved him instantly. This person also knows that if he does not repent and believe he will certainly go to hell forever—and deserve it. This particular perishing sinner is utterly orthodox, convicted of the wrongness of his sin, but unwilling to repent and forsake it. He is unsaved and he knows it. He knows that if he were born of God he would enter the kingdom of God—something which practicing homosexuals do not do (see 1 Corinthians 6:9).

What Is at Stake

This is no mere ivory tower concern. It is not an esoteric debate among theologians; the antinomian threat is everywhere. Antinomianism has penetrated, and in many cases permeated, many evangelical churches in America. This false gospel is even spread by missionaries in foreign lands. A Reformed lawyer friend now serving with our military in a foreign land has given me permission to use here a letter he recently wrote to me.

Dear Dr. Gerstner,

I am a lawyer serving with the U.S. Air Force in Madrid, Spain. . . . [M]y beliefs are now firmly in the Reformed camp.

Living in Madrid, I have made the acquaintance of several missionaries. They are fine Christian people fighting a tough battle here in Spain. One of them is a graduate of Dallas Theological Seminary. We often get together and study the Bible and discuss theology. We were studying Hebrews and as you can guess, "easy believism" reared its head.

His position is as follows: 1) You can have Jesus as Savior and not Lord. 2) Salvation and discipleship are not the same thing. 3) Repentance means to change your mind about Jesus, not about sin. 4) Christians can fall away and not come back, and if they then die they will go to heaven. 5) He keeps telling me that if I believe as I do (that repentance does lead to a changed life and a changed mind about sin, and that a true Christian will not abide in sin), I cannot have assurance because I sin every day. 6) Calvin and Luther have an "insane" view of sin and, besides, they were "bad" people.

My own study of Galatians and the Reformers has strengthened my belief in *sola fide*. Are we now Judaizers adding conditions to the pure gospel? Paul says that we can only live right with God by faith in Him and by His empowering presence. On some of your tapes you have spoken out against the "dispensational" heresy. I seem to remember on one of your tapes stating that these people failed to make a distinction between necessary and meritorious works, but you moved on rather quickly. What's the deal?

Ryrie and Hodges are conservative theologians. It seems to me that they are trying to change their theology to fit reality (many so-called Christians don't live holy lives) rather than trying to change reality by their theology.

Any help or insight would be sincerely appreciated.

Respectfully yours,
John W. Gunderson

We have shown by this survey of history, past and present, that Dispensationalism is another gospel. The stakes are indeed high, for the church faces a direct challenge from within Protestantism to the integrity of the gospel message.

If Luther had to proclaim to the church of the sixteenth century that justification is by faith alone and not by meritorious works, we must protest to the church, as she approaches the twenty-first century, that justification is by a LIVING and not by a DEAD faith!

CONCLUSION

We have now examined the Dispensationalism of yesterday and today. We have found that Dispensationalism is virtually the same today as yesterday. There have been some variations, of course, but none are essential. There are many varieties (to use an expression from natural science), but no new species.

We have seen that, although Dispensationalism claims to be four-point Calvinism, it is, in reality, consistent Arminianism. This spurious Calvinism denies all five points of Calvinism. Its "total depravity" is not total because this allegedly depraved person is, nonetheless, able to exercise faith. Dispensational "unconditional election" is actually an election conditioned on foreseen faith. The dispensational denial of "limited Atonement" (to which it admits) destroys the possibility of any true Calvinism. Dispensational irresistible grace is, upon examination, nothing of the sort. Finally, and perhaps most important, Dispensationalism rejects the Calvinistic and scriptural doctrine of the perseverance of the saints in favor of an utter travesty—the "eternal security" of the sinner.

We have also seen that Dispensationalism is, at best, dubious evangelicalism. All of its distinctive doctrines undermine, either explicitly or implicitly, the salvation which is to be found only in Jesus Christ. Its understanding of a "dispensation" undercuts the Biblical doctrine of grace in any dispensation. Its notion of "prospective salvation" in the Old Testament is very different from salvation in Jesus Christ, and the alleged kingdom offer to the Jews dishonors the Lord whom the dispensationalist claims to serve. The dispensational distinction between Israel and the church, rather than distinguishing law and grace, denies grace completely, maintaining as it does that there is more than one way of salvation. Finally, and perhaps most obviously, the Antinomianism inherent in Dispensationalism places souls in jeopardy by teaching that a man may have Christ as Savior but not as Lord, that good works are an option for the Christian, even that a person may totally cease to believe in Christ and still be saved.

Charles Ryrie concluded his well-known book, *Dispensationalism Today*, with an appeal to fellow Christians to recognize the validity of Dispensationalism alongside their own interpretations. Anything other than that seems ungracious to Dr. Ryrie. Dispensationalists consider their theology Christian, and other Christians should concur in that judgment. People, including dispensationalists, should be taken at face value, their views accepted as what they say they are.

Consider the illustration he cites. "Neither the older nor the newer dispensationalists teach two ways of salvation, and it is not fair to attempt to make them so teach."[1] If we have shown anything in this present volume, it is that Dispensationalism does teach more than one way of salvation—and that in doing so it teaches no salvation at all. If that is true it is fair so to charge. Indeed it is absolutely imperative precisely because we love dispensationalists and value their souls and the souls of those they reach.

We do not wish to be ungracious. Neither do we wish to be naive. What Dr. Ryrie overlooks here is the crucial difference between utterance and intention. There may be a great difference between the two, as everyone recognizes. What Ryrie or anyone says and what he intends to say may be poles apart. We will believe that dispensationalists do not intend to teach two ways of salvation until it becomes clear that individual dispensationalists do understand the criticism, that they cannot answer it, and that they still go on, for whatever reason, teaching the doctrine.

On the other hand, the church is not called to spare false doctrine and false teachers because of the possible intentions of those who teach such doctrines. Any student of church history is quite aware that many heretics have been very sincere in their error. The standard of judgment is fidelity to God's inerrant Word. The Apostle Paul's charge to Timothy expresses this well:

> Preach the Word; be prepared in season and out of season; correct, rebuke and encourage—with great patience and careful instruction. For the time will come when men will not put up with sound doctrine. Instead, to suit their own desires, they will gather around them a great number of teachers to say what their itching ears want to hear. They will turn their ears away from the truth and turn aside to myths. (2 Timothy 4:2-4, NIV)

---

1. Ryrie, *Dispensationalism Today*, p. 207.

My plea to all dispensationalists is this — show me the fundamental error in what I teach or admit your own fundamental error. We cannot both be right. One of us is wrong — seriously wrong. If you are wrong (in your doctrine, as I here charge), you are preaching nothing less than a false gospel. This calls for genuine repentance and fruits worthy of it before the Lord Jesus Christ whom we both profess to love and serve.

Soli Deo Gloria!

APPENDIX

DISPENSATIONALISM AND COVENANT THEOLOGY

D ispensationalists like to contrast themselves with covenant theologians. They seem to view these two systems as the two available alternatives. Covenant theologians, on the other hand, have been among the most trenchant critics of Dispensationalism. For this reason it is necessary to pay some more attention to the dispensational case against Covenant theology.

The two systems are substantively very different, although there are some surface similarities. Both systems make much of the covenants in Scripture. What the dispensationalist means by a dispensation is, in a formal sense, what covenant theologians mean by *covenant*. Dispensationalists number seven or so, while covenant theologians commonly refer to only two (with the covenant of redemption in the eternal background). Beneath this formal similarity lie deep differences. Covenant theology recognizes two overarching covenants which frame God's dealings with man—the covenant of works and the covenant of grace. The covenant of works was established between God and Adam in the Garden and promised eternal life on condition of obedience. That covenant of works was broken in the Fall and is no longer in effect—it being replaced by the covenant of grace. The covenant of grace is between Christ and the believer who accepts (believes) His salvation. Covenant theology traces this single covenant of grace throughout Scripture. Although it was administered in various ways throughout the Old and New Testaments, covenant theologians agree on one crucial point—that there is one covenant of grace (although a number of administrations) and thus only one way of salvation.

Charles Lincoln attempts to prove the correctness of dispensational versus covenantal theology. His work on the covenants is the best dispensational presentation of the subject I have seen.[1] It contains the fullest array of arguments against the unity of the covenant of grace, the so-called "all-time covenant." They are impressive, well articulated, and as cogent as the material permits. If this attack on Covenant theology can be successfully refuted, Covenant theology ought, in the process, to be vindicated in the minds of dispensationalists. I will examine all sixteen of Lincoln's arguments in some detail.

First of all, Lincoln asserts that there is no Scripture that sets forth such a covenant. We concede this point only as we admit that no Scripture sets forth the Trinity explicitly. When the Jehovah's Witnesses makes this charge against the truth of the Trinity, the dispensationalist joins the covenantalist in proving that Scripture does implicitly, and most emphatically, teach that doctrine. If the dispensationalist would follow the same method here, he would join with the covenantalist on this point also and maintain that the *concept* of the covenant of grace is spread throughout the pages of Scripture. It is true that the term "covenant of grace" is not used and the precise definition of Reformed theologians not articulated. But, is that the same thing as saying that "no Scripture sets forth such a covenant"? Does the Scripture not set forth the idea that God gave His Son to die as a sacrifice for our sins and that, when we accept that sacrifice, we are saved by that grace? When the dispensationalist says that there is no way of salvation in any dispensation except the way of the blood of Jesus Christ, is he not affirming the "all-time covenant of grace"? Is he not therein showing that the covenant of grace is not only not untenable, but is absolutely indispensable? Does the dispensationalist, in other words, have any objection to the covenant of grace except the absence of the very expression itself? As Van Harvey writes, "all Biblical Theology is, in a loose sense, 'Covenant Theology.' "[2]

Lincoln's second argument is that such a covenant of grace has not been recognized in the history of the church. With this second argument we also agreeably disagree. Just as the Bible does not use that type of phraseology, so also the church, until modern times, has not generally used that type of terminology. Just as truly as the Bible

---

1. Charles Fred Lincoln, "The Development of the Covenant Theory," *Bibliotheca Sacra* 100 (1943):134–163.

2. Van Harvey, *A Handbook of Theological Terms* (New York: Macmillan, 1979), p. 61.

teaches the covenant of grace without using that particular language, so also the church has always held to the covenant of grace, even when it has not employed that language. If the dispensationalist is sincere in saying that Old Testament believers are saved in Jesus Christ, then he does so, implicitly, as well.

Third, Lincoln contends that there is no teaching about it in the Protestant confessions until a century after the Reformation. This is both somewhat correct (in a formal sense) and historically misleading. There can be no doubt whatsoever that John Calvin (1509–64) strongly affirmed the unity of the covenant of grace.[3] Ulrich Zwingli (1484–1531) was virtually a covenant theologian proper (his argument for infant baptism presupposes the unity of the covenant of grace), and his successor, Heinrich Bullinger, indubitably was.[4] Bullinger, indisputedly a covenant theologian, does not use the word "covenant" in his *Second Helvetic Confession* of 1566. Anyone reading the fifteenth chapter of this confession nevertheless would never doubt that it expressed Covenant theology. Thus, there can be no doubt that the unity of the covenant of grace was strongly affirmed by Reformed theologians from the earliest period of the Reformation. It is implicitly taught in the earlier confessional documents and explicitly mentioned in the later confessions.

Fourth, Lincoln contends that covenantalism leads to the ignoring of the church covenants which occupy a large place in the Bible. Admittedly, there are many covenantal enactments in the Bible that are not especially developed in Covenant theology. The reason for this is that they do not represent fundamental theological concepts but specific agreements on particular occasions. Covenant theology is in no way opposed to these.

Here again, Lincoln has failed to do his historical homework. As a matter of fact, where Covenant theology has been most widely accepted, covenants of this character are most in evidence. The Scots, for example, are famous for their Covenanters. They were called "Covenanters" because of the church and national religious covenants which they made. It is not coincidental that they were covenant theologians in the sense in which we are discussing that term here. Seventeenth-century New England Congregationalism is an even more notable illustration of the propensity of covenant theologians to make church covenants.

---

3. Calvin, *Institutes*, II.10.1–6.
4. See Ulrich Zwingli, "Of Baptism" in *Zwingli and Bullinger*, ed. G. W. Bromiley (Philadelphia: Westminster, 1953), pp. 129–175. On Bullinger, see Leonard J. Trinterud, "The Origins of Puritanism," *Church History* 20 (1951):37–57; and J. Wayne Baker, *Heinrich Bullinger and the Covenant* (Athens, Ohio: Ohio University Press, 1980).

Fifth, Lincoln contends that Covenant theology leaves no place for Israel's national hopes. This is a more significant argument. Some covenant theologians do believe that Israel will return to the land God had promised her. Many covenant theologians believe in a general conversion of Israel in the end-time in accordance with their understanding of Romans 11:26. Many covenant theologians do *not* believe in either of those future hopes, but the point is that their belief or disbelief in Israel's future hopes of land and/or salvation does not grow out of their Covenant theology. It depends upon their understanding of the Biblical teaching and promises about the future of national Israel. It is an exegetical matter and not a theological implicate.

Dispensationalists do believe, of course, in both these future hopes of Israel. They think that any covenant theologian who thinks otherwise is in error. What we are saying to Lincoln here is that, even if these covenant theologians are in error, it is not because of their Covenant theology, which is the point he is attempting to make, but because of their exegesis.

The sixth reason, that Covenant theology does not allow any place for the distinctive position of the church, is ambiguous and therefore not cogent. Its ambiguity lies in the words *distinctive* and *church*. If Mr. Lincoln means that Covenant theology has no distinguishing position for the present-day church, he is speaking incorrectly. Covenant theology maintains that there is a great *modal* difference between the church in this dispensation and the church of the older dispensation.

This difference was stated most sharply in the words of Jesus regarding the greatest member of the church in the old dispensation—John the Baptist. Our Lord said that, though John the Baptist was the greatest born of woman, he was less than the least in the kingdom of heaven (see Matthew 11:11). That did not mean that he was not in the church. That did not mean that he was not a spiritual person. All that it does mean is that, positionally speaking, his benefits as the greatest of all in the old dispensation were incomparably less than the benefits of the least in this much richer dispensation. Covenant theologians stress the theme of Paul in 1 Corinthians 10 where he emphatically states that the church in this dispensation is in a much more glorious condition than she was in the dispensation of the law. In Galatians 3, Paul sees Old Testament church members as children; in this dispensation, those same children have grown up.

Dr. Lincoln, being a dispensationalist, probably means "unique" or "qualitatively different" by the word "distinctive." It is perfectly true that Covenant theology has no place for the notion that the church in this age is distinctively unique—that she never existed before Pentecost. Since it has been proven that that is also the Biblical doctrine, this is an argument in favor of and not against Covenant theology.

Seventh, Lincoln maintains that Covenant theology's spiritualizing hermeneutic vitiates the truth of God. Against this favorite dispensational argument we need only refer the reader back to chapter 6 of the present volume where the matter has been treated in great length.

Eighth, Lincoln alleges that Covenant theology errs in making the church the covenant people of God, whereas Scripture attributes that designation only to Israel. Here, we admit the criticism as a form of praise. Covenant theologians do believe that Israel is the only covenant people of God. But Israel, as we have seen, is not an earthly "herd of swine"—she is the church of God in the earlier dispensation. The church today is the Israel of God in this dispensation in which we live. "Israel," in the sense in which dispensationalists mean that term, is not the covenant people of God in any dispensation. The true Israel of God is indeed the church and the people of God in all dispensations.

Ninth, Lincoln contends that Covenant theology "applies a false definition of the word dispensation, making it to mean a mode of administering the covenant of grace."[5] We have no quarrel with this statement except for the word *false*. If that word were deleted and the word *true* put in its place, we would have an accurate statement of what a dispensation actually is. This we have shown in great detail above.

Lincoln's tenth allegation, that Covenant theology obliterates the distinctions of each dispensation, is simply false. Covenant theology does recognize and set forth the "distinctives of each dispensation." The difference is simply that the covenant theologians call these "distinctives" "modal" but not "substantive differences."

The very form of the eleventh argument against Covenant theology, that it "mixes" law and grace, is another argument in its favor. Covenant theologians recognize that law and grace exist side by side in both the Old and New Testaments. It also recognizes that law and grace must be *distinguished* in both dispensations. Dispensationalism, on the other hand, *separates* law and grace rather than *distinguishing* them. By separating the two along testamental lines, the dispensationalist fails to recognize the proper role of both in both Testaments. Dispensationalism not only does not "mix," but actually divorces law and

---

5. Lincoln, p. 136.

grace so as to make the separated law an implicit form of legalism and the separated grace an explicit form of Antinomianism.

Twelfth, Lincoln states that covenant theologians fail to recognize the dispensations for what they are, and so accuse dispensationalists of teaching more than one way of salvation. We have proven at great length in the body of this book that dispensationalists do teach more than one way of salvation. Here we simply refer the reader back to Scofield's definition of a *dispensation* as "a period of time during which man is tested in respect of obedience to some *specific* revelation of the will of God."[6] If the word *testing* is to have any meaning at all, it is involved in the way of salvation.

Lincoln's thirteenth point is that Covenant theology misconstrues Ephesians 3:2, which passage allegedly makes the "present the exclusive time of grace stewardship."[7] We cannot believe what we are reading. Surely Dr. Lincoln does not want to suggest that, because the word *oeconomia* has the definite article, the Apostle Paul had a monopoly on the stewardship of grace?

Here we see that Lincoln's Dispensationalism forces him to assume that there is more than one way of salvation, whether he admits to it or not. At this point, Lincoln seems to have more in common with the consistently dispensational Bullingerites than with more moderate dispensationalists. Covenant theology maintains (and most dispensationalists claim to believe) that there has only been one way of salvation in all dispensations. We all agree, furthermore, that that one way has been by grace. If we all agree that there has been only one way, and that the way of grace is in all dispensations, then certainly it is obvious that, whatever Paul means by Ephesians 3:2, he is not claiming that he alone was a proclaimer of the only way of salvation from the time the first saint was redeemed until the last.

Lincoln's fourteenth point, that Scripture mentions at least an "old" and a "new covenant" (which roughly correspond to the two Testaments) as proof that there are at least two contrasting covenants, is a heavy point but it does not help Lincoln's cause. Sufficient to say here, by way of refutation, that whatever lingering problems in reconciliation there may yet be, the old covenant by which Israel was saved was the blood of Jesus Christ and faith in it, which technically is nothing less than the covenant of grace. The way we are saved in the new covenant is by the covenant in the blood of Jesus Christ and faith in that

---

6. *Scofield Reference Bible*, p. 5.
7. Lincoln, p. 137.

blood. Whatever the differences are, they are not differences in essence. Rather, they are nonessential or modal. So Dr. Lincoln is quite wrong in saying that there are "at least *two contrasting covenants*" of *grace*.

The sixteenth reason, that John 1:17 shows that after Christ came, "grace is so manifested as to become the only way of approach to him," is essentially the same as the fifteenth, so we consider them together.[8] It was the grace of Jesus Christ, the dispensationalist and covenantalist alike affirm, that saved people in the Mosaic era, just as it is the grace of Jesus Christ which saves people in the Christian era. If dispensationalists are going to insist that there is one way of salvation in all dispensations, then we are going to have to hold them to that claim. If they do hold to their own claim, then they cannot say (as Lincoln is suggesting here) that this *new* way is "the only way of approach to him," as if it were essentially a different way from other dispensations. Lincoln himself seems to recognize that we cannot say that. Consequently, he qualifies the statement by indicating that it is a *clearer* way and a more *open* way, but not really a different way after all. It is almost as if, with the final argument of this array, Dr. Lincoln himself lets the covenantal truth out.

In summary, let us say that, in spite of all his many arguments, Lincoln has not shown that the "all-time covenant of grace" is untenable. The speciousness of his many contentions shows that a true concept of the covenant of grace, whether by that name or any other, is lacking in Dr. Lincoln (and in Dispensationalism generally). To talk about one, two, or three covenants is almost academic when it is noticed that Dispensationalists do not have the one indispensable covenant of grace—the only way of salvation.

It is not merely that they reject the proper Reformed way of formulating this concept of salvation, but that they lack this concept of salvation in any formulation. In spite of all the dispensational protestations to the contrary, dispensations (if they mean what their definition says) have to be testings for salvation. If persons met those tests, then presumably they would be acceptable to God. Since they were sinners, this must imply that they were saved from their sins thereby. That does indeed make an all-time or any-time covenant of grace untenable.

That there is no covenant of grace in dispensational theology is most evident when it is lacking even in their dispensation of grace. The covenant of grace (because it is a covenant) does require something of man. This non-meritorious requirement is the same in both dispensa-

---

8. Ibid., pp. 137–138.

tions — a working faith. Since Dispensationalism is demonstrably antinomian, it does not require anything of man for salvation — even faith.
Call it covenant of grace or not, the only way of salvation is by faith
in Jesus Christ, and Dispensationalism does not require genuine faith
in Jesus Christ for salvation. All it asks for is a "profession" of faith —
which is hardly the same thing as Biblical saving faith in Christ.[9]

9. I am not unaware that dispensationalists are asserting, more and more commonly
today, that they do not teach merely nominal faith. However, assertion is not proof.
When Dispensationalism does truly give up mere nominalistic faith for a working
faith, Dispensationalism will be Dispensationalism no more.

INDEX

ABOUT THE AUTHOR

J ohn H. Gerstner is Professor emeritus of Pittsburgh Theological Seminary, is Associate Pastor of Trinity (PCA) Church in Johnstown, Pennsylvania, and is currently theologian-at-large at Ligonier Ministries. He is a lecturer on the Bible at Geneva College. He has been a visiting professor at Trinity Evangelical Divinity School since 1966 and is adjunct professor of theology at Reformed Theological Seminary and adjunct professor at Knox Theological Seminary. He holds a B.A. from Westminster College, an M.Div. and Th.M. from Westminster Theological Seminary, and a Ph.D. in Philosophy of Religion from Harvard University.

Dr. Gerstner has published many books, audio and video tapes, and numerous articles in theological journals and magazines. He was a pastor for ten years and a professor of church history at Pittsburgh Theological Seminary (1950–80) and still preaches and lectures around the world. He and his wife of fifty years, Edna, reside in Ligonier, Pennsylvania.

COLOPHON

The typeface for the text of this book is *Times Roman*. In 1930, typographer Stanley Morison joined the staff of *The Times* (London) to supervise design of a typeface for the reformatting of this renowned English daily. Morison had overseen type-library reforms at Cambridge University Press in 1925, but this new task would prove a formidable challenge despite a decade of experience in paleography, calligraphy, and typography. *Times New Roman* was credited as coming from Morison's original pencil renderings in the first years of the 1930s, but the typeface went through numerous changes under the scrutiny of a critical committee of dissatisfied *Times* staffers and editors. The resulting typeface, *Times Roman*, has been called the most used, most successful typeface of this century. The design is of enduring value to English and American printers and publishers, who choose the typeface for its readability and economy when run on today's high-speed presses.

Substantive Editing:
William B. Evans

Cover Design:
Steve Diggs & Friends
Nashville, Tennessee

Page Composition:
Thoburn Press
P.O. Box 2459
Reston, Virginia 22090

Printing and Binding:
Maple-Vail Book Manufacturing Group
York, Pennsylvania

Dust Jacket Printing:
Strine Printing Company
York, Pennsylvania